MILITARY THREATS

Recent Titles in Contributions in Military History

American Sea Power in the Old World
The United States Navy in European and Near Eastern Waters, 1865-1917
William N. Still, Jr.

A Hollow Threat: Strategic Air Power and Containment Before Korea
Harry R. Borowski

The Quest for Victory: The History of the Principles of War
John I. Alger

Men Wanted for the U.S. Army: America's Experience with an All-Volunteer Army Between the World Wars
Robert K. Griffith, Jr.

Bullets and Bureaucrats: The Machine Gun and the United States Army, 1861-1916
David A. Armstrong

General John M. Palmer, Citizen Soldiers, and the Army of a Democracy
J. B. Holley, Jr.

History of the Art of War: Within the Framework of Political History, The Middle Ages
Hans Delbrück, translated by *Walter J. Renfore, Jr.*

"Dear Bart": Washington Views of World War II
Glen C. H. Perry

Fighting Power: German and U.S. Army Performance, 1939-1945
Martin van Creveld

Two If by Sea: The Development of American Coastal Defense Policy
Robert S. Browning III

Hitler's Luftwaffe in the Spanish Civil War
Raymond L. Proctor

The Antagonists: A Comparative Combat Assessment of the Soviet and American Soldier
Richard A. Gabriel

MILITARY THREATS

A Systematic Historical Analysis of the Determinants of Success

Peter Karsten, Peter D. Howell,
and Artis Frances Allen

Contributions in Military History, Number 36

GREENWOOD PRESS
WESTPORT, CONNECTICUT • LONDON, ENGLAND

Library of Congress Cataloging in Publication Data

Karsten, Peter.
Military threats.

(Contributions in military history, ISSN 0084-9251 ;
no. 36)
Bibliography: p.
Includes index.
1. War. 2. Military art and science.
3. International relations. I. Howell, Peter D.
II. Allen, Artis Frances. III. Title. IV. Series.
U21.2.K37 1984 355′.02 83-8552
ISBN 0-313-23825-1 (lib. bdg.)

Library of Congress Catalog Card Number: 83-8552
ISBN: 0-313-23825-1
ISSN: 0084-9251

First published in 1984

Greenwood Press
A division of Congressional Information Service, Inc.
88 Post Road West, Westport, Connecticut 06881

Printed in the United States of America

10 9 8 7 6 5 4 3 2 1

We dedicate this book to the memory of Prince Karl Max Lichnowsky, German ambassador to Britain in 1914, whose sound advice and tocsins might have prevented the outbreak of World War I had they been heeded by his government; and to diplomats of his calibre throughout the world today.

Contents

Tables

Preface

In the fall of 1962, two of the authors of this study were in school; the other was serving as an officer on the USS *Canberra*. On October 22 President John Kennedy reported to the nation and the world the presence of Soviet missiles in Cuba; he ordered a blockade of that island and demanded that the Soviets withdraw the missiles. The Organization of American States (OAS) gave its belated sanction to the American action.

The *Canberra* was the command ship of the blockading force, but we all sensed the universal danger: a threat had been issued; a line had been drawn. How would the Soviet leadership respond? Would the two powers find their way back from the brink? Or would the world be plunged into nuclear darkness?

Almost twenty years later, in a potentially less ominous but ultimately more tragic crisis, Argentine troops seized the Falkland (Malvinas) Islands, and Britain threatened to remove "the invaders" by force unless they withdrew speedily. Punctuating the threat, British warships, with troops embarked, made their way south in the Atlantic. The United Nations Security Council, the Organization of American States, and Britain's European allies condemned one or the other of the parties. Another threat had been issued.

The threat to use military force is a terribly grim and awesome business, raising, in our minds, several rather fundamental questions. Is the threat justified? Are the interests that the threatener feels to be endangered worth the risk of war? And what of the target? Are its interests or its prestige so at risk that it cannot acquiesce? If it calls the threatener's bluff, can the threatener find a face-saving way back from the brink? Will the target provide the way, or will its response be intransigent, its recourse war?

Threats are serious business and deserve attention. Some must inevitably be issued, for nations are still sovereign, disputes still arise, and no universal force exists that can resolve them all. We may not approve of this ineluctability, but we must acknowledge it. Threats, in any case, are to be preferred to preemptive attacks. Some threats must still be issued, but others should not, unless one is indifferent to the loss of life. Some should not be issued because they have little chance of success. That is one of the unanticipated findings of our study. We asked no more complex a question than why some threats succeed and others fail. But in concluding that some of those failures *should* have been foreseen by those who issued the threats, we found another reason for our study, even if we cannot recall specifically discussing it when we began.

Ours was little more than the social scientists' curiosity. To be sure, we sensed that our work was also that of the policy analyst—the search for better *policy*, as well as better theoretical understanding of policy. But for some time we thought of the relevance of our study only with apprehension, because we did not like to think of ourselves as servants of power, devising formulas to produce "better" threats. Our self-pride then amazes us now. No study of threats, however much more sophisticated or complete than ours, could succeed in giving to a national leadership any more than some ideas as to "what mattered" or how to proceed, given certain circumstances. None of these ideas, moreover, would supplant the particular conditions that prevail in any threat environment, independent of how deftly one manages the crisis. That is to say, if one does not threaten the right target for the right reasons, it may not matter how well one does it. But more of this within.

Direct military threats made by one power, or a coalition of powers, have for some time been the subject of attention of scholars and policy analysts. However, the existing literature dealing with direct military threats is either purely theoretical in character or is based on the analysis of a relatively small number of cases, and often the specific threat is subsumed in a broader study of policymaking or crisis management. (This literature is the subject of chapter 1.) Such studies can, of course, be insightful, and, as we think we have shown, some of them are. But we felt that one could not accept any of the hypotheses thereby generated regarding the success or failure of threats unless all such hypotheses (and, indeed, some others, implicit in the relevant variables) were subjected very specifically to verification through systematic analysis of a statistically sufficient number of actual cases. That is what we have attempted herein.* Our methodology is described briefly in chapter 2 and in appendix 1.

In chapter 3 we address (and, on the basis of our evidence, answer) the following questions: What are the general characteristics of the "typical" direct military threat? What types of threats succeed, under what circumstances? What sorts of threats lead to war? Did threats issued in the pre-nuclear past differ in outcomes from those of the nuclear present? In that present, have threats made by the United States differed substantially from those made by the Soviets,

*J. David Singer was referring to inquiry into "the causes of war," but his call in 1970 for scholars "to put the independent variable(s) in operational form, gather the necessary data," and engage in "multi-variate analysis" seemed to apply to our interest in the successful threat as well (Singer, "From *A Study of War* to Peace Research," *Journal of Conflict Resolution* 16 (December 1970).

Chinese, or British? And finally, can we say anything of the long-term consequences of these threats?

The concluding chapter summarizes our findings, compares them to the conventional wisdom, and tests those findings by asking how well they predict the outcome of six additional historical cases. We also attempt to apply our findings to a theoretical futuristic scenario, altering the character of several variables, in order to suggest the significance of what we have done. As the study drew to a close, events in Poland and in the Falkland Islands caught the attention of the world, and from the perspective of mid-1982, we added some observations on these crises, as they also seemed logical and telling tests of some of the key findings of this study.

Artis Frances Allen drafted the "Yugoslav scenario," described briefly in the final chapter (and available at nominal cost to interested readers). Peter Howell wrote the first draft of chapter 1 and is conducting a more specific, separate analysis, which is limited to "hard" data (allowing equal internal analysis, utilizing population figures, economic data, numbers of manpower and military hardware, and the like), referred to in chapter 2 and appendix 1. Peter Karsten conducted the analysis of the coded data cards and the questionnaire (appendix 2) and wrote the first draft of the preface, chapters 2, 3, and 4, and the appendices. But all three of us conducted the research, engaged in the coding of each case history, and prepared the select bibliography; and each read and suggested revisions to each chapter.

We are indebted to several colleagues and friends but want particularly to acknowledge the stimulation and support provided by Joseph Coffey, former Director of the Center for Arms Control and International Security Studies at the University of Pittsburgh, who set this study in motion, persuaded us to conduct it, and offered friendly advice and support throughout. We want also to thank Raymond Hinnebush of the College of St. Catharine's, who, while associated with us at an early stage of this project, had a substantial hand in the shaping of our research design. We are also grateful to Charles Gochman, Constance Rae, and Phil Sidel of the University of Pittsburgh, Paul Schroeder of the University of Illinois, Stephen Kaplan of the Brookings Institution, Patrick Morgan of Washington State University, and Timothy McKeown and Michael Solomon of Carnegie-Mellon University for their useful advice and criticism offered at various stages of the project. Of course, no one whose help we are hereby acknowledging is to be held responsible for any of our errors of omission or commission herein.

MILITARY THREATS

1

An Introduction to the Subject: Precision, Imprecision, and Theoretical Models

Military power has always been one of the most important devices utilized by states to achieve their goals within an international system. As an instrument of power, military force has not been limited to actual armed conflicts, but it has frequently been used as a threat to influence the behavior of another state. In the threat environment, it is the proposed or potential damage that could be inflicted by a nation's armed forces rather than the actual defeat of an opposing military force that provides the basis for attaining a diplomatic objective. Threats to employ force as a means of securing a goal can be either direct or indirect. Indirect (or "systemic" or "potential") threats are an inherent feature of international systems populated by states that enjoy substantial military capabilities. An effective military system gives a nation the constant potential to formulate precise direct threats or actually to employ violence in pursuit of a desired end. But as long as the threat of violence remains indirect or unspecified, as long as the threat is not linked to the performance of some specific action by the target, the pressure exerted by military force remains covert, ill-defined, and amorphous.

Indirect threats are implicit in the military capabilities of a nation, and such threats are sometimes associated with conflict. This conflict does not refer to overt hostilities, but to an antagonistically competitive process of state interaction. This process is characterized by a degree of structure and stability to the conflict. Thus, while the states may be in opposition on a number of issues, the pattern of the conflict remains reasonably constant, and, consequently, the behavior of the respective states can be anticipated with some accuracy. In such situations, the violence potential of the opposing military forces would act as a deterrent to certain types of behavior without any of the actors formally enunciating a threat. Military power compels decisionmakers automatically to include some consideration of the potential costs of a military conflict when selecting a course of action. In this fashion, indirect threats act to restrict the range of acceptable options. Hence, it seems clear that indirect threats are included in the decisionmaking process. However, the actual degree of pressure exerted by military capabilities alone is extremely difficult to determine with any precision. The major function of indirect threats is to deter certain types of issues from being raised, and it is often unclear whether a power's failure to raise certain issues or to seek certain goals was the result of the indirect threats or because the state's decisionmakers were influenced by other factors. Consequently, it is sometimes not easy to surmise whether the power would have sought the goal in question had it experienced an environment less threatening.

While we are aware of the presence of these indirect, or "background," threats, we have chosen to focus this study on the use of direct threats to obtain specific diplomatic objectives. Rather than providing a structure or background to international relations, these threats are linked to clearly stated objectives and require a reaction from the target within either a specified or, at least, an implied time span. (In the event that a time limit is not formally included in the threat, a sense of urgency would still meet this requirement.) Thus, direct threats are more precise and more temporally limited than indirect threats. Moreover, they occur in different types of situations. Indirect threats are generally associated with stable periods of conflict, while direct threats are most frequently found during crises. During a crisis, the preexisting pattern of relations among states breaks down, and the international structure becomes very fluid. The crisis involves an identifiable break in the pattern of interstate relations and creates the possibility that the system or subsystem may experience sudden and noticeable alterations in its structure and organization.

In terms of individual states, the crisis may involve new sets of relationships that could involve substantial costs to the actors. It is this combination of risks and opportunities, afforded by the temporary fluidity of the international system during a crisis, that provides military threats with their appeal. Threats derive a substantial part of their effectiveness from the fact that all international conflicts, except wars of extermination, retain some degree of interdependence among the parties involved, at least in the sense that there are limits to actor behavior in the crisis.[1] There is a range of outcomes, from the "ideal" to the minimally tolerable objectives of each nation, that encompasses potentially acceptable solutions. The extent to which the actual outcome will favor a particular interest reflects the power each nation can bring to bear on the issue. Power, in this sense, is the ability to induce another state to perform an action that it would not do voluntarily. Nations use force and threats of force as diplomatic tools to structure the bargaining process in a manner favorable to their particular interests. The military threat, then, represents one aspect of the broader use of violence in diplomacy. It is an effort to use military power so that otherwise unobtainable goals may be reached without actually fighting.[2]

Threats are considered effective if, at least in the calculations of the target country, they increase the dangers associated with a proposed action or nonaction to the point where the probable costs exceed the probable gains. Theoretically, the skillful use of threats would structure the decisionmaking of the opponent so that only the desired calculations about costs and benefits were applicable to the decision. In such cases, the threatener would be able to secure its objective of compelling the target to engage in (or deterring the target from performing) some specified form of behavior without incurring the cost of military action. In this type of usage, the threatener not only influences the target's behavior through direct threats, but it also threatens indirectly by proposing to raise the level of international tension and thereby raise the danger of an even broader conflict.[3]

While these uses of threats have been a part of traditional diplomacy, the development of aerial warfare and the deployment of nuclear weapons have accelerated the systematic study of the utility of threats as a diplomatic tool. The destructive power of the weapons and the imbalance between the effectiveness of the delivery and defense systems have made it possible to threaten a country's economy and population without first defeating its military forces. Nuclear weapons appeared to have created the possibility of issuing at the inception of a crisis the type of threats that in the past had been possible only after inflicting a military defeat. This superiority of offensive weapons focused attention on the need to develop a strategy for using atomic weapons to deter nuclear attacks and to influence other states in less critical situations; that is, a strategy to utilize nuclear weapons as traditional tools for exercising diplomatic power.

The Eisenhower Administration formulated the doctrine of Massive Retaliation as a single strategic formulation that could be applied simultaneously to both nuclear and subnuclear crises. The effort to use the threat of a massive nuclear strike against the Soviet Union as a means of deterring small-scale wars and insurrections demonstrated the tremendous difficulties that are inherent in trying to establish too direct a link between the destructive power of the new weaponry and effective diplomatic power. Massive Retaliation was an inadequate strategic concept for a number of reasons. It was based on a highly questionable set of assumptions concerning the monolithic nature of the Communist movement and, correspondingly, overestimated the degree of Russian control over all types of international disorder. A more important flaw in the concept lay in the belief that the threat of nuclear attack might serve as an effective response to minor provocations. For anything less than a major threat to American security, the disparity between the provocation and the response could make the threat seem incredible. Moreover, if such threats were utilized against another nuclear power and if they appeared credible, the probability of a preemptive strike could increase tremendously.[4]

By the 1960s, the increase in Soviet nuclear strength and the conceptual limitations of Massive Retaliation led to significant shifts in American thinking about the role of military power in international relations. From 1962 to the present, the United States has argued that the balance of nuclear forces guarantees Assured Destruction in the event of a war with the Soviet Union. The vulnerability of both superpowers is seen as placing sufficient restraints on both nations' behavior to obviate the likelihood of nuclear war. Rather than eliminating the role of military pressure in international affairs, this balance of nuclear power suggests an expanded role for conventional forces.[5] Given the size of existing nuclear forces, conventional military action may be able to operate beneath the umbrella of strategic mutual deterrence. An international system may be operating that is analogous to that of the nineteenth century—that is, a polycentric world in which major powers avoid large-scale war among themselves while actively utilizing military threats and peripheral warfare as instruments of diplomatic suasion.[6] In fact, the rough outline of such behavior is suggested by the general restraint shown by the Soviet Union and the more powerful United States in a number of post–World War II crises and conflicts, though the United States *did* employ nuclear suasion on several occasions.

The increase in conventional capabilities during the Kennedy Administration reflected an appreciation of the continuing—indeed, the expanded—importance of conflicts that are well below the nuclear threshold. The doctrine of Flexible Response was intended to provide the president with a much wider range of options than were available under Massive Retaliation. However, the shift in thinking was based more on an awareness of the shortcomings of Massive Retaliation than on a clear theoretical view of the role of conventional weapons as instruments of influence. There remains a need to develop a theoretical framework that will establish the degree of risk inherent in efforts at coercive suasion.[7]

Most of the theoretical discussions of military threats have been strongly influenced by the concepts and models developed in the field of strategic deterrence. In this area, the absence of an empirical base for studying nuclear war has forced deterrence thinkers to rely on simulation, analogies from game theory, and decisionmaking models. Consequently, the theories have tended to be highly abstract and deductive and have relied greatly on assumptions postulating the rationality and motives of the decisionmakers within both the threatening and the target countries. It is no derogation of the inventiveness and insight of their creators to say that "Chicken," "Prisoner's Dilemma," and "Critical Risk" (among others) are models of decisionmaking that presume cost-benefit analysis, good communications, and accurate perception on the part of the decisionmakers. While nuclear deterrence *could* reflect the theoretical model, conventional-level crises may be more complicated. At the subnuclear level, nations may possess a much wider variety of options and outcomes. Not only can the threats be escalated, but it may also be possible to introduce a wider and more effective array of allied powers in a position to exert influence in the situation.[8]

Despite the different types of behavior addressed by theories on the diplomatic utility of threats, there is a substantial consensus on the basic outline of what is necessary for successful coercion. Analysts have assumed that all nations base their decisions on a cost-benefit analysis for each alternative course of action. If national behavior can be reduced to efforts to maximize identifiable gains and minimize risks or losses, then the function of the threat is to convince the decisionmakers in the target state that the costs, less benefits, attendant to a proposed course of action (or nonaction) will be greater than the anticipated benefits, less losses. In general, there are three ways by which military threats can establish a cost-benefit ratio favorable to the coercing state. The threatener can attempt to deny the objective to the target, destroy the value of the objective, or inflict costs either in the target's acquisition of the objective or in some other areas that are greater than the benefits the target would receive from the objective in question.[9] The common factor to all three forms is that the threatener must be able to limit the range of alternatives available to the target to those that involve an unfavorable ratio of costs to benefits.

Of all the assumptions made by theorists concerned with threats, the rationality of the decisionmaking process may be the most important. Unless there were some predictability to the manner in which nations could be expected to respond to threats, such measures would be perilous and uncertain forms of international relations. In terms of the decisionmaking model, the response to a military threat involves a careful examination of the probability of incurring measurable costs and benefits for the entire range of alternative actions. The model specifies that the threat will be successful as long as the costs, less benefits, to the target, given the probability of the threat being enacted, exceed the benefits, less losses, accruing if the threat is not enacted.[10] Clearly, this model can provide a guide to policy formulation only to the extent that it represents the actual decisionmaking formulations of a target during situations of external threat. In late December 1853, the British and French governments threatened Russia with war by sending their fleets into the Black Sea and clearly warning the Russians that they were not to attack Turkish warships, nor sail from their ports until further notice. The combined Franco-British armada was overwhelmingly superior to the Russian Black Sea Fleet, and several leading statesmen felt that the Tzar would see the folly of defiance. Lord Palmerston wrote to his fellow cabinet minister, Lord Clarendon, the foreign secretary:

> As to our good cousin Nicholas, I scarcely expect that he will declare war against England and France for so polite an attention as a request that he will not expose his Black Sea fleet to the various dangers which might beset their ships if they left their good anchorage at Sebastopol. . . . seeing that "all autocrat" as he is, he is yet a man; he will become reasonable in proportion as he finds that his difficulties and dangers will increase by his remaining unreasonable; and when he finds England and France in earnest and determined to defend Turkey, he may possibly feel that he has nothing to gain, and may have something to lose by the continuance of his war [with Turkey].

The problem was that Nicholas was not the "rational actor" that Lord Palmerston believed him to be. Or, to put it differently, Palmerston and the Tzar had different notions of what was "reasonable" and what was not: what one could give up and what one could not. Within two months, the Crimean War was under way.[11]

Consider another historical example. In 1889 Italy's prime minister (and foreign minister), Francesco Crispi, appears to have engaged in just such a cost-benefit analysis. He perceived certain signals and behavior by the French Government and military to represent a threat to Italy. What to do? Crispi gave the matter constant attention and thought, and he wrote his war minister on July 10: "No statesman can possibly wish for war and I myself even less than another, because I am aware that we are not sufficiently strong, and even were we so, I should not dare to face the consequences of a conflict whose results no one can foresee."[12]

This certainly seems to be an excellent example of the "rational actor" at work. Crispi assessed his capabilities and adjudged the risk of damage to be unacceptably high. He clearly regarded the threat as real and the probability of French attack to be substantial. Hence, he expressed a clear preference for negotiation. The trouble with this "excellent example" (and the reason we mention it) is that it was all wrong! There simply *was* no French threat. As Raymond Cohen and others have demonstrated, Crispi was utterly paranoid and imagined a worst-case scenario of French belligerence and menacing that did not exist![13] If a paranoid statesman can appear to be acting "rationally" in accord with the cost-benefit model, what *is not* "rational"? Is it possible that a rational actor can behave in a paranoid (or even a psychotic) manner? Leaders faced with a real threat may reason as did the Kaiser in 1914, when, angered by the aligning of Britain with Russia and France, he observed that "we may be destroyed, but England shall at least lose India!" Perhaps the Kaiser was simply "irrational"; alternatively, "rational" and "irrational" have little meaning in this context.

The attribution of rationality to the decisionmaking process presumes that the parties on each side of the threat possess full information. However, it is not clear that military decisions can be made in a purely rational manner. Linking ends and means requires adequate information, a system capable of assimilating and organizing the information, and a governmental structure capable of implementing the decision in a relatively short period of time.[14] Even if these conditions are present normally, there is no guarantee that these conditions would be operative during a crisis. It is possible that a decisionmaking system may either be glutted with a flow of information that exceeds its capacity or that the threat situation might alter the regular flow of information in such a manner that the system could be starved for information.[15] Moreover, these problems are not restricted to the target. The requirements for adequate information are just as stringent for the threatener. A rational use of military threats must be based (as we shall see) on an awareness of the values assigned to the variables in the target's calculations. Hence, if either the threatener or the target suffers from any problems in terms of its flow of information, the ability of both parties to make decisions rationally would be affected.

For the decisionmaking model accurately to depict the real world, the rationality of the crisis managers must operate without being impaired by the crisis itself. Yet the impact of the crisis may impede the formulation of a rational response to a threat. During periods of high tension, decisionmakers tend to adopt simplified cognitive structures; goals are reduced, and the range of perceived alternatives shrinks.[16] This suggests that the target may have increased difficulty in recognizing signals and communications, particularly if the threat requires an innovative response. As a consequence, the ability to solve problems rationally may decline or break down completely during a crisis.[17] There is also a tendency for a crisis to accentuate the competitive aspect of a relationship at the expense of the cooperative features. This shift of emphasis may reduce the capacity for decisionmakers to control the course of events or, at least, may create the perception that events are moving beyond their control.[18] Hence, whatever problems are normally associated with predicting the course of events and logically selecting appropriate actions can be complicated simply by tension, to say nothing of the complex character of the crisis situation itself.

The problem of choosing a proper response to a threat is complicated further by the fact that costs, risks, and benefits are not fixed values, but fluctuate throughout a crisis. Thus, if a nation issues a threat to deter a target nation from performing some specific act, the issuance of the threat automatically increases the risks and gains for both parties. The target has a limited range of choices: it may accede to the threat; it may ignore or defy the threat; or it may try to influence the threatener by some form of counterthreat. In the event that the threat is ignored or defied, the threatener must decide whether or not to enact the penalty. Whatever costs the target's action originally posed for the threatener, they are now compounded by two factors. First, carrying out the threat clearly involves costs associated with the military action. Second, a decision against carrying out the threat not only allows the target to achieve its original objective but by doing so in the face of the threat, enables the target to obtain additional benefits. Having the threat proven to have been a bluff could weaken the prestige of the threatener and, by implication, detract from the credibility of future threats. Finally, it should be noted that the decision about fulfilling the threat is discrete from the original decision to issue it, regardless of the planning that preceded the threat. The threat and the defiance automatically alter some elements of the international system, and the threatener must decide whether fulfilling the threat is still in its national interest.

The shift in values for the components of the cost-benefit analysis is similar for the target. Whatever course of action the target had intended to pursue initially would have to be recalculated to take into account the threat. Also, to the extent that the target is able to generate support for a decision to issue counterthreats, the relative value of the variables would change, and the calculations of all parties would have to expand to include the new variables associated with the target's actions. Furthermore, abandoning an announced course of action under direct pressure involves costs in addition to those directly involved with foregoing the anticipated benefits. Such a change of plans would involve a loss of prestige both at the international level and, perhaps, at home for specific groups within the target state. The international consequences of yielding to pressure might be quite similar to those incurred by a state that is unwilling or unable to enforce its threats: loss of prestige and diminished influence. The result of these changing values is to force decisionmakers constantly to recalculate the risks and gains throughout the crisis.

Given the shifting nature of the variables, the need for information about the values of the target might be vital to one thinking of issuing a threat. It also appears necessary that a potential threatener be clear about its own values both at the outset of and throughout the crisis. Yet, in practice, both types of information can be vague or ambiguous. Frequently, neither side's objective or goals become evident until after the crisis develops. For example, prior to the Korean War, few of the eventual participants seemed to appreciate the interests of the other actors. In the case of the United States, the importance of Korea was not stressed until after the fighting started. The North Korean attack led the Truman Administration to link Korea to other foreign-policy issues and to domestic political pressures for a more vigorous policy against the Communists. Situations that are characterized by such lags in identifying the national interest indeed pose several problems for any assumptions made prior to the crisis concerning the nature of a rational response.[19]

The assumption of rationality also includes a view of the target's decisionmaking process as a unitary system. That is, decisionmaking is seen as taking place within a system of shared goals and values that enables the system to function as if it were a consistent and rational individual. The existence of factions proposing conflicting or simply different objectives within the decisionmaking body would automatically make the process of selecting an appropriate response to a threat more complex and therefore more unpredictable. Moreover, it is difficult to conceive of a society that is not characterized by organized political groups, by bureaucratic interests such as the foreign service, the military services, and various organized economic interests, or, in extreme cases, by groups attached to an outside power. The ability of a state to respond rationally to a threat may depend on the severity of the disagreements among such organized pressure groups and the strength of the respective groups themselves.

It should be noted that there is no a priori reason to assume that a substantial degree of internal factional conflict would necessarily incapacitate the decisionmaking process within the target state. The magnitude of the factional impact may be determined by the nature of the threat and the needs of the factions themselves. A broad-range threat from an outside source could induce domestic factions to submerge their differences and cooperate in the face of a common danger. However, the emergence of this increased cohesion and solidarity is by no means certain. A different type of threat, even to the same country, could produce exactly the opposite effect, especially if the threatened action might produce concrete benefits for specific factions. Thus, neither the presence nor the absence of active factions provides—*inter alia*—an indication of whether or not a threat would be effective. A decision preceded by bitter factional strife could result in a policy of resistance as readily as it might produce acceptance of the terms of the threat. It seems reasonable to expect that a severely factionalized state would experience extreme difficulty in selecting any response. In such a case, the refusal or inability of the target to alter its behavior in accordance with the threat may have little to do with rational weighing of costs and benefits assumed by the threatener. Moreover, the lack of response could easily be misread. If the threatener assumes a single decisionmaker in the target, then no response could indicate defiance. Such a misinterpretation would seem to be particularly likely in cases where the threat required a positive response from the target.[20]

An example of the effect factions might have on rational decisionmaking in a crisis might be seen in the fruitless efforts of the Carter Administration to secure the release of the American hostages in Iran. It appears that the hostages had become a significant symbolic issue in a domestic Iranian power struggle. Decisions by the Iranian Government do not appear to have conformed to the rational decisionmaking model. The militants holding the hostages, the Imam Khomeini, and the moderates (represented by Bani-Sadr) may, all or in part, have come to regard any change in the hostages' situation as imposing unacceptable political costs. Under such circumstances, a threat might well provoke no action at all from a highly factionalized target.

Even if both the threatener and the target operate without serious factional conflicts and do not have significant gaps in their information, different cultural values could produce behavior in one country that might be unanticipated in another. The response to a threat may be culturally determined, and the decision in such instances would be justified by reference to internal social norms, not to universally accepted rules of evidence and method.[21] The infusion of particularistic cultural values into the selection of a response to a threat creates a decisionmaking process that involves more than merely the calculation of potential rewards and punishments associated with the threat. Yet the salience of these cultural values may vary among the members of a policymaking body, and therefore it is difficult to predict their strength in a particular situation.

The target's decisionmaking process might also include some consideration of the perceived alternatives for goal attainment. Although these alternatives may lie outside of the immediate threat environment, they may, nonetheless, have a strong bearing on the target's response.[22] Moreover, the target may have a cluster of goals involved in a crisis situation, all of which would enter the calculations regarding the proper behavior to meet the threat. Hence, while each state may seek to maximize its goals, if goals and benefits are culturally determined, actions that are logically consistent when judged by the standards of a particularistic set of social norms may be considered irrational by the criteria used in other decisionmaking systems. In this vein, J. David Singer has suggested, for example, that different societies could tolerate dramatically high levels of destruction. A country with a large, relatively unproductive population might accept very great losses. Similarly, highly authoritarian regimes may enjoy enough control over the society consciously to incur tremendous losses.[23] Thus, when the German leadership refused to believe that the Serbian crisis could not be ''localized,'' and also refused to believe British warnings that she would intervene on the side of France and Russia, Europe was plunged into war. The Kaiser, who might have defused matters in late July, instead became resigned, stubborn, and morose, and spoke of holding the line ''whatever the cost.'' Moreover, the involvement of issues containing highly charged ideological, moral, or other cultural values may be conducive to the social acceptance of high levels of damage.

In addition to these general societal values, questions involving personal honor, prestige, or the political position of the leadership are seldom included in models of decisionmaking unless such factors are explicitly included in the decisionmaking process itself. These nonrational factors relate to personal, not social, benefits and may be implicit, exerting an influence on the behavior of the leadership by affecting the types of information utilized.[24] In this vein, it could be argued that national-security managers have as a group adopted and internalized a mode of behavior and a set of values that produce a limited ability to process certain types of information. Using Vietnam as an example, Richard Barnet has described these values as consisting of *machismo*, a belief in the efficacy of military force, and a view that presumes behavior to be limited to crude responses to pleasure and pain. These values are then reinforced by a life-style that stresses long hours of work in an environment that restricts the number and variety of people with whom the policymakers come into contact, that limits the range of alternative sources of information, that produces bureaucratic loyalties, and that attempts to diminish cognitive dissonance. The result, in the case of Vietnam, was for the national-security managers to ignore information, even from within the State Department and the Central Intelligence Agency, that questioned the effectiveness of the policies being followed.[25]

Given the tremendous emphasis on rationality in theories of the diplomatic uses of coercion, it is not surprising that a great deal of attention has been focused on communications between the threatener and the target. Obviously, threats must be received and understood before a rational response can be formulated within the context of those threats, and if the threat is to be successful, the target must believe that the probability that the threat will be enacted is high enough to warrant a serious response. For example, the concern of some with the process of communicating a believable commitment to use force reflects an appreciation of the ambiguities inherent in diplomatic correspondence and even in prior treaty arrangements. It would be a rare treaty that was drawn so tightly that there was not any doubt about each nation's responsibilities and willingness to fulfill its respective obligations. In fact, as Bruce Russett has pointed out, the historical record provides little support for the credibility or sanctity of treaty commitments. In numerous cases, immediate definitions of national interest superseded treaty obligations.[26]

Commitments can be divided into two categories: situational and nonsituational. The former represents commitments derived from a nation's conception of its national interest in a particular situation. The decision to act is not based on "legalistic" commitments, but on the identifiable interests threatened in the crisis. Hence, such commitments exist independent of formal treaty obligations. Treaties may reflect conditions under which a nation might wish to defend its interests, but in this view, the obligation to act comes primarily from the issues involved in the crisis, not from the treaty. In this type of commitment, a state might have ties and obligations to non-allied nations that could be more binding than ties augmented by treaties. Nonsituational commitments are based heavily on formalized obligations. The nonsituational view of commitments posits certain national interests that are embedded in the international structure. Such interests transcend transitory shifts and have a stability that makes binding prior commitments a rational measure. Moreover, the fulfillment of publicly made nonsituational commitments can lend credibility to other types of commitments. If a state makes a point of fulfilling its treaty obligations, it could enhance the believability of its threats.[27]

Whatever the nature of the commitment, the threat must be communicated and believed before coercion can affect the target's behavior. Since crises may be accompanied by serious alterations in the normal flow of information, the verbal statement of the threat may not be sufficient. This may be especially true if either a lack or a surplus of information creates conflicting signals. In such cases, the threatener might strive to impart the utmost clarity in its communications and might reinforce its messages by different credibility-establishment gestures. Gestures such as a partial or general mobilization or the deployment of troops in a threatening manner may be intended to indicate the seriousness with which the issue is viewed by the threatener, but they also increase the costs to the threatener of not carrying out the threat in the face of the target's refusal to accede to the demands. Furthermore, vague threats may signal concern and increase the likelihood of military action, but since they are inherently more difficult to analyze than precise warnings, they could lead to undesired military action.[28]

There is a consensus among theorists concerned with decisionmaking in response to military threats that the clarity with which the threat is communicated is positively related to the success of the threat. This is, of course, the case, to a certain obvious extent. The target must perceive a threat and relate it to the action desired by the threatener in order to formulate a rational response. However, while clear communication seems necessary in the logical structure of the model, it does not necessarily operate in the same manner in actual crisis situations. For example, a vague or ambiguous threat may successfully signal the threatener's interests, while the lack of clarity could reduce the costs to the target of complying with the conditions of the threat.

Clarity, in and of itself, is not a sufficient precondition for a successful threat. The threat may be clearly formulated and delivered, but it will not be effective unless the target believes that the threatener intends to follow through. The credibility of the threat may stem in part from the target's evaluation of the military capacity and resolve of the threatener. An effective threat may depend on the threatener's military capacity to inflict the proposed damage (or to have a "reasonable" chance of doing so). A threat that exceeded a nation's known military capacity would seem to be innately unbelievable. However, while the lack of military power might render a threat ineffective, possession of the requisite capacity does not insure that the target will believe the threat.[29]

In situations marked by substantial risks to both parties, establishing the credibility of the threat may be quite difficult. A number of theorists, among whom Thomas Schelling and Herman Kahn are the most prominent, argue that success in establishing one's credibility lies in implementing maneuvers that so bind the threatener that any options other than enacting the threat are eliminated. In essence, credibility is thus translated into another set of cost-benefit relationships. If the costs of not fulfilling the terms of the threat are greater than the costs associated with the proposed military action, then the threat should be believable. According to this analysis, freedom of action during a crisis is a rather moot benefit. Gains attributable to increased flexibility may be more than offset by the loss of credibility due to the threatener's freedom *not* to implement the threat. Rationality, in the sense of being able to consider new options throughout the crisis, may be viewed as dysfunctional. Once a nation decides to threaten, gains can be maximized by utilizing what has been termed the "rationality of irrationality." By causing the threat to appear to be irrevocable unless specific conditions are met, the threatener, it is argued, increases its credibility and, consequently, increases the likelihood of the threat's being successful.[30]

In this vein, Kahn used the analogy of the game of "chicken," in which two drivers demonstrate their resolve and *machismo*—both related to crisis management—by driving speeding automobiles toward one another until one driver loses his nerve and swerves to avoid a collision. Kahn argues that the game is roughly analogous to coercive diplomacy and that the game can be "won" by communicating to the opponent an irrevocable commitment not to swerve. Kahn suggests gestures such as visibly drinking a bottle of whiskey, severing the brake lines, and throwing the steering wheel out of the window as a means of demonstrating one's resolve. As with Schelling's argument, these actions have the effect of shifting the entire burden of decision to the target. The threatener has established the only conditions under which the "game" can be played. Thus, even if it would be foolhardy to fulfill the threat if the effort at coercion failed, this ceases to be an option for the threatener. Only the target can make the decisions that will avert the threatened action and the consequent damage to both parties. In effect, the irrevocable commitment also reduces the target's freedom of action. The nature of the commitment limits the target's options to accepting or rejecting the conditions put forward by the threatener. As long as the target bases its decision on a cost-benefit analysis, Kahn argues, it would have no rational choice but to accept the terms of the threatener.[31]

The irrevocable commitment also is intended to eliminate the potential costs to the threatener from the calculations of the target. The cost-benefit decision-making model ordinarily assumes that each nation seeks only to maximize its own relative gains. As such, the threatener's costs become part of the equation only to the extent that they might raise questions about the credibility of the threat. Thus, if Kahn and Schelling are correct, there does not have to be an asymmetry of costs in favor of the threatener; coercion can be effective even if the nation issuing the threats would incur greater damage than the target.[32]

There may be a number of shortcomings to these views of the value of irrevocable commitments. Schelling and Kahn assume adequate knowledge of the opponent's values and intentions. If the target enters a crisis willing to fight on a particular issue, the use of an irrevocable commitment as a diplomatic tactic may simply make war inevitable. Moreover, the strategy would appear to be equally valid for both sides in a dispute. If both parties engaged in the "rationality of irrationality," war would again appear to become inevitable. Finally, the assumption that such an irrational threat had been conveyed clearly to a target may not always be a sound one. Decisionmakers are forced to operate on the basis of judgment, both with regard to the intentions of their opponents and the clarity with which their signals were received. A misreading of information might erode the basis for the utilization of an irrevocable commitment as a tactic.[33]

Given the importance of credibility in the rational-actor analytic model, some argue that an inverse relationship may exist between the severity of the threat and the probability that it will be enacted. The target's calculations might include the extent of the proposed damage in the likelihood that the threatener will enforce its threats. Thus, a threat that proposes massive destruction but that has a low probability of becoming enacted may still be an effective use of coercive diplomacy. However, as the discrepancy between the provocation and the threatened damage increases, there may be a corresponding decline in the credibility of the threat, since larger threats may carry greater costs for the nation issuing them. Consequently, it might be argued that one should increase the severity of the threat only if the increase in threatened damage compensates for the decline in the probability of the threat being enacted according to the calculations of the target. Symbolically, the reasoning could be expressed as $\frac{\Delta T}{\Delta P}$, where P = the percentage change in the probability of the threatener fulfilling the threat, and T = the percentage change in the amount of damage threatened. If $\frac{\Delta T}{\Delta P}$ is greater than one, increasing the size of the threat would be effective.

Despite the apparent mathematical precision of the rational analytic model, it may not be a satisfactory guide to international behavior during a period of crisis. A number of the explicit and implicit parts of the models of coercive diplomacy based on rational decisionmaking can be reformulated in a manner that would allow them to be tested by examining historical use of threats of force for political purposes. For example, the distinction between compellence and deterrence may provide an insight of but modest value in the determination of crisis behavior. It has been argued that compellence and deterrence ask different things of the target and thereby involve different considerations on the part of the target's policymakers. Yet, in one sense, both uses of threats are coercive in that they both demand that the target perform an act, because either complying with or defying a threat involves a conscious decision. It is not the coercion itself but the difference in what is asked of the target that suggests that it is easier to deter than to compel. The argument is based on the assumption that it is cheaper for the target to accede to a deterrent rather than a compellent threat since the costs of abandoning something currently enjoyed or stopping or reversing a policy under way are presumably greater than the costs of not initiating a contemplated action. Future benefits, it is said, can always be discounted and do not have the same levels of institutionalized support as do established policies.

The distinction between the costs involved in complying with deterrent as compared to compellent threats may be analytically useful, yet in practice, it may be extremely difficult to distinguish any difference in costs. There is no reason to assume that a contemplated action may not enjoy more support from established bureaucratic interest groups within the government, organized pressure groups outside of the government, or public opinion than an unpopular existing policy. Shifts in the constellations of groups supporting proposed and existing policies are endemic features of democratic political systems and are present to a lesser degree in all systems. The need to justify policy decisions may make it easier in some instances to comply with a compellent threat if the magnitude and clarity of the threat can be used to legitimize the decision. In such a case, policymakers can argue that they have no rational choice but to accede to the threatener's demands.

For example, suppose we consider two hypothetical threat situations. In country A, a group has just risen to power following a highly emotional and popular campaign for an irredentist foreign policy. Country B might have an existing policy that enjoys the intense support of a minority of the population with a majority that is either indifferent or mildly opposed. Imagine that only the supporters of B's policy may be characterized by a high degree of intensity in their commitment. Given these situations, might it not be more difficult and "costly" for the leadership in country A to yield to a deterrent threat concerning its irredentist ambitions than for country B to yield to a compellent threat aimed at an existing policy? In fact, the compellent threat might even facilitate the abandoning of the potentially dangerous policy by B's leaders. Given only minority support, albeit intense, the outside threat might enable the leadership to plead that it had no feasible alternatives and thus placate or silence its domestic critics.

These problems appear to be present regardless of whether one is considering public or secret forms of either type of coercion. The critical factor is probably not whether the threat is compellent or deterrent, public or secret, but the strength of the values placed on the issue by the target country. As such, on a theoretical level, the distinction between deterrence and compellence offers little in the way of adding any precision to the general propositions about cost-benefit analysis as the basis for policy formulation during a crisis.[34]

These theoretical shortcomings may stem from the cold war environment within which most of the theories were formulated. The assumption that the United States has been upholding the existing international order against the expansionist tendencies of the Soviet Union and her allies would interject a bias in the evaluation of the values assigned to an issue by the contending parties. If one posits a conservative state protecting the status quo from an opponent that is basically opportunistic, the threats of the conservative state tend to be classified as deterrent, and the values assigned to the dispute by the target would also be modest since they stem from opportunist and expansionist impulses and would appear to be peripheral to the vital interests of the target. Classification of a threat as "deterrent" or "compellent" is, in many cases, highly subjective since such classifications involve perceptual judgments by the analyst that may not correspond to those of the actors in the crisis. There is, then, no necessary agreement among the parties involved in a threat situation as to whether a threat is deterrent or compellent. The policymakers of both the threatener and the target may interpret the nature of the threat according to their respective nation's needs and interests. If these evaluations stem from substantially different perspectives or value judgments, what may appear to be the epitome of deterrence to one state may be viewed as simple aggression (compellence) by the target.

The problems involved in moving from the general model of cost-benefit decisionmaking to a precise and workable proposition—such as the distinction between deterrence and compellence—are common to most of the hypotheses generated by such models. Moreover, the deductive nature of rational models fails either to support or refute many traditional views concerning the political uses of force. For example, suppose that one is concerned about the effectiveness of redeploying parts of one's armed forces to support a threat. Were such tactics instrumental in determining the outcome of a threat in the past? If so, are they still instrumental? Rational decisionmaking models offer rather feeble guidance for such questions. Tactics such as moving troops about may be effective if they enhance the credibility of the threat or if they convince the target that the cost-benefit ratio is in favor of the threatener, but it is theoretically possible that such force movements are irrelevant or even counterproductive (if they provoke a preemptive strike). If we assume that the target is familiar with the military capabilities of the threatener, then *extraneous* force movements may be superfluous.

Similarly, the discussions of diplomatic maneuvering during a crisis have not produced an unambiguous consensus. The emphasis on rational cost-benefit analysis—especially the more extreme versions such as those of Schelling and Kahn—places a great deal of importance on retaining the initiative during the crisis. Bargaining during a crisis is described as a process wherein the actors sequentially respond to one another in a series of alternating and discrete decisions. To paraphrase Oran Young, policymakers should be seeking the initiative that forces their opponent to initiate. That is, the goal of the policymaker is to structure the threat environment in such a manner that the opponent's only rational alternatives are either to concede or to formulate a novel and unanticipated response. Such an innovative response would reverse the roles played by the actors, and the original threatener would be forced to abandon its initial goals or match the target's response with a similarly creative new policy. Success occurs when one side is unable to formulate an effective response and is forced to select a policy that only minimizes its losses. The end result of this positional maneuvering is a situation analogous to many chess endgames. The location of the pieces on the board may provide equal security for each player, but whichever player has to move fatally weakens his position.

This type of analysis has been used fruitfully to explain a number of crises. For example, the 1948 crisis over Berlin appeared to follow the pattern of diplomatic maneuvering described above. If one assumes that neither the Soviet Union nor the United States wanted to fight to maintain its position vis-à-vis Berlin, then the ability to structure the other country's decisionmaking matrix was the critical factor in determining the outcome of the crisis. Thus, the initial Russian ploy of closing the highways presented the United States with the unpalatable choice of forcing passage along the highways, presumably with a high risk of war, or of acquiescing to the Soviet interpretation of the status of Berlin. The Berlin Airlift provided a dramatic reversal of the necessity for choice. The success of the airlift forced the Russians to choose between attacking the planes—a choice that almost surely meant war—or accepting the American presence in Berlin. The keys to the outcome were that neither side was willing to take too high a risk of war, and that whenever the alternatives became limited to war or retreat, the side that had to make the decision lost.

As the preceding discussion suggests, there are a number of problems inherent in some assumptions about the decisionmaking process. The arguments concerning rationality, access to information, and the establishment of credibility are derived from game theory, simulation, and logical deductions. However, in the real world, it may be that the values used in the decisionmaking formula are idiosyncratic and unpredictable by cost-benefit analysis alone. The subjective and perceptual nature of factors such as benefits or risks raises the possibility of distortion and misunderstanding. This would be especially true to one seeking to anticipate the full value an opponent may place on a particular item or issue in a dispute. Moreover, the target may fail to appreciate the full importance of some issues and interests until after the onset of the crisis. Finally, states may hold attachments to certain values that are absolute—that is, it may be impossible to devise a threatened level of damage that would produce a surrender. The slogan "I'd rather be dead than Red," which enjoyed some currency during the 1950s, expressed both a rather naive oversimplification of the range of alternatives facing the United States and a desire for a foreign policy based on the sort of moral absolutes that would obviate the relevance of the models of coercion based on cost-benefits analysis.

Instances in which states have behaved on the basis of absolute and unyielding attachments to certain values have occurred frequently enough to suggest some modification of the cost-benefit component of the rational decisionmaking model. Efforts to affect the target's cost-benefit analysis sometimes fail miserably. During the Roman wars with Philip V of Macedon in 200 B.C., the city-state of Abydos futilely utilized a series of coercive diplomatic tactics that fulfilled almost all the requirements specified by modern "Chicken" theorists. Philip besieged this coastal city that was allied with Rome indirectly, through an alliance with Rome's ally, Athens. The Abydians responded to the attack by consciously trying to alter the cost-benefit ratio for Philip's venture. First, the Abydian soldiers took an oath to fight to the death. Second, they piled the city's treasures on a cliff and swore to dump them into the ocean as soon as the walls were breached. Finally, the old men took an oath—which was clearly intended to be binding according to the cultural standards of the period—to kill all the women and children and then commit suicide if the Macedonian attack was successful. The initial gesture was obviously intended to raise the costs of conquering the city beyond what Philip was willing to pay. The latter two tactics were intended to reduce the value of the objective should Philip continue the attack. The thrust of both approaches might have been to restructure Philip's cost-benefit analysis to the point where continuing the attack would have been unprofitable. All these measures were communicated to Philip, and we may assume that Philip regarded the oaths as credible, for Livy writes: "The king, astounded by this . . . , checked the assaults of his soldiers and announced that he would give them 3 days in which to die." Despite the efforts of the Abydians and the additional information Philip may have acquired during the course of the battle, the Macedonians continued the attack, and the fact that the Abydians' threat was credible (they did themselves in as advertised) was no deterrence to Philip's swords. What the Abydians did not give sufficient weight to was the fact that their city was strategically important to Philip because it controlled the Pontic grain trade and his access to Asia Minor, located, as it was, at the mouth of the Dardanelles.[35] Philip could not be deterred by the threat of self-destruction of treasure and potential slaves; it was not these that were crucial to him in his struggle with Rome. Perhaps the threatener must be able to damage something the target wants badly in order to deter him from doing something that the target does not want to be done.

The rather valiant assumptions underlying the rational analytic model of decisionmaking lead to a thorny set of theoretical and practical problems. Consequently, a number of alternative models of decisionmaking have been offered, stressing two major areas of policymaking in which the rational-actor model is either modified or rejected. The first area stresses structural features of the decisionmaking process. The features include the presence of domestic politics, bureaucratically determined loyalties and perceptions, and the limitations on possible policy options imposed by organizational capabilities. Second, many theorists have focused on the psychological impact of stress on the decisionmaking process. It is argued that during periods of high tension, individuals adopt a pattern of resolving perceived value conflicts that is at odds with the criteria necessary for rational cost-benefit analysis.

Graham Allison's organization process model depicts both the range of possible policies and the form in which the chosen action is actually implemented as being determined by the nature of governmental organizations. Rather than a monolithic decisionmaker, there are a number of competing organizations, all of which have their own specific goals. Yet, all of these organizations share certain common features. They resolve complex problems by disaggregating each problem into simpler form and assigning problem segments to different parts of the organization. Both the overall organization and the subunits develop standard operating procedures for performing their normal functions. These procedures are designed both to produce an efficient performance of standard tasks and to enhance the growth and autonomy of the organization.

The presence of these organizations seriously compromises the system's ability to function as a rational actor. Information is channeled according to standard operating procedures and may or may not be adequate during a particular crisis. The organizational procedures tend to be rigid, are designed for routine tasks, and may not be suited to respond to exceptional events. Consequently, any requests for unusual information or for the implementation of an unusual job will probably not be implemented efficiently. The result is to preclude a rational analysis of a full range of options and to restrict the leadership's choices to preformulated plans and capabilities. That such conditions can generate serious dilemmas can be illustrated by considering the problems posed by the German war plans for the Kaiser before World War I or by the problems faced by the Tzar in choosing between full mobilization and no mobilization.[36]

The bureaucratic model describes policy outputs as the result of bargaining among bureaucratic interest groups. Members of the organizations internalize the values or norms of the organization. This then takes on a form of ideological thinking that identifies the national interest with the interests of the particular organization. The result is a lack of rational analysis and a tendency to apply standardized responses to certain stimuli. Since each organization operates in an environment in which it competes for funds, prestige, and influence, it is under strong pressure to act decisively in order to expand its interests at the expense of other organizations. In this sense, the "armed forces exploit and search for external enemies to overwhelm their domestic foes."[37]

Clearly, this competition has an identifiable effect on the information that passes through the bureaucracy to the leadership. It is invariably selective and always is presented in the form of an argument. The result is to reduce the decisionmaking function to building a coalition among competing interests. The resulting policy may satisfy the participants, but it hardly comports with the requirements of the rational analytic model.[38]

Other theorists have argued that the stress associated with a crisis produces a psychological reaction that precludes the rational analysis of the costs and benefits. Crises present all decisionmakers with an indifference curve—a trade-off between two desired goals: avoiding war and gaining a particular objective. A crisis occurs whenever these goals are interactive and negatively related. In that case, the probability of achieving one goal reduces the likelihood of achieving the other.

Psychological pressures may induce cognitive processes that structure incoming information according to nonrational criteria. Given the uncertainty of a crisis situation, the central goal of the decisionmaker is to simplify the environment. The trade-offs between important values create a cognitive dissonance that is resolved by denying that the trade-off exists. No indifference curves are formed; no probabilistic judgments are made; and no formal analysis is made of the consequences of proposed actions. The goals sought by the policymaker are segmented and pursued sequentially. If the crisis is severe enough to prevent the segmentation of the goals, the individual may retreat and perceive the course of events as being so powerful that there is only one possible policy to adopt. This is, in fact, almost exactly the process Ole Holsti observed in his analysis of the 1914 crisis.[39]

If crisis behavior actually follows the cognitive model, the theory seriously undercuts the validity of deterrence theories based on rational models. The tendency, according to cognitive theorists, is for a state to refuse to negotiate. Having denied the existence of a values trade-off, leaders behave as if they can pursue both goals simultaneously. The result tends to be ultimatums instead of diplomatic exchanges based on a recognition that each country has its values ranked on an indifference curve. Clearly, if both countries are led by individuals using cognitive in lieu of rational processes, the danger of war is increased tremendously. Thus, Jack Snyder argues that John Kennedy's definition of the risks in Cuba led directly to the confrontation with the Soviet Union. By claiming that a refusal by the United States to risk nuclear war over the missile issue would increase the risk of war in the future, Kennedy not only resolved the trade-off problem but also guaranteed an ultimatum rather than negotiating a quid pro quo.[40]

Given the logical problems inherent in the rational analytic model and the presence of cogent conflicting theories, does rational decisionmaking offer a worthwhile guide to the crisis behavior of states? Perhaps the first step in assessing this question is to relax some of the more extreme assumptions concerning perfect information, communication, and the cost-benefit analysis of alternative policies. In their extreme form, these assumptions would obviate the possibility of coercive diplomacy as a form of interstate behavior. If states had perfect information and were capable of rationally analyzing the consequences of all the possible outcomes, and were assured that other states were equally rational, no one would ever have to issue a threat. Each state would be able to predict accurately reactions to a policy and, given the common knowledge of the cost-benefit ratios, would never initiate a policy that would not be successful. In short, the extreme assumptions underlying deterrence theory negate the reasons for its implementation.[41]

It is possible to relax the assumptions about perfect information and still retain some of the explanatory power of the model. If a decisionmaker lacks perfect information about the elements of a crisis, a threat may provide additional information about the potential costs present in a conflict situation and about the values of other states.

Relaxing the assumptions raises the question as to whether or not the theory is robust enough to withstand altering its logical structure. This problem could be approached in two ways. One could merely revise the *theories* of coercive diplomacy. Such refinement could capture most of the complexities of the situation and might clarify the specific circumstances under which coercive diplomacy could be effective, but it will still leave one with *theories*.[42]

A second approach, and the one adopted in this study, is to shift the form of the question from a theoretical to a behavioral proposition. Instead of asking what a rational response might be, the focus would be on how states have actually behaved in a given set of circumstances. Theoretical propositions about coercive suasion can be reformulated as hypotheses and tested by examining the historical use of military threats as diplomatic tools.

BEYOND MODELS AND THEORIES

Theories of coercive diplomacy cannot be verified as long as these theories remain abstract and deductive. The models posit cost-benefit analysis as the most important feature of the decisionmaking process, and, as a consequence, they emphasize rationality, communication, and commitment. Formulations based on these considerations, however, may not resolve conflicting values assigned to the decisionmaking formula. The problems can be at least partially resolved by testing the theories developed in the literature in a systematic, empirical fashion. The historical record provides us with a number of instances where nations tried to use military threats to advance their interests. Consequently, it may be possible to determine systematically the degree to which the various components of the rational decisionmaking model have actually operated during crises. Rather than *assuming* values, *postulating* degrees of credibility, and such, the hypotheses concerning policymaking during a crisis can be reformulated to focus on actual perception and actual behavior. In essence, the form of the question raised shifts from asking what a rational response might be to asking what policymakers have actually perceived and how nations have actually behaved in a given set of circumstances. As J. David Singer recently observed, ''the 1960s saw a great deal of [theoretical] research that was 'low on relevance',' ' because ''many peace researchers found 'the light better' under the laboratory lamp post than down the dimly lit street of international history.'' ''Dimly lit'' it is, indeed, but it is a street that researchers are increasingly frequenting.[43]

One simply cannot ''prove'' most hypotheses on the basis of a single historical event. If one's objective is to foster theoretical propositions of general applicability, individual examples can do little more than to clarify the hypotheses.[44] A more effective use of the historical record would treat the past as a means of testing propositions about crisis behavior. Both the rational decisionmaking models and the specific propositions concerning crisis behavior that have been derived from these models can be operationalized and tested in a systematic and empirical fashion, as can other hypotheses. Such shortcomings as have hitherto preoccupied us with the rational models and their subpropositions (such as the question of the distinction between deterrence and compellence, the importance of shifting forces, and the importance of maintaining the diplomatic initiative) may be interesting and of theoretical use (that is, useful as theory), but in and of themselves they do not refute any hypotheses. Only a systematic study of a number of threats can do that.

It is possible that a careful examination of past crises may point up conditions under which different aspects of the theoretical arguments may operate and conditions under which they are inoperable. Moreover, many of the existing theories appear to rest on implicit historical assumptions, which may or may not hold up under critical examination. Perhaps assumptions concerning the causes of World War II may be the most pervasive. However, the connection between the failure of the major powers to respond to Hitler's aggression and the outbreak of the war may not represent either the most frequent cause of war or the most common type of situation in which military threats may be employed. The degree of universality enjoyed by such propositions can only be established after such assumptions have been made explicit rather than implicit and have been subjected to some type of verification.[45]

The possibility also exists that as long as the work on coercive diplomacy remains abstract, there is a danger that theoreticians may be studying false issues. For example, the rational decisionmaking model seems to require clear and precise information in order to operate properly. A threat that is imperfectly delivered is not likely to be perfectly effective. Statesmen have known this for some time, of course. The stress on clear communications may miss the possibility that diplomats could be profiting by deliberately reducing the clarity of their threat in a particularly appropriate situation. Without systematic examination of crisis behavior, it would be very difficult to determine the degree to which communication problems have affected the outcome of a crisis.

The number of threats studies is, of course, quite important if one is engaged in the systematic testing of hypotheses. Some scholars have let too small an N suffice. Graham Allison, for example, asks a bit too much of his N when he writes: "never in history (i.e., in one of the five cases I have examined). . . ."[46] The probability that no one of five cases should have behaved as the hypotheses that Allison was testing had predicted is, by any reckoning, unlikely, but it does not warrant the phrase "never in history." Glenn Snyder and Paul Diesing examined sixteen crises "as a data source for the empirical development of general theory" in *Conflict Among Nations*.[47] However, only two of these crises ended in war, which necessarily leads one to question the universality of such generalizations as they offer regarding the causing of war or its avoidance. Richard Ned Lebow has, more recently, explored some twenty-six crises, "described only so far as they are useful or necessary to document theoretical propositions."[48] Lebow's list includes five threats that were mere justifications for hostilities; hence, only twenty-one of his cases are of use in learning why some true threats end in war and others do not. Neither Lebow nor Snyder and Diesing ask precisely our question: What accounts for the successful threat? Nor do they suggest, as we do, that the number of cases they examine enable them to identify any statistically significant correlations.[49] They are careful to speak only of the "development of general theory" or of "documenting theoretical propositions." Nonetheless, they sometimes clothe these propositions with an air of verity when they illustrate them with historical examples. As such, they permit the *incautious* reader to infer that their propositions are, in fact, the ones that would be derived from analysis of known crises. Since they distinguish their own "derived" theory from the "pure" theory of writers like Thomas Schelling, they may appear to be claiming something approaching universality and general explanatory power for their propositions. In any event, their views on threats are, in our view, the most sophisticated of any in the literature. As such, we shall refer to them from time to time, in agreement or disagreement.

We are not as modest, methodologically, as either Lebow or Snyder and Diesing. We analyzed statistically some seventy-seven threats and then tested our findings against six additional threats, and we *do* maintain that our findings enable us to say which of a number of theoretical propositions tend to be the more powerful in accounting for why some threats succeed and others fail. Our confidence is simply a matter of numbers—that is, statistical techniques exist that identify those propositions with the greater "powers of prediction." We do not claim to be able to predict with certainty the outcome of any *current* crisis (though we shall conclude by speaking of two recent events that our findings explain—the Solidarity crisis in Poland and the Falkland Islands crisis), but we do claim to have identified, with more certainty than any other analysis to date, the particular conditions that, if present, render threats more or less likely to fail. Certain conditions are simply more critical than others in the threat environment. As we shall indicate, some of these were not fully appreciated to date, and this appreciation may constitute our primary contribution to the field.

Some may question one or another aspect of our statistical analyses. We encourage such readers to consider the examples we offer (in the fashion of Lebow, Snyder, George, and others) in illustration of each statistical finding. These, at the very least, would indicate that our findings have idiosyncratic applicability. In other words, if you doubt the scientific strength of our methodology and analysis, at least allow that they are suggestive, and view our findings accordingly—as illustrated hypotheses, whether proved or unproved.

NOTES

1. Thomas C. Schelling, *The Strategy of Conflict* (Cambridge, Mass.: Harvard University Press, 1960), p. 5.

2. Ibid., pp. 6-52; J. David Singer, "Inter-National Influence: A Formal Model," *American Political Science Review* 57 (June 1963):421.

3. William W. Kaufmann, "Force and Foreign Policy," in *Military Policy and*

National Security, ed. Kaufmann (Princeton: Princeton University Press, 1956), pp. 233-67; Singer, "Inter-National Influence," pp. 420-30.

4. Bernard Brodie, *Strategy in the Missile Age* (Princeton: Princeton University Press, 1959), pp. 248-63; Bernard Brodie, "Anatomy of Deterrence," *World Politics* 2 (January 1950):173-92; William W. Kaufmann, "The Requirements of Deterrence," in *Military Policy*, ed. Kaufmann, pp. 12-38; Alexander George and Richard Smoke, *Deterrence in American Foreign Policy: Theory and Practice* (New York: Columbia University Press, 1974), pp. 21-34.

5. Michael D. Salomon, "American Strategic Thinking," University of Pittsburgh, Center for Arms Control and International Security Studies, Occasional Papers (July 1977).

6. Kaufmann, "Force and Foreign Policy," pp. 233-67.

7. George and Smoke, *Deterrence in American Foreign Policy*, pp. 41-45.

8. Ibid., p. 74.

9. Thomas W. Milburn, "What Constitutes Effective Deterrence?" *Journal of Conflict Resolution* 3 (June 1959): 138-45; Glenn H. Snyder, *Deterrence by Denial and Punishment*, Research Monograph No. 1, Woodrow Wilson School of Public and International Affairs, Center for International Studies (Princeton: Princeton University, 1959).

10. "If the opponent has an option for challenging the status quo that seems to him likely to advance his interests at an acceptable cost-benefit ratio, deterrence can fail even in the presence of a credible U.S. commitment." George and Smoke, *Deterrence in American Foreign Policy*, pp. 59-60, 526. Similar formulations may be found in Bruce Russett, "The Calculus of Deterrence," *Journal of Conflict Resolution* 7 (June 1963):97-109; and in Clinton F. Fink, "More Calculations About Deterrence," *Journal of Conflict Resolution* 9 (March 1965):54-65.

11. H.W.V. Temperley, *England and the Near East: The Crimea* (Hamden: Archon Books, 1964), p. 382. Consider also German Admiral von Tirpitz's gleeful remark, August 1, 1914, upon hearing the inaccurate report that Britain had decided to remain neutral in the war with France that Germany's threat to Russia seemed to have provoked: "The risk theory worked!" Harry F. Young, *Prince Lichnowsky and the Great War* (Athens, Ga.: University of Georgia Press, 1977), p. 116.

12. Quoted in Raymond Cohen, *Threat Perception in International Relations* (Madison, Wis.: University of Wisconsin Press, 1979), p. 41.

13. Ibid.

14. J. David Singer, *Deterrence, Arms Control, and Disarmament* (Columbus: Ohio State University Press, 1962), pp. 8-9.

15. Oran Young, *The Politics of Force: Bargaining During International Crises* (Princeton: Princeton University Press, 1968), pp. 23-31; George and Smoke, *Deterrence in American Foreign Policy*, pp. 71-82; Glenn H. Snyder, "Deterrence and Power," *Journal of Conflict Resolution* 4 (June 1960):167-71.

16. Thomas W. Milburn, "The Concept of Deterrence: Some Logical and Psychological Considerations," *Journal of Social Issues* 17 (1961):3-11.

17. Singer, "Inter-National Influence," pp. 428-29. Cf. Richard Ned Lebow, *Between Peace and War* (Baltimore: Johns Hopkins University Press, 1981).

18. Young, *Politics of Force*, p. 19.

19. Snyder, "Deterrence and Power," pp. 167-71.

20. Singer, "Inter-National Influence," pp. 428-29; George and Smoke, *Deterrence in American Foreign Policy*, pp. 7-182.

21. Singer, *Deterrence, Arms Control, and Disarmament*, p. 9.

22. Milburn, "Concept of Deterrence," pp. 3-11.

23. Singer, *Deterrence, Arms Control, and Disarmament*, p. 31.

24. Martin Patchen, "Decision Theory in the Study of National Action: Problems and a Proposal," *Journal of Conflict Resolution* 9 (June 1965):164-76.

25. Richard J. Barnet, *The Roots of War* (New York: Atheneum Publishers, 1972), pp. 95-136.

26. Russett, "Calculus of Deterrence," pp. 97-109.

27. Franklin B. Weinstein, "The Concept of a Commitment in International Relations," *Journal of Conflict Resolution* 13 (1969): 39-56.

28. Morton A. Kaplan, "The Calculus of Nuclear Deterrence," *World Politics* 2 (October 1958):40.

29. Singer, *Deterrence, Arms Control, and Disarmament*, p. 57.

30. Thomas C. Schelling, *Arms and Influence* (New Haven: Yale University Press, 1961), pp. 35-39, 87-89, 116-25; Schelling, *Strategy of Conflict*, pp. 1-30, 38-43, 119-30, 137-39; Snyder, "Deterrence and Power," p. 171.

31. Herman Kahn, *On Escalation: Metaphors and Scenarios* (New York: Praeger, 1965), pp. 9-51, 57-61.

32. Ibid; Schelling, *Strategy of Conflict*, pp. 21-37, 110, 111, 119–61; Snyder, "Deterrence and Power," p. 171.

33. Stephen Maxwell, "Rationality in Deterrence," Institute for Strategic Studies, *Adelphi Paper* No. 50 (1968), pp. 4-18; Philip Green, *Deadly Logic: The Theory of Nuclear Deterrence* (Columbus: Ohio State University Press, 1966), pp. 157-211; Marc Pilisuk, *International Conflict and Social Policy* (Englewood Cliffs, N.J.: Prentice-Hall, 1972), pp. 92–107.

34. See Edward Luttwak, *The Political Uses of Sea Power* (Baltimore: Johns Hopkins University Press, 1974), pp. 25–26, for a similar argument. Cf. David Baldwin, "Power Analysis and Word Politics," *World Politics* 31 (Jan. 1979):188–92.

35. Snyder, *Deterrence by Denial and Punishment; Livy*, trans. Evan Sage, vol. 10 (Cambridge, Mass.: Harvard University Press, 1935), pp. 55–57; F. W. Wallbank, *Philip V of Macedon* (Cambridge, England: Cambridge University Press, 1940), p. 133.

In fairness to Glenn Snyder, we must point out that his most recent study reports that none of the sixteen crises he and his colleague studied included a "committing threat" (that is, a "Chicken" game). Snyder and Paul Diesing, *Conflict Among Nations* (Princeton: Princeton University Press, 1977), p. 214. The Abydos case was the only such "Chicken" threat we uncovered. "Chicken" is an exceptionally uncommon game in the real international arena. Henry Kissinger *implies* that he was engaging in such a game with the Soviets in October 1973 by ordering a "Red Alert" when he writes of the action: "Two could play at Chicken." (*Years of Upheaval* [Boston: Little, Brown], p. 589.) But his public remarks over the next several days, assuring all that the "Red Alert" was *not* intended as a nuclear threat, significantly undercut his own evaluation of the measure.

36. Graham T. Allison, *Essence of Decision: Explaining the Cuban Missile Crisis* (Boston: Little, Brown, 1971); Graham Allison, "Conceptual Models and the Cuban Missile Crisis," *American Political Science Review* 63 (1969):689–718.

37. Colin Gray, quoted in Patrick Morgan, *Deterrence: A Conceptual Analysis* (Beverly Hills, Calif.: Sage, 1977), p. 65.

38. Morton H. Halperin, *Bureaucratic Politics and Foreign Policy* (Washington, D.C.: Brookings Institution, 1974); Charles E. Lindblom, *The Intelligence of Democracy: De-*

cision Making Through Mutual Adjustment (New York: Free Press, 1965), especially chaps. 2, 3, 4, 5; Allison, *Essence of Decision,* pp. 144–84; Allison, ''Conceptual Models,'' pp. 705–18.

39. John D. Steinbruner, *The Cybernetic Theory of Decision: New Dimensions of Political Analysis* (Princeton: Princeton University Press, 1974); Steinbruner, ''Beyond Rational Deterrence: The Struggle of New Conceptions,'' *World Politics* 28 (January 1976):233–45; Jack L. Snyder, ''Rationality at the Brink: The Role of Cognitive Processes in Failures of Deterrence,'' *World Politics* 30 (April 1978):345–65; Ole Holsti, *Crisis, Escalation, War* (Montreal: McGill–Queen's University Press, 1972), pp. 7–25.

40. Jack Snyder, ''Rationality at the Brink,'' pp. 350–65.

41. Morgan, *Deterrence*, pp. 79–82.

42. For an excellent effort to refine the theories of rational decisionmaking and coercive diplomacy, see Morgan, *Deterrence,* passim.

43. J. David Singer and associates, *Explaining War: Selected Papers from the Correlates of War Project* (Beverly Hills, Calif.: Sage, 1979), p. 13. Quincy Wright was among the first to consult history in studying crises; Singer's Correlates of War Project is the most ambitious, but one also must note the important work of scholars like Bruce Russett, Alexander George, Glenn Snyder, Oran Young, and R. Ned Lebow in this regard.

44. This is not to say that such studies cannot do these sorts of things quite well. For example, we regard Glenn Paige's *The Korean Decision* (New York: 1970), Ole Hosti's *Crisis, Escalation, War,* and Charles Lockhard's *The Efficacy of Threats in International Interaction Strategies* (Beverly Hills, Calif.: Sage Professional Papers in International Studies, vol. 2, series No. 02–023, 1973) as exceptionally provocative and insightful ones, albeit each deals with but one crisis.

45. Evan Luard, "Conciliation and Deterrence: A Comparison of Political Strategies in the Interwar and Postwar Periods," *World Politics* 19 (January 1967):167–89; Jonathan Knight, "Risks of War and Deterrence Logic," *Canadian Journal of Political Science* 6 (March 1973):21–36.

46. Allison, *Essence of Decision,* p. 262.

47. Snyder and Diesing, *Conflict Among Nations,* p. 4.

48. R. Ned Lebow, *Between Peace and War,* p. 5.

49. One recent study of interstate threats that does make such a claim is Bruce Bueno de Mesquita's *The War Trap* (New Haven: Yale University Press, 1981). He analyzes some ninety threats (as well as a larger number of other crises and interventions) from the nineteenth and twentieth centuries, testing a sophisticated rational-actor model (though only with ''hard'' equal-interval data on actual capabilities, formal alliances, and distances), but he does not ask our questions either. His ''success-failure'' dependent variable is dichotomous (ours is a four-point ordinal scale). And ''success'' to him does not mean that war was not waged; ''success'' refers to the threatener's attaining his objectives, with or without war (our ''objectives only'' version of the outcome variables). Hence, he finds such factors as actual military capabilities to be of consequence where we do not.

2

Methodology

A prerequisite for studying the political utility of coercive diplomacy is to restrict the universe of possible threats to a manageable number. We decided to limit the study to military threats, even though such threats are only one of a nation's instruments for exerting pressure in the international arena. Theoretically, one might compare military threats to purely economic, moral, or diplomatic sanctions. With the appearance of Klaus Knorr's *The Power of Nations* and *Power and Wealth,* it seemed to us that economic threats had been satisfactorily examined, and we decided to look only at threats with a military dimension. A number of these also included economic coercion, to be sure, and we were interested in knowing whether that appeared to make a difference, but we saw no need to repeat Knorr's insightful analysis. We accept his findings: economic coercion alone succeeds but rarely.[1]

Others have discussed those political uses of military forces that are designed to reassure, assuage, or persuade allies and neutrals.[2] We recognize the potential value of such studies, but we decided against the inclusion of such categories in our analysis. We would concern ourselves exclusively with crises involving military threats.

While all crises faced by a state may not involve formal military threats, we must nonetheless begin with a definition of an "international crisis" as a means of establishing threshold conditions for considering individual instances of coercive diplomacy. We like Michael Brecher's distinction between the conceptual and the operational aspects of a crisis.[3] On the conceptual level, a crisis involves a structural change in the external environment faced by the state. The change must be of sufficient magnitude to convince decisionmakers that important values are being endangered and that some sort of response must be devised. Expressed in operational terms, the crisis would involve four necessary conditions:

1. A recognition of an unanticipated change in the external environment;
2. A perception of the external change as a threat to values held by decisionmakers;

3. A high probability of military hostilities;
4. A finite time limit in which to formulate a proper response to the threat.[4]

The first three points appear to be self-explanatory; however, the fourth may require some amplification. Finite, in this case, means short or limited only in the sense that the decisionmakers perceive themselves to be operating under temporal constraints. What is important is that decisions in crises are reached under pressure, generated by the decisionmakers' belief in a time limit, not necessarily by a predetermined period of time such as is generally specified in an ultimatum. (Hence, given the relatively subjective nature of the concept and the varied communication problems faced by pre–twentieth-century policymakers, we allowed the concept of a finite period some operational flexibility for cases in the more distant past.)

Our next task was to decide what we meant by a threat, and what would make that threat a success or a failure. For our purposes, a threat occurred only if leaders of one or more powers signaled clearly (either in public or in private) a willingness to use military force against one or more other nations in order to deter them from doing something or to compel them to do something. We decided that a statesman's vague or general remarks that bore no particular relation to any issue, dispute, or object of contention; that did not appear to be aimed with timeliness or urgency at any particular target nation or nations; or that sought to procure no particular behavior with any substantial immediacy would not qualify. The movement or mobilization of troops, warships, or aircraft in the course of the crisis was not absolutely necessary, though such movement would certainly serve to verify evidence that statesman X's more or less oblique remarks were intended to threaten, and such movements could serve as the equivalent of such remarks if they were unambiguously threatening in character.[5] We assessed the clarity and consistency of the communication of the threat's objectives and means of implementation and noted any time limits imposed.

A threat that was ignored or rejected "failed," even if the threatener decided to back up its warning with muscle and won its objectives by force of arms, because we decided that a threat can be said to "succeed," either wholely or in part, only if the threatener's objectives are at least partially attained without recourse to fighting. We equated the threat that is followed by war with the bluff that was called. This mixes apples and oranges, to be sure, but on the level with which we were primarily concerned—the threat environment—these two types of threats have one preeminent thing in common: they failed to obtain political objectives by the mere *threat* to use force. And in that sense, though they may be "apple" and "orange," they are still "fruit." (Nonetheless, we did separately code the degree to which the threatener's objectives were attained when force *was* used, in order that the outcome of our cases could also be ordered in terms of the attainment of the threatener's objectives alone.)[6]

Inasmuch as we restricted ourselves to threats actually made in the real world between national powers, we ignored three potentially useful, but fundamentally different, universes—gang (or street) wars, civil wars, and threats that were considered by policymakers but never issued. American leaders considered making a military threat to the Soviets in 1948, when the Soviets challenged their access to West Berlin, and they did order the repositioning of some U.S. air units, but, essentially, they decided against reliance upon military threats, opting for the less menacing Berlin Airlift instead.[7]

Recently, a note in President Harry Truman's own handwriting, part of a journal he kept while in the White House, came to light. Dated January 27, 1952, it read in part:

> It seems to me that the proper approach [to the communist enemies in the Korean War] now would be an ultimatum, with a 10-day expiration limit, informing Moscow that we intend to blockade the China coast—and that we intend to destroy every military base in Manchuria, including submarine bases, by means now in our control [nuclear weapons], and if there is further interference, we shall eliminate any ports or cities necessary to accomplish our peaceful purposes.
>
> This means all-out war. . . . This is the final choice for the Soviet government to decide whether it desires to survive or not.[8]

Despite these intentions, President Truman issued no such threat. Further consideration of this course of action must have led him to consign the notion to the "ash-heap of history." As such, while the moment is fascinating and well worth analysis, we shall not dwell on it here, for it was "a thought rejected."

To restrict ourselves to threats actually issued, we are aware that we could consequently say little about the causes of threats, for such a study would have to explain why certain proposed threats were *not* issued before it could say why other iterated threats *were*. But we simply are not asking that question. We are rather concerned with knowing why certain actual threats failed, and why others succeeded. Consequently, our universe of cases is composed entirely of threats *not* rejected as inappropriate or unfeasible by policymakers; it is composed of threats actually made.

This is not to say that we ignored the other universe, composed of potential threats considered but rejected. On the contrary, we are fully aware of the likelihood that the characteristics of the two categories—threats considered but rejected as measures by policymakers, and threats considered and implemented—differ considerably. Consequently, our findings will be of only limited value to a policymaker who is *considering* making a threat,[9] for we can say little of why some decisionmakers have decided against such a course of action. If a policymaker were to turn to our findings and decide that his threat would succeed because the variables we identify as the more important ones in explaining the success or failure of the threat all appeared to favor his state in the crisis in hand, he might awake the next morning to discover his "hand called" or, worse, to find himself at war. The reason for his chagrin would be that several of the variables in our statistical models do not contain much variation in the strength of the values that we gave for the status or intentions of the threateners in our case analyses; all had comparably high (or low) values. That is, certain things appear to be given; one rarely issues a threat unless these conditions are present (or absent). (More on this in the next chapter.) It will suffice now to repeat that we shall only be able to discuss why actual threats have failed or succeeded, not why they were made in the first place.

The cases consist of instances in which one or more major powers threatened one or more distinct target nations, where the bonds between the targets or threateners were such that the threat could be said to represent all or to affect each uniformly. In the course of a crisis, the target of the initial threat sometimes offered its own counterthreat. This occasionally posed a problem in case selection, but we generally found that as the crisis became pronounced, the powers tended to become more identifiably "target" or "threatener." If the character of the threat differed substantially among the target nations, if the targets themselves were dissimilar in their responses, or if a distinct counterthreat drew its own distinct response, each threat might be coded as a separate case. In a few instances, such as the Second Peloponnesian War, the outbreak of World War I, the Corfu crisis of 1922-1923, the crises that began with Munich and ended in World War II, Lebanon in 1958, and the Laos and Berlin crises in 1961, two or more separate targets were coded, as one threat led to another, thus creating more than one case from what others might call the same crisis. But this was rare, and for reasons to be provided later, only these six crises retained their character as discrete units after the process of weighting cases was completed. Given the importance that has been accorded four of these six crises by scholars and statesmen alike, we felt that this double-counting was not unwarranted.[10]

How were the cases chosen? We wanted to code a substantial (statistically worthwhile) number of cases from both the modern, post–1945 nuclear age and the pre-nuclear past in order to see whether any features of the threat environment differed from one era to the other. Locating a substantial number of codable cases in the pre-nuclear past was more difficult than we had expected, given the number of variables for which we sought codable information.[11] Most historians have not asked the same questions we were asking, or have not gathered, in a convenient place and form, the information we sought.[12] And, of course, some information, such as that pertaining to the perceptions of the state actors of one another's interests, capabilities, and intentions, was simply unavailable—either buried undiscovered in a foreign archive or forever lost. After consulting treatises, bibliographies, and texts, and seeking the aid of professional colleagues,[13] we identified some forty-five codable past cases.

This list of cases from the past is, of course, shorter than it could conceivably be, but we feel that it is satisfactory for three reasons. These cases were sufficiently important to receive adequate scholarly attention, and, as such, they *may* have had more influence in the shaping of opinions as to "what will work and what won't'' than threats that have not been amply recorded and discussed. More significant, since a prime goal of this study is to learn which independent variables best "predict" or offer the "maximum likelihood estimate" of the success or failure of a threat, we felt that an excessive number of cases from the premodern era would not be appropriate. Many analysts assume that cases drawn from the modern era of high technology and rapid communication are more likely to be predictive of the future than those drawn from the distant past, or even the more recent pre-radio or pre–rapid-firing eras (a notion, by the way, that our findings largely do not substantiate). Moreover, we were aware of a number of other theoretically codable threats (for example, England versus Holland, 1672; Italy versus Turkey, 1911) that we did not code because we agreed that the central feature of these threats, both of which led to war, was the severity of the demands made and the general intransigence of the threatener—that is, the threat was essentially a pretext for war. We had already determined (in a preliminary analysis) that this intransigence was most significant,[14] but we thereupon decided to suppress the significance of these sorts of cases. We had ''discovered,'' and we hereby report, the obvious: the intransigence of the threatener's leadership can lead to war.[15] Having unearthed this truism, we saw no value in adding more of these sorts of cases to our *N*. In short, we coded until further coding appeared unfeasible, inappropriate, or unnecessary.

A similar survey of the literature and consultation with experts produced some thirty-two codable cases from the nuclear age.[16] In this instance, our sources of information (some of them quite highly placed and informed) lead us to believe that our sample is very close to being the total universe of such modern cases involving major powers. Table 2.1, organized chronologically, constitutes our list of cases.

Our system was that one individual assumed primary responsibility for the study of a case while the others read more selectively. After an initial twenty- to thirty-minute description of the case, accompanied by the distribution of a one- or two-page synopsis, the case leader answered questions, citing directly from essays or books brought to the coding room, and the group then collectively coded the case, arguing to a consensus agreement any differences of opinion regarding the coding of a particular variable.

Our codebook ''grew like Topsy'' from an initial sortie of fifteen to ninety-three ordinal and eighteen nominal independent variables. These variables were designed for several functions: to gauge the objectives of the threatener(s) and target(s), to measure the interests of the parties and to describe their decision-making, to measure relative capabilities, to deal with the tactics employed, to record the various perceptions held by one power of the other in the course of the crisis, to deal with the clarity and accuracy of the threat transmission, to examine the external environment, and to measure changes in the foregoing variables during the course of the crisis, as well as to measure and describe the outcome (five dependent variables). (Table 2.2 is a listing and brief description of these variables, organized by category, each with its potential values.) Most

Table 2.1
CASES
(ARRANGED CHRONOLOGICALLY)

Weight of Case	Outcome Ranking*	File No.	Threatener(s)	Target(s)	Date	At Issue (in brief)
PRE-NUCLEAR PAST						
1.300	4	55	Athens	Potidaea	431 B.C.	Suzerainty/Sovereignty
1.300	1	57	Sparta	Acanthus	431 B.C.	Grape crop
1.300	4	56	Athens	Melos	416 B.C.	Suzerainty/Sovereignty
0.780	4	76	Rome	Carthage	218 B.C.	Iberia
0.650	4	62	Rome	Macedon	200 B.C.	Greece
1.300	1	68	Vikings	France	A.D. 845	Gold
1.300	4	54	Mongols	Khwarazm	A.D. 1218-19	Sovereignty
0.975	4	69	England	France	A.D. 1415	Poitou and Picardy
1.300	2	42	France	Florence	A.D. 1495	Florentine forts
1.625	3	67	Britain	Russia	A.D. 1719	Sweden
1.300	1	60	Britain	King of Two Sicilies	A.D. 1742	Naples
1.625	2	66	China	Vietnam	A.D. 1770	Suzerainty
1.625	4	70	Prussia	Austria	A.D. 1778	Bavaria
0.975	4	41	Britain	Egypt, France	A.D. 1839-40	Syria
0.975	4	77	Britain	China	A.D. 1840-41	Opium

1.300	1	46	Britain	United States	A.D. 1846	Oregon Territory
1.625	2	71	Austria	Prussia	A.D. 1850	Hesse-Kassel
1.300	4	37	Britain, France	Russia	A.D. 1853	Walachia/Moldavia/the Straits
0.650	4	48	Austria	Kingdom of Sardinia	A.D. 1859	Lombardy
0.650	4	36	Prussia, Austria	Denmark	A.D. 1863	Schleswig-Holstein
0.975	2	72	United States	France	A.D. 1865-66	Mexico
0.520	4	50	Prussia	Austria	A.D. 1866	Holstein/Hesse/Saxony
0.975	4	33	France	Prussia	A.D. 1870	Leopold's candidacy
0.325	3	49	Russia	Turkey	A.D. 1877	Istanbul/the Straits
1.625	4	58	Britain	Egypt	A.D. 1882	Suez Canal
0.325	4	52	Japan	China	A.D. 1895	Korea
1.625	1	73	United States	Britain	A.D. 1895-96	Boundary between Venezuela and British Guiana
1.300	1	53	Russia, Germany, France	Japan	A.D. 1896	Liotung Peninsula
0.650	4	47	United States	Spain	A.D. 1898	Cuba
1.300	4	34	Britain	Boers	A.D. 1899	Boer sovereignty
1.625	1	74	Austria	Serbia	A.D. 1908-09	Bosnia-Herzegovina
1.040	2	65	Britain	Germany	A.D. 1911	Morocco
0.975	2	43	Austria	Serbia	A.D. 1913	Serbian access to sea

Table 2.1 Continued

Weight of Case	Outcome Ranking*	File No.	Threatener(s)	Target(s)	Date	At Issue (in brief)
PRE-NUCLEAR PAST						
0.325	4	44	Austria	Serbia	A.D. 1914	Serbian sovereignty
1.625	4	45	Russia	Austria, Germany	A.D. 1914	Serbia
0.650	4	35	United States	Mexico	A.D. 1914	Tampico
1.300	2	59	Japan	China	A.D. 1915	"21 Demands"
0.975	3	38	United States	Germany	A.D. 1916	Neutral rights on seas
0.624	3	51	Britain	Turkey	A.D. 1922	Chanak/Turkish sovereignty
0.980	4	63	Italy	Greece	A.D. 1923	Corfu
1.300	2	64	Britain	Italy	A.D. 1923	Corfu
1.300	1	40	Germany	Britain	A.D. 1938	Czechoslovakia
1.300	1	39	Germany	Czechoslovakia	A.D. 1939	Czech sovereignty
0.325	4	75	Germany	Poland	A.D. 1939	Danzig/Polish sovereignty
0.300	4	61	Britain	Germany	A.D. 1939	Poland
POST-NUCLEAR PRESENT						
1.040	1	22	United States, Iran	Soviets	A.D. 1946	Azerbaijan
0.780	2	20	United States, Yugoslavia	Soviets	A.D. 1950-51	Yugoslav sovereignty

0.975	4	26	China	United States	A.D. 1951	Chinese security (Yalu River)
1.625	4	15	United States	Cambodia	A.D. 1956	Cambodian independence
1.300	3	29	Soviets	Poland	A.D. 1956	Polish leadership
0.520	2	31	Soviets	Britain, France	A.D. 1956	Suez
0.585	4	13	United States, Turkey	Syria	A.D. 1957	Syrian posture
1.625	4	24	Soviets	United States	A.D. 1958	Berlin/German treaty
1.300	2	16	United States	China	A.D. 1958	Quemoy
0.104	2	2	United States	Soviets	A.D. 1958	Lebanon
1.040	3	18	United States	United Arab Republic	A.D. 1958	Lebanon
1.625	1	14	United States	Ecuador	A.D. 1960	Andean border with Peru
1.040	1	9	United States	Dominican Republic	A.D. 1961	Trujillo
1.300	2	7	United States	Soviets	A.D. 1961	Berlin/German treaty
1.625	3	25	Soviets	United States	A.D. 1961	Berlin/German treaty
1.040	3	1	United States	Soviets	A.D. 1961	Laos
1.300	3	17	United States	North Vietnam	A.D. 1961	Laos
1.625	1	30	Britain	Iraq	A.D. 1961	Kuwait
1.300	2	4	United States	Soviets	A.D. 1962	Cuba/missiles
0.975	3	27	China	India	A.D. 1962	Himalayan border
0.390	4	10	United States	North Vietnam	A.D. 1965	Troops in South Vietnam

Table 2.1 Continued

Weight of Case	Outcome Ranking*	File No.	Threatener(s)	Target(s)	Date	At Issue (in brief)
POST-NUCLEAR PRESENT						
1.300	4	28	Soviets	Czechoslovakia	A.D. 1968	Soviet suzerainty
0.325	2	21	United States, Yugoslavia	Soviets	A.D. 1968	Yugoslav sovereignty
1.300	4	3	United States	North Korea	A.D. 1968	USS *Pueblo*
0.390	2	19	United States	North Korea	A.D. 1969	EC-121
1.300	1	32	Soviets	Ghana	A.D. 1969	Soviet vessel
0.520	1	8	United States	Syria	A.D. 1970	Jordan/Palestinians
0.520	4	5	United States	India	A.D. 1971	Pakistan
0.780	4	11	United States	North Vietnam	A.D. 1972	Truce talks
1.625	2	12	United States	Soviets	A.D. 1973	Middle East tensions
0.312	4	6	United States	Cambodia	A.D. 1975	SS *Mayaguez*
0.650	2	23	United States, Kenya	Uganda	A.D. 1976	Kenya

*Explanation of ranking:
1 = total success w/o warfare
2 = substantial success w/o warfare
3 = partial success w/o warfare
4 = failure (no success, or warfare)

Table 2.2
VARIABLES

I. ORDINAL VARIABLES, BY CATEGORY

A. Interests

1 (& 2). Extent of interest the threatener (and, separately, the target) had in the object or area of contention by virtue of its location in the threatener's (or target's) sphere of influence. (1-10) scale

3 (& 4). Degree to which the location of the object or area of contention was considered of strategic-military importance by the threatener (and, separately, by the target). (1-10 scale)

5 (& 6). Degree to which the crisis, defined broadly, carried fairly immediate consequences for the military security of the threatener (and, separately, of the target). (1-10 scale)

7 (& 8). The worst-case extent of physical risk that the target (and, separately, the threatener) felt it would suffer in the event the crisis ended in bloodshed, the *likelihood* of such bloodshed being disregarded in calculating this cost-risk variable. (1-10 scale)

9 (10, 11, & 12). Extent of target's economic investments, as a percentage of all the target's foreign investments, in the threatener (and, separately, the extent of the threatener's investment in the target; the target's in the area of contention; and the threatener's in the area of contention). (1-10 scale)

13 (14, 15, & 16). Extent of target's markets, as a percentage of all the target's foreign markets, in the threatener (and, separately, the extent of the threatener's markets in the target; the target's in the area of contention; and the threatener's in the area of contention). (1-10 scale)

17 (18, 19, & 20). Degree to which the target relied on critical resources imported from the threatener (and, separately, the degree to which the threatener relied on such resources from the target; the target, on resources from the area of contention; and the threatener, on resources from the area of contention). (1-10 scale)

21 (& 22). The degree to which the crisis affected the economic viability of the target (and, separately, of the threatener). (1-10 scale)

23 (& 24). Degree to which a commitment made in the international arena by the target (or threatener) was viewed as being important or at stake in the crisis ("commitment"). (1-10 scale)

25 (& 26). The extent of the threatener's (and, separately, the target's) identification with the area of contention by virtue of any historical, ethnic, or colonial ties. (1-10 scale)

27 (& 28). The degree to which the target (and, separately, the threatener) regarded the crisis as one in which moral or ideological issues were at stake. (1-10 scale)

29 (& 30). The degree to which the target (and, separately, the threatener) regarded itself as having important "political power" interests, whether they were questions of sovereignty or aggrandizement, at stake in the crisis. (1-10 scale)

31 (& 32). The degree to which one or more bureaucracies within the target (and, separately, within the threatener) were at odds in the crisis with the key decisionmakers regarding policy matters because the policies of the leaders were at odds with the interests of that bureaucracy or bureaucracies. (1-10 scale)

33 (& 34). The degree to which the leader of the target (and, separately, the leader of the threatener) regarded his personal leadership interests as being imperilled by the crisis. (1-10 scale)

B. Objectives

35 (& 36). Type of objective of the threatener (and, separately, of the target), ranging from status quo to radical revision of international scene. (1-5 scale)

37 (& 38). Degree to which the threatener's (and, separately, the target's) objectives in the crisis were of unlimited or uncompromising nature in the crisis. (1-5 scale)

39. Degree to which the threatener was uninterested in a negotiated settlement of the crisis ("warmonger" weight variable). (1-5 scale)

C. Capabilities

40. Ratio of population of target coalition and threatener coalition. (1-5 scale) (1 = threatener substantially larger than target, 2 = threatener slightly larger than target, 3 = threatener and target about equal, and so on.)

41. Ratio of GNP of target and threatener. (1-5 scale)

42. Ratio of nuclear-force levels of target and threatener. (1-5 scale)

43. Ratio of conventional tactical forces of target and threatener. (1-5 scale)

44. Ratio of effectiveness of the political systems in the target and the threatener in mobilizing resources and support for government policies. (1-5 scale)

45. Ratio of the degree of cohesiveness (versus factionalization) among elites in the target and the threatener. (1-5 scale)

46. Ratio of the stability of the regimes in the target and the threatener. (1-5 scale)

47. Ratio of the degree to which the top decisionmakers were secure within the target and the threatener. (1-5 scale)

48. Ratio of the ability of the target and the threatener to penetrate and attract elite "clients" or friends within each other's decisionmaking system. (1-5 scale)

49. Ratio of the "commitments" record (that is, the history of a willingness to live up to foreign promises, at whatever expense) of target and threatener. (1-5 scale)

50. Ratio of the degree to which the formal or informal alliance systems added to the support of the target and the threatener. (1-5 scale)

51. Ratio of the leverage that the target (or threatener) had over the other by virtue of the economic dependency of the one on the other. (1-5 scale)

52. Ratio of the leverage that the target (or threatener) had over the other by virtue of the military dependency of the one on the other. (1-5 scale)

53 (& 54). Extent to which the populace supported the policies of the threatener (and, separately, of the target) in the crisis. (1-5 scale)

55. Ratio of threatener's overall capabilities to target's (smallest-space analysis-generated variable) (1 = highly unbalanced in threatener's favor, and so on.)

D. "Situational" Variables

56. Level of regional tensions. (1-5 scale)

57. Degree to which "the lay of the land" or nature of the disputed terrain had effect on the suitability of the operations of the contenders. (1-3 scale) (1 = more suitable for threatener, 2 = even, and so on.)

58. Degree to which distance from the scene of operations had effect on the fortunes of the contenders. (1-3 scale)

59. Degree to which the climate of international opinion tended to legitimize the objectives of one or the other of the contenders. (1-3 scale) (1 = legitimizes threatener's objectives, 2 = even or no legitimation of either, and so on.)

60 (& 61). Record of previous threatener (and, separately, target) operations in the area. (1-4 scale) (1 = goals substantially achieved, and so on.)

62. Character of world system at time of crisis (bipolar-multipolar). (1-5 scale) (1 = extremely bipolar, and so on.)

63. Degree of importance of crisis to world balance-of-power systems. (1-5 scale) (1 = essentially unimportaant, and so on.)

E. Clarity and Accuracy of Threat

64 (& 65). Clarity of communications between threatener and target (and, separately, between target and threatener) regarding goals. (1-4 scale) (1 = message transmission always clear and consistent, 2 = message transmission generally clear and consistent, and so on.)

66 (& 67). Clarity of communications between parties regarding means. (1-4 scale)

68 (& 69). Clarity of communications between parties regarding time limits (if applicable). (1-4 scale)

70. Degree to which target understood threat (''target understands'' weight variable). (1-5 scale)

71. In deterrence cases, the degree to which we were satisfied that the deterrence took place—that is, that the target's response was a function of the threat itself and not of some other external variable or variables (the ''true deterrence'' weight variable). (1-5 scale) (1 = quite sure that deterrence took place, 5 = quite sure that target never intended to act, and that threat does not explain target behavior.)

F. Tactical Variables

72 (& 73). Degree to which the threatener's (and, separately, the target's) initial selection of tactics left itself further options. (1-5 scale)

74. Degree to which the ''initiative'' was maintained by the threatener or the target throughout the crisis. (1-3 scale) (1 = generally maintained by threatener, 2 = about as often by each, 3 = generally maintained by target.)

75. Suitability of tactical forces, if any, put forward by the threatener in conveying the threat in terms of what it would have taken to force the target militarily to observe the demands of the threatener. (1-10 scale) (1 = no forces deployed, 2 = only about a quarter of what would be needed deployed, 3 = about half of what would be needed deployed, . . . 10 = over twice as much as would be needed deployed.)

76 (& 77). Extent of display of perception by threatener (and, separately, by target) that its interests were affected by the crisis. (1-5 scale) (1 = high display, . . . 5 = no display.)

G. Perceptions Held by One Power of the Other in the Crisis

78 (& 79). Threatener's (and, separately, target's) perception of the degree of importance of the interests the target (threatener) felt were at stake in the crisis. (1-5 scale) (1 = threatener perceived target's interests in the crisis to be considerable, and so on.)

80 (& 81). Target's (and, separately, threatener's) perception of objectives that the threatener (target) had in the crisis. (1-5 scale)

82 (& 83). Threatener's (and, separately, target's) perception of the target's (threatener's) overall capabilities. (1-5 scale)

84. Target's (and, separately, threatener's) perception of the credibility of the threats (promises) offered in the crisis. (1-3 scale)

H. ''Change'' Variables

86 (& 87). Change in rigidity of objectives of threatener (and, separately, of target) in the course of the crisis. (1-3 scale) (1 = more flexible, and so on.)

88 (& 89). Change in strength of target's (and, separately, of threatener's) capabilities in the course of the crisis. (1-3 scale) (1 = increase, and so on.)

90 (& 91). Change in threatener's (and, separately, in target's) perception of the magnitude of its interests involved in the course of the crisis. (1-3 scale)

92 (& 93). Change in target's (and, separately, in threatener's) perception in the course of the crisis of the importance of the interests the threatener (target) felt were at stake in the crisis. (1-3 scale)

I. Consequences of Threat

1, 2, & 3. Degree to which threatener's objectives were attained and threat "succeeded." (1-7 scale) (1 = no war, objectives totally attained; 2 = no war, objectives substantially attained; 3 = no war, objectives partially attained; 4 = no war, no objectives attained; 5 = war, objectives totally attained, and so on.) (4 through 7 recodable as "failure.")

4. Degree to which the threat affected the long-range (future) relations between the threatener and the target (either by causing the target to become *more* or *less* accommodative to the future policies of the threatener). (1-5 scale) (1 = target became very accommodative in future, and so on.)

5. Degree to which the threat affected the long-range (future) ability of the threatener to get the target to do what it wanted done. (1-5 scale) (1 = strongly increases ability of threatener, . . . 5 = strongly increases propensity of target to resist threatener.)

II. NOMINAL VARIABLES

1 (& 2). Type of interest the threatener (and, separately, the target) perceived to be of prime importance in the crisis (among the following: economic interests; political power interests [prestige, sovereignty]; ideological-moral interests; military security interests; "commitment"—"identification" interests).

3 (& 4). Specific type(s) of any military rewards and/or punishments used by threatener (and, separately, by target) in the course of the crisis. (24 categories)

5 (& 7). Specific type(s) of economic rewards and/or punishments used by threatener (and, separately, by target) in the course of the crisis. (18 categories)

7 (&8). Specific type(s) of political rewards and/or punishments used by threatener (and, separately, by target) in the course of the crisis. (20 categories)

9 (& 10). Specific type of diplomatic technique(s) employed by threatener (and, separately, by target). (6 categories)

11 (& 12). Specific type(s) of "credibility-establishment gestures" used by threatener (and, separately, by target) in course of crisis. (7 categories)

13 (& 14). Type of change(s) in capabilities of threatener (and, separately, of target) in course of crisis. (6 categories)

15. Type of regime of target. (4 categories) (1 = traditional oligarchy/dictatorship, 2 = constitutional pluralist, 3 = bureaucratic modernizing, 4 = revolutionary modernizing.)

16. Date of crisis. (1-4 scale) (1 = earliest case to fall of *ancien régime* and emergence of mass armies [1790]; 2 = 1791 to World War I; 3 = World War I to Hiroshima; 4 = Hiroshima to present.)

17. Character of the behavior demanded of the target by the threatener. (3 categories) (1 = deterrence only, 2 = demands action under way be stopped, 3 = compellence only.)

18. Name of threatener. (4 categories) (1 = U.S., 2 = USSR, 3 = China, 4 = other. Included simply to enable us to isolate U.S. threats and Communist threats.)

of these variables were derived from hypotheses developed in the literature on threats.[17] But some (such as one noting the degree to which the threatener itself initially intends that war ensue) were added as we proceeded and perceived additional hypotheses that ought to be included.[18]

We shall not state here each and every hypothesis incorporated into these independent variables, as such a list would merely repeat the self-evident information in Table 2.2. But a few examples may be in order. The very first of the ordinal variables, A.1, is included to test the hypothesis that, all other things being equal, threats will succeed when the threatener has extensive interest in the area of contention in the crisis by virtue of that area's being located in the threatener's acknowledged sphere of influence. Similarly, variable E.64 is designed to test the hypothesis that, all other things being equal, threats will succeed when the communications between threatener and target are always clear and consistent.

Nor will we illustrate the way each and every one of our hypotheses-variables were made operational. In many instances, that process is all too obvious; we gathered information about trade, population, GNP, conventional-force levels, distances, and the like, and coded appropriately. But some of the variables consist of more subjective issues, such as the perception that the threatener's leaders had of the target's capabilities or interests, the perception that the target's leaders had of the credibility of the threat, the perception that the target's (or the threatener's) leaders had of the risks of physical and economic damage its nation might incur in the event of war, or other such subjective matters. Perhaps it is incumbent on us to provide some illustrations of how we used evidence in determining the proper ordinal value to assign to these sorts of variables in a particular case.

Let us begin by considering a passage in a letter that the French ambassador to Britain, François Guizot, wrote to the Duc de Broghie on September 23, 1840, for the French cabinet's consideration. Tensions between Britain and France were high as a consequence of their equally vigorous support of different sides in a Turko-Egyptian war. The British were on the verge of threatening war with France if France persisted in encouraging the Egyptian leader's aggressive policies in Syria. (Indeed, the threat was issued only a few weeks after Guizot penned these thoughts, and its consequence was the French monarch's dismissal of the hard-line French premier, Adolphe Thiers, and his replacement by none other than Guizot himself.) Guizot's thoughts, then, are one indication (there are others, quite comparable) of the views of the French leadership. Guizot begins with the central question:

> Should France go to war in order that the Pasha of Egypt keep Syria?
>
> Obviously, this is not a sufficiently large interest to become a cause of war. France, which did not go to war to liberate Poland from Russia and Italy from Austria, cannot reasonably do so in order that Syria should be in the hands of the Pasha rather than those of the Sultan.

The war would be either oriental or naval, or continental and general; if naval, the disparity of forces, damages, and risks are uncontestable. If continental and general France could only sustain it by giving it a revolutionary character, that is to say by abandoning the honest, sage and useful politics that she has followed since 1830, and by transforming the alliance itself from four powers into an enemy coalition.[19]

Note that Guizot compares Egypt unfavorably to Poland and Italy. Consequently, we suspect that we should assign a low-degree number to variable A.26, the extent of the target's identification with the area of contention by virtue of any historical, ethnic, or colonial ties. Guizot also judges the physical risk that France would suffer to its naval and maritime interests in the event of war, which provides us with evidence relevant to the coding of variable A.8, and, finally, we notice Guizot's reference to the ''revolutionary character'' that a full-fledged war (with Britain's continental partners to the July 15 convention regarding Turkish rights—Austria, Prussia, and Russia) would have to take. Hence, we know that Guizot saw the possibility of a coalition acting against France, evidence relevant to our coding of variable C.50. Guizot's *disapproval* of such a ''revolutionary character,'' consistent with his conservative disposition, is information we will want in determining the extent to which France regarded the crisis as one in which ideological issues were at stake (variable A.28). Obviously, one must consult other evidence as well in determining the appropriate values for each of these variables,[20] but this account may explain how we could derive useful information from one document.

Since we have begun illustrating our method by discussing evidence pertaining to the Syrian crisis of 1840, let us continue with some other documents relevant to that crisis. Throughout the winter, spring, and summer of 1839–1840, the French prime minister, Adolphe Thiers, issued one statement after another of his government's commitment to the Egyptian pasha, Mehemet Ali. What change, if any, did this generate in the British Government's objective (checking the rise of Mehemet Ali) during the course of the crisis (variable H.86)? Lord Palmerston, the British foreign minister, answers the question in a letter to Sir Henry Lytton Bulwer, British chargé in Paris, on August 31, 1840:

Does Thiers imagine that such menaces and revilings that he has been pleased to deal out through his irresponsible organs have made the slightest change in our determination and intentions? If he does, he has yet much to learn as to the character and habits of the English nation.[21]

Thiers tried to learn of England's resolve through Ambassador Guizot and a German noblewoman who frequented the salons of British society. Guizot and his associate had considerable luck in penetrating the Whiggish elements of Lord Melbourne's coalition cabinet (variable C.48). When Guizot praised certain Whig peers for their friendliness in early 1841, Lord Palmerston observed:

What a painful picture does the [former] French Ambassador give of the British Cabinet, when he quietly relates his cooperation with different members of it for the purpose of thwarting the Secretary of State for Foreign Affairs and to prevent him from promoting and securing the interests of England; and how much must Privy Councillors have kept the secrets of the Cabinet when Guizot says that he knew about everything from day to day that passed in our deliberations.[22]

Let us offer another illustration from a different crisis. On August 23, 1958, the Communist Chinese Government began to shell Quemoy and broadcast threats in an attempt to dislodge Nationalist Chinese from the offshore island. The United States immediately began resupplying operations and signaled a willingness to defend the Nationalist positions with "all the force at its disposal." Within two weeks, the Communists had cut back on their shelling, deterred. How do we know that the Communist Government was deterred? On September 5 Chairman Mao delivered a speech to a meeting of party leaders:

At present we only have hand mortars and grenades. War with hydrogen and atomic bombs naturally can be feared and can make people die. Because of this we oppose fighting. . . . I simply did not calculate that the world would become so disturbed and turbulent [as a consequence of the shelling of Quemoy].[23]

In these remarks we detect evidence of assessments of costs and risks (variable A.8) of the target's perception of the threatener's capabilities (G.83) and of the degree to which we may be assured that deterrence took place (the "true deterrence" weight variable, E.71).

Another example concerns the variable measuring the threatener's "political power" interests. In December 1877 the British Government appears to have believed that its prestige was at stake (variable A.30) in a confrontation that was developing between Britain and Russia. How did we surmise this? We noted that in mid-December Queen Victoria spoke of the need to stand up to Russia lest Britain be rendered a "subservient, second-rate, cotton-spinning power." We also noted the remark of the foreign secretary, Lord Derby, regarding the prime minister, Disraeli. In late December, Derby (who would eventually resign rather than press Russia as hard as the cabinet wanted) complained that Disraeli "believes strongly in 'prestige.'"[24]

Our two final examples address the question of credibility. How did we know how to code the variable that recorded whether the target perceived the threat to be credible? The first example is that of the Polish reaction to the Nazi demands regarding Danzig and the Polish Corridor in the summer and fall of 1939. Difficult as it may be to believe now, both Beck, the Polish foreign minister, and Gluchowski, the deputy minister for war (the central Polish figures in the crisis), doubted that the Germans would fight. Gluchowski told a British diplomat that the "Wehrmacht was a great bluff, since Germany lacked the trained reserves to maintain standards." Hence, Poland was, "naturally," capable of resisting.[25]

Some forty-one years earlier, on October 1, 1898, Sir Edmund Monson, the British ambassador to France, reported to his government remarks the French foreign minister, Theophile Delcassé, had made to him regarding the Fashoda crisis (see discussion of this crisis in chapter 4). The "national honour" was at stake, Delcassé had said, and he was unable to order Captain Marchand to withdraw from Fashoda without a quid pro quo from Britain. "As to the possibility that M. Delcassé was 'bluffing,'" Monson wrote to Lord Salisbury, "I am bound to say that I believe he . . . thoroughly meant what he said."[26] Lord Salisbury might not believe Delcassé, and we would have to ascertain Salisbury's views separately, but his chief informant on the resolve of the French *did* believe the foreign minister; of that much we can be sure.

Before moving to the results of our analysis, let us challenge the reader to scan the variables listed in Table 2.2 and to jot down a list of those four or five variables the reader suspects to be the strongest predictors of the success or failure of threats. One of the potential criticisms of a study like ours might be that we simply "rediscover the obvious." That is, of course, easily said after a reader *knows* which variables our analysis identified as predictors. But a prior glance at our list of variables should reveal that there are a substantial number of "obvious" predictor-candidates, and, as we shall see in chapter 4, a dozen high-ranking policymakers whom we interviewed did *not* choose several of the variables that we identified as predictors, and *did* identify others that we did not find significant.

Those interested in an account of our statistical analysis may turn to appendix 1.

NOTES

1. Klaus Knorr, *The Power of Nations* (New York: Basic Books, 1975) and *Power and Wealth* (New York: Basic Books, 1973). We shall note such parallels we found with Knorr's work at the appropriate place. Suffice it to say now that we did find parallels.

2. See, especially, Barry Blechman and Stephen S. Kaplan, *Force Without War: U.S. Armed Forces as a Political Instrument* (Washington, D.C.: Brookings Institution, 1978). This study, while insightful, is of limited value because its analytic methodology is limited to simple correlations of dependent and independent variables while generally not controlling the independent variables.

3. Michael Brecher, "Toward a Theory of International Crisis Behavior," *International Studies Quarterly* 21 (March 1977):39–74.

4. For similar definitions of crises, see Charles F. Hermann, "Some Issues in the Study of International Crisis," in *International Crisis: Insight from Behavior Research*, ed. C.F. Hermann (New York: Macmillan, 1972), pp. 3–17; James Robinson, "Crisis: An Appraisal of Concepts and Theories," in *International Crisis*, ed. Hermann, pp. 20–35; and Glenn Snyder and Paul Diesing, *Conflict Among Nations: Bargaining, Decision Making, and System Structure in International Crises* (Princeton: Princeton University Press, 1977), pp. 6, 210–18.

5. We did not become aware of Charles Gochman's definition of an interstate threat until after completing the study, but we find it compatible with our own. Gochman's words are: "an explicit verbal statement by a high official on behalf of a member state for other than strictly defensive purposes; or, an overt mobilization of armed forces by a member state, during periods of dispute or high tension, clearly directed against another

member state for other than strictly defensive purposes.'' Gochman, ''Status, Conflict and War: The Major Powers, 1820–1970'' (Ph.D. diss., University of Michigan, 1975), quoted in Bruce Bueno de Mesquita, *The War Trap* (New Haven, Conn.: Yale University Press, 1981), p. 99.

6. It would seem to go without saying that this concern with the outcome of a threat should be of utmost significance to any analysis of the subject, but one recent extensive quantitative study of nuclear-era American threats simply correlated actions taken in the post-1956 era with different ''desired objectives.'' The authors felt that this would provide ''information that can assist decision-makers and planners in selecting action options,'' even though that study ''does not provide an assessment of the efficacy of the actions for achieving the objectives''! (Your objectives are A, B, and C? Then be advised that, in the past, American policymakers with such objectives who issued threats took actions X, Y, and Z. Of course, the threat may have failed altogether—indeed, war may have ensued—but that's another matter!) Indeed, the methodology employed by these analysts causes us, necessarily, to be highly suspicious of one of their findings—that ''repositioning air power in crises involving communist adversaries is a highly visible and relatively low cost manipulation of force to achieve a desired outcome.'' Repositioning air power may very well be a ''highly visible'' and inexpensive gesture, but their study simply does not even ask whether such a gesture has achieved desired outcomes. Policy Sciences Division of CACI, Inc. Federal, *Executive Aid for Crisis Management: Technical Report* (May 1978) (prepared for Advanced Research Projects Agency), pp. 4–5, 14–18.

7. Dean Acheson, *Struggle for a Free Europe* (New York: Norton, 1971), p. 17. Some believe that this repositioning (of ninety B-29s) constituted a threat; we do not. The B-29s chosen were not capable of delivering nuclear weapons, and the most competent analysts of the crisis have concluded that the Soviets must have known this. Harry Borowski, *A Hollow Threat: Strategic Air Power and Containment Before Korea* (Westport, Conn.: Greenwood Press, 1982), p. 127, quotes General George Kenney, SAC's commander: ''We don't seem to be using [the ninety B-29s] as a club. Perhaps in time the Russians will figure that as long as we don't mention them around the green table, that they are no good [that is, non-nuclear] anyhow.'' (Kenney to General Ennis Whitehead, August 9, 1948, Whitehead Files, Simpson Historical Research Center, Maxwell Air Force Base.) Cf. Gregg Herken, *The Winning Weapon: The Atomic Bomb in the Cold War, 1945–1950* (New York: Vintage, 1982), p. 259.

8. Reported by Francis Loewenheim in the *Houston Chronicle*, August 10, 1980.

9. This troubles us; we feel ambivalent about such advice. Although we are interested in threats as a field of inquiry, we regard them as hazardous, sometimes immoral courses of action for nations to take; but we allow that there are occasions when threats are entirely appropriate.

10. In this regard, those who doubt that the three threats issued during the Second Peloponnesian War are regarded as instructive by statesmen may be reminded that Thucydides was the standard diet of most Western curricula in the early modern and modern ages, and that, recently, the former director of the CIA, Admiral Stansfield Turner, placed Thucydides in the forefront of the curriculum while he was president of the Naval War College.

11. Needless to say, we were not able to find sufficient information on every variable in each case to enable us to use it; in the event that these gaps were few and far between, we simply coded ''no data'' and included the case. But where the gaps were substantial, we did not include the case.

12. We are not alone in noting this problem. See Klaus Knorr, ed., *Historical Dimensions of National Security Problems* (Lawrence, Kans.: University of Kansas Press, 1976), pp. 3–4. But the several data collections that students of international relations have been gathering over the years (conveniently listed in Dorothy LaBarr and J. D. Singer, *The Study of International Politics* [Santa Barbara, Calif.: Clio Books, 1976]) were useful.

13. We particularly thank Paul Schroeder of the University of Illinois, Cho-yun Hsu of the University of Pittsburgh, and Raymond Hinnebush of The College of St. Catharine's.

14. Kendall's rank-order correlation coefficient of our success-failure variable and our "intransigence" variable was − .377, statistically significant to the .001 level.

15. After our analysis had reached its second draft, R. Ned Lebow's *Between Peace and War* was published, and we noted that he also describes crises in which the threatener's intransigence and demands made its threat a virtual excuse for war. (Lebow's term is "justification of hostility." Others might call it "warmongering.")

It is also worth noting that such crises appear in theoretical form as well. The "Big Bully" model is one wherein the threatener really wants war. (See, for example, Glenn Snyder and Paul Diesing, *Conflict Among Nations* [Princeton: Princeton University Press, 1977], pp. 46–47.)

16. In fact, we eventually analyzed six more cases to test our findings (chapter 4), and occasionally considered several other "marginal" cases in describing those findings (chapter 3). Hence, we may be said to have used well over eighty cases, but only seventy-seven were coded, weighted, and used in the initial analysis.

17. As was indicated in chapter 1, there were many theoretical and several empirical sources that we considered in the preparation of our codebook. We shall not repeat these here. But we did find that two scholars had conveniently gathered many of the relevant hypotheses. These are K. J. Holsti, "The Study of Diplomacy," and Glenn Snyder, "Conflict and Crisis in the International System," both in James Rosenau et al., *World Politics* (New York: Free Press, 1976), pp. 299–305, 700–720.

18. Thus, J. David Singer writes: "The more data a creative social scientist has ready at hand, the more likely he is to come up with critical insight; nothing is as suggestive of hypotheses as data and correlation matrices." Singer, "From *A Study of War* to Peace Research," *Journal of Conflict Resolution* 14 (December 1970): 539.

19. François Guizot, *Mémoires pour servir à l'histoire de mon temps,* 8 vols. (Paris: Michel Lévy Frères, 1858–67), 5:371. We coded the British threat in August 1840 to Mehemet Ali's Egypt, not the later threat to his French ally, hence this Anglo-French crisis is offered here merely as illustration.

20. For example, we take note of King Louis Philippe's remark to Saint-Aulaire in late July 1840: "Basically, [Thiers] wants war, and I don't; and if he leaves me no alternative, I will break him rather than break with all Europe." T.E.B. Howarth, *Citizen-King* (London: Eyre and Spottiswoode, 1961), p. 265.

21. Sir Charles Webster, *The Foreign Policy of Lord Palmerston, 1830–1841*, 2 vols. (Cambridge, England: The University Press, 1935), 2:701.

22. Ibid., p. 730.

23. Allen S. Whiting, "New Light on Mao, Quemoy, 1958: Mao's Miscalculations," *China Quarterly* 62 (June 1975):265, 268.

24. Richard Millman, *Britain and the Eastern Question* (Oxford: Clarendon Press, 1978), pp. 338, 347.

25. Quoted in Raymond Cohen, *Threat Perception in International Crises* (Madison,

Wis.: University of Wisconsin Press, 1979), p. 110. Cf. Robert B. Parker, *Headquarters Budapest* (New York: Farrar and Rinehart, 1944), pp. 86–95.

26. Ronald Robinson and John Gallagher, *Africa and the Victorians* (London: St. Martin's Press, 1961), p. 372.

3

Success and Failure: Results of a Statistical Analysis of Seventy-Seven Weighted Cases

> People do not act as they ought. You calculate a little too much upon nations and individuals following reason, right and a just view of their own interest. I do not say that these are not the great considerations which actuate individuals, but there are other motives which exercise at least equal power and influence. . . . you mistake [King] Louis Philippe's character if you suppose that he will act [in the Syrian crisis] solely according to his interest and not from passion. He has a great deal of Jemappes* left about him still.

Lord Melbourne, the British prime minister, to Lord Palmerston, the foreign minister, August 25 and September 3, 1840.

Recall that we are asking the following questions: What are the general characteristics of the "typical" military threat? What types succeed and what types fail, under what circumstances, with what interests at stake, what sorts of actors, and why? What sorts of threats lead to war? Did threats issued in the pre-nuclear past differ in characteristics or outcomes from those of the nuclear present? And, in that present, have threats made by the United States (nearly 70 percent of our present threats) differed in characteristics or outcomes from those made by the Soviets, Chinese, or British (that is, by our other "present" cases)? Finally, what have the long-term consequences of these threats been?

Let us begin with a consideration of the first of these questions.

GENERAL CHARACTERISTICS OF THE "TYPICAL" THREAT

There was nothing "typical" about many of the dimensions of our seventy-seven weighted[1] threats. The cases spread themselves with considerable even-

*Jemappes, a French victory over the antirevolutionary European coalition in 1792 in which Louis Philippe, in command of French forces, rallied them from a panic-stricken retreat and led a daring counterattack.

handedness over spectra representing the level of interests of the parties in their spheres of influence, the importance in the crisis of commitment or of morality, the relative effect on the parties of alliance systems or of the degree of factionalization among the policymaking elites, the effect of the nature of the terrain in the theatre of operations on the parties, the type of behavior alteration demanded by the threatener, and the outcome itself, to mention but a few dimensions.

With regard to the last two mentioned variables, some specifics may be of interest. Almost half of the weighted threats could be characterized as acts of pure compellence, only one of four as an act of pure deterrence. (The remaining 27 percent were either of mixed character or were characterized by the demand that the target withdraw from action under way but not yet completed.) Compellence appears to have been more common a phenomenon than deterrence.[2] Perhaps this is due in part to the fact that we were studying only the more explicit threats, or perhaps it is due to the fact that deterrence requires *anticipation* of undesired target behavior, something that is often impossible to do. In any event, the figures should not be read as evidence that the typical threat is imperialistic or aggressive in character, for some acts of compellence (eight of thirty-six) are themselves designed to *check* aggression and to force a return to the status quo ante. One thinks here of the British threat to Russia in 1719 as Peter's forces threatened to overwhelm Sweden and destroy the balance of power in the Baltic; the Russo-French-German threat to Japan in 1896 after that nation's crushing rout of China; the British threat to Italy in 1923 upon Mussolini's seizure of the Greek island of Corfu; and the American threat to the Soviet Union in 1962 regarding the missiles in Cuba. In fact, when one characterizes the nature of objectives of the threateners on a "status-quo–revisionist" scale (1–5), one finds that 34.7 percent are "thoroughly status quo" in nature and 18.5 percent are "essentially status quo," while only 38.6 percent are either "essentially" or "thoroughly" revisionist in character. (Some 8.1 percent are of mixed or ambiguous character.)

Our threats spread themselves out nicely on the success-failure spectrum. Some 39.1 percent were "failures" (that is, the threats resulted either in war or a calling of the bluff); another 11.5 percent were "partially" successful (the threatener attained *part* of its objectives); while 21.9 percent were "substantially" successful; and 27.5 percent were "totally" successful.

There were variations to be found. But there were also some significant similarities. For example, both the threatener and the target tended to have high political power interests (of sovereignty or prestige) at stake in the crisis—that is, they tended to fall at the upper end of a spectrum that estimated the extent to which the political power interests of the one or the other were imperilled by the crisis.

Part of this result seems quite logical. It seems reasonable to assume that nations do not issue threats unless they perceive their prestige or sovereignty to be at stake. Moreover, the very act of issuing a threat may cause a state to regard its prestige as being on the line. (In any event, it is a rare power that does not

Table 3.1
EXTENT TO WHICH POLITICAL POWER INTERESTS ARE AT STAKE IN CRISIS (IN PERCENTAGE OF WEIGHTED CASES)

	(High) 1	2	3	4	5	6	7	8	9	(Low) 10	Totals
Estimates by threatener of its interests at stake	17.1	24.5	22.6	10.7	11.6	6.0	4.9	0.6	0.0	2.0	100
Estimates by target of its interests	26.4	33.9	22.5	6.9	1.3	2.1	2.8	0.0	4.0	0.0	100

gain prestige in the event that its threat leads to the securing of all or most of an objective without actual fighting.) It does not follow that *all* such threats need necessarily evoke anxieties concerning sovereignty or prestige within the chambers of the target's decisionmakers. Were the threat vague or concerned with peripheral matters, or were the target stronger than the threatener, the threat need not evoke such anxieties. But threats do not generally involve peripheral interests of the target (which may be precisely why they are deemed necessary). Since every threat involves the risk of military conflict, a target state is invariably confronted with a dilemma: if it decides to yield to the threat, it may lose face; if it ignores or confutes the threat, it may lose its entire sovereign body. And only about three in ten of our threats were uttered in an ambiguous fashion (an important category, as we shall see). Threats are generally quite clear, particularly with regard to the goals of the threatener (though less often with regard to its means of carrying them out).[3] (See Table 3.2.)

The target is rarely stronger than the threatener,[4] for our cases were limited to threats issued to targets possessing similar or smaller military capabilities; our threateners were always major powers, while our targets were not. Hence, it is not surprising that threatener coalitions tended to be decidedly more populous, economically powerful, and militarily mighty than their targets. (See Table 3.3.)

The target was generally more aware of the risks to itself in the event that the crisis ended in war than was the threatener. (See Table 3.4.) The threatener was much more likely to regard its relative capabilities as sufficient to secure its

Table 3.2
CLARITY OF THREATS
(IN PERCENTAGE OF WEIGHTED CASES)

	(Clear and Consistent) 1	(Sometimes Unclear, ambiguous, inconsistent) 2	(Unclear, Inconsistent) 3	(Communi-cation channels inoperative) 4	Totals
Regarding goals	71.6	27.3	0.7	0.4	100
Regarding means	59.4	34.5	5.7	0.4	100

objectives in the crisis than was the target. (See Table 3.5.) This was one reason why many targets believed that they had substantial political power interests at stake. George Kennan has argued that

> most small or militarily-inferior nations are sensible enough to recognize that there is nothing to be gained by yielding to blackmail of any sort from stronger ones, because the demand acceded to today will merely be followed by another one tomorrow. . . . a study of the behavior of governments in the face of a large disparity in military power would probably reveal that as a general rule the smaller and weaker the country, the more sensitive its government to any hint of military pressure being applied against it, and the more ready its resistance to . . . pressure . . . from the stronger power.[5]

Raymond Gastil immediately denied the validity of Kennan's hypothesis,[6] which appeared to run counter to the common wisdom, but one author of this book offered some support for Kennan's hypothesis in a study of accommodation, which appeared to show that states that chose to accommodate threateners were not disproportionately weaker than those threatening them.[7] However, inasmuch as that study was restricted to *accommodative* responses to threats, it did not constitute a true testing of the Kennan hypothesis, for that would require that one know the ratio of accommodative and confrontative acts of both weak and strong states in receipt of threats. The present study provides us with such ratios, and they appear to indicate that, if Kennan may be overstating his case when he argues that smaller and weaker states are *more* ready to reject threats than

Table 3.3
RELATIVE STRENGTHS OF PARTIES
(IN PERCENTAGE OF WEIGHTED CASES)

	(Threatener Considerably Higher Than Target) 1	2	(About same) 3	4	(Target Considerably Higher Than Threatener) 5	Totals
Population ratio	30.2	26.0	32.0	9.9	1.6	100
GNP ratio	36.9	29.0	23.3	9.6	1.2	100
Available conventional force ratio	19.6	51.0	15.5	13.5	0.4	100
Nuclear weapons ratio (in percentage of the (30) modern weighted cases in which nuclear weapons were held by one or more parties)	68.9	11.7	6 .1	10.2	3.1	100

larger, more powerful ones, he seems closer to the truth than Gastil. Kennan's main premise is that small states are not ready-made patsies; Gastil's, that they are. When we examine the correlation of either the population, GNP, or military forces ratios of threatener and target with the success-failure variable (Tables 3.6, 3.7, and 3.8), we find no evidence that weaker or smaller states are more likely to yield to threats than are stronger, larger states. This is, of course, a remarkable statement, and it may be explained by one of our findings: the importance of the degree to which the target's goals were limited. Weak targets appear to be intransigent as often as strong ones. (But more on this in a moment.)

There were other similarities among the threats that we studied. Most (60.6 percent) occurred in moments of regional warfare or high regional tension, tension that had usually given rise to the threat itself. Similarly, both parties generally did much to demonstrate that they had interests at stake in the crisis.

Table 3.4
PHYSICAL COSTS-RISKS TO PARTIES IN THE EVENT CRISIS ENDS IN WAR (IN PERCENTAGE OF THE WEIGHTED CASES)

	(High)									(Low)	Totals
To target	16.7	19.6	5.4	13.7	8.9	6.0	15.8	12.2	2.6	0.0	100
To threatener	10.4	5.8	0.3	3.2	3.4	13.3	10.1	20.1	29.4	4.0	100

(See Table 3.9.) The targets generally regarded the threats as credible—that is, in 69.5 percent of the cases, the targets appeared to believe that the threateners *did* intend to fight if their demands were not met. (In only 8 percent of the cases did the targets appear to believe that the threat lacked credibility. The remaining 22.5 percent of the cases did not belong to either of these clear-cut categories.)

Table 3.5
PERCEPTIONS BY PARTIES REGARDING RELATIVE CAPABILITIES (IN PERCENTAGE OF WEIGHTED CASES)

	(Much Stronger Than Opponent) 1	2	(About Same) 3	4	(Much Weaker Than Opponent) 5	Totals
Threatener's perceptions	29.3	41.2	13.0	16.5	0.0	100
Target's perceptions	1.6	14.3	21.3	44.9	17.9	100

Table 3.6
RATIO OF POPULATION OF THREATENER AND TARGET BY SUCCESS OR FAILURE OF THREAT (IN PERCENTAGE OF WEIGHTED CASES)

	Threatener Substantially More Populous	Threatener Slightly More Populous	About Same	Target Slightly More Populous	Target Sub-stantially More Populous	Totals
Objectives totally obtained w/o war	33.9	17.5	36.6	12.1	0.0	100
Objectives substantially obtained w/o war	33.9	22.8	32.8	10.6	0.0	100
Objectives partially obtained w/o war	20.2	19.4	46.4	14.0	0.0	100
Failure	29.6	35.8	24.2	6.5	3.9	100

Kendall's Rank-Order

Correlation Coefficient= -.014

And, finally, the cases had in common the fact that there were rarely any substantial trading or investment relationships between the contending parties or with any contended-for third party, nor were the contending parties importing any critical resources from one another or from any contended-for third party. This is not to say that economic interests were *always* irrelevant, for they clearly were central to a few cases (such as the Spartan threat to the grape vines of Acanthus in 431 B.C.). Rather, it indicates that trading or investment partners rarely threaten one another militarily. Threats to the economic viability of the target that do not imply inherent losses to the threatener are another matter. The Spartan threat implied the long-term devastation of the Acanthan economy, while Sparta, which had no significant trade with Acanthus (an Athenian League city-state), ran no economic risks in the crisis. It is the *absence* of any economic

Table 3.7
RATIO OF GNPs OF THREATENER AND TARGET BY SUCCESS OR FAILURE OF THREAT (IN PERCENTAGE OF WEIGHTED CASES)

	Threatener Sub-stantially Higher	Threatener Slightly Higher	About Equal	Target Slightly Higher	Target Sub-stantially Higher	Totals
Objectives totally obtained	39.2	12.1	43.3	5.4	0.0	100
Objectives sub-stantially obtained	26.5	42.9	17.5	13.2	0.0	100.1
Objectives partially obtained	25.6	60.4	0.0	14.0	0.0	100
Failure	43.0	25.2	19.1	9.8	2.9	100

Kendall's Rank-Order

Correlation Coefficient= -.108

ties that serves as a predictor of trouble, as Bruce Russett has shown.[8] The British trade relationship with Germany in 1914 is sometimes cited to demonstrate that such relationships are no bar to conflict. They are certainly no *absolute* bar, but George Hunt was surely closer to the truth when he wrote of the seventeenth-century wars of North American Indians:

> Tribes fought only their direct competitors. Trader fought trader and hunter fought hunter, but trader and hunter never fought each other. The trader, moreover, was always anxious to mediate between warring tribes to further the cause of peace, and thereby the interests of commerce.[9]

Secretary of State Cordell Hull sensed the same principle when he wrote of the coming of World War II in his autobiography:

> Yes, war did come, despite the trade agreements, but it is a fact that war did not break out between the United States and any country with which we had been able to negotiate

Table 3.8
RATIO OF CONVENTIONAL MILITARY STRENGTHS OF THREATENER AND TARGET BY SUCCESS OR FAILURE OF THREAT (IN PERCENTAGE OF WEIGHTED CASES)

	Threatener Sub- stantially Stronger	Threatener Slightly Stronger	About Equal	Target Slightly Stronger	Target Sub- stantially Stronger	Totals
Objectives totally obtained	11.0	70.2	0.0	10.8	0.0	100
Objectives Sub- stantially obtained	10.1	39.7	43.4	4.2	2.6	100
Objectives partially obtained	20.2	52.0	5.4	22.4	0.0	100
Failure	29.2	40.9	20.0	9.8	0.0	99.9

Kendall's Rank-Order
Correlation Coefficient= -.051

a trade agreement. It is also a fact that, with very few exceptions, the countries with which we signed trade agreements joined together in resisting the Axis. The political line-up followed the economic line-up.[10]

Factor analysis and nonparametric correlation revealed another noteworthy characteristic of our cases: in the course of the crisis, the threatener's demands sometimes (15.1 percent of the cases) became more flexible and compromising. Under these circumstances, the threatener's decisionmakers tended to regard the target's interests as more substantial than they had originally thought them to be. The obverse was also true.[11] That is, as a crisis deepened, sometimes (19.5 percent of the cases) the threatener felt it had to become more inflexible, and it simultaneously tended to regard the target's alternatives to be more flexible than its own. This is essentially what Ole Hosti had hypothesized on the basis of the study he and his colleagues conducted of the origins of World War I.[12]

Table 3.9
EXTENT OF DISPLAYS BY PARTIES OF THE INTERESTS AT STAKE IN CRISIS (IN PERCENTAGE OF WEIGHTED CASES)

	(Considerable Display)			(Negligible Display)		
	1	2	3	4	5	Totals
By threateners	42.7	28.3	21.6	7.1	0.4	100.1
By targets	41.7	41.5	9.4	5.8	1.6	100

SUCCESS OR FAILURE: THE FULL SAMPLE

Before describing the results of our statistical analysis of the seventy-seven weighted cases, we feel that it is seemly to offer a few *caveat*-like observations. In the first place, our findings concern seventy-seven weighted cases, hardly the total universe of threats issued by major powers over the past two thousand years. However, our subset may still be said to represent the total universe, and our generalizations may therefore effectively apply to future threats. How so? The subset constitutes nearly the total universe of cases from the nuclear age and those for which information was available from the past. Hence, we believe these conditions qualify the subset to speak for other cases and to provide us with generalizations based on well-established statistical tests.

In the second place, we note that idiosyncratic features abound in such an analysis as this. While we list, in approximate order of magnitude, a number of variables or factors that appear to account for the success or failure of threats, we are well aware that any *single* threat may stand or fall because of a single variable or factor that may be unimportant in other cases. Almost anything is possible, given the multiplicity of potential causes and the prominence of the human element. Nevertheless, we believe that some generalities are deductible from our analysis, and that those independent variables with the larger Kendall's and maximum likelihood estimate (MLE) coefficients that are statistically significant are those that will be important in one way or the other in most threats. As such, the findings constitute an advance on what we already ''knew'' about military threats. Nevertheless, despite our attempts at rigor, in the final analysis, we were still short of accounting totally (in a statistical sense) for the success or failure of all the threats. The amount of variance in the dependent variable, explained by our independent variables, ranged from about 58 percent to about 68 percent (depending on the statistical technique employed and the set of cases being examined),[13] which is to say that given information regarding any single uncoded threat as complete as that utilized in our seventy-seven coded threats, we could "predict" the success or failure of such a threat only with a probability of about two out of three. This assumes that we would have as much and as detailed information regarding both contenders as we had in each of the coded cases. All these cases were, more or less, in the past, and, consequently, we had available to us information (often substantial) about the interests, objectives, capabilities, tactics, and perceptions of both contenders—information such as is usually unavailable in the eye of a crisis itself.

In the third place, we offer the standard *caveat*: correlation is not the same as causality. Some independent variables may be *correlated* with the dependent, "success-failure" variable, but may not be responsible for the success or failure of the threat. This *caveat* becomes increasingly warranted, since we shall begin the report of our findings with such a variable. This variable, with a perfectly respectable Kendall's rank-order correlation coefficient (.24, statistically significant to the .01 level) and the second most statistically significant maximum likelihood estimate coefficient (significant to the .009 level) in our analysis of the seventy-seven cases, *may* be noncausal in character.

This predictor relates to the "climate of international opinion." All other things being equal, when the climate of international opinion tended to operate in a manner that "legitimized" the threatener's goals, the threat tended to be successful. This was certainly the case in 1923, when Britain successfully challenged Italy's behavior in the Adriatic Sea and brought the Corfu affair to the attention of the League of Nations. It describes the Soviet reaction to pressure in the United Nations for the withdrawal of her forces from Iran in 1946. It also describes the situation in December 1960, when the newly elected president of Ecuador's demands for a portion of the Peruvian Andes were rebuffed by a successful threat from the United States, with the support of the Organization of American States. That organization may have helped the United States again in October 1962, when it endorsed the American blockade of Cuba. From a negative perspective, in 1962, the Chinese, who had virtually *no* international support, proved unsuccessful in deterring India from encroaching on her Himalayan borders. (China's threats failed to deter India, in part, because Nehru felt he had the "moral support" of much of the world.)[14] The negative perspective is also evident in the case of "Rolling Thunder," a series of aerial raids and pauses increasingly unpopular in world circles, which the United States unsuccessfully used intermittently, from 1965 to 1968, to compel North Vietnam to stop its support of the National Liberation Front by threatening to resume the bombing. Other examples might be given, but they would not prove anything unless it were simultaneously established that the weight of that international opinion, pressing down against the threatener (or, more frequently, the target), actually caused that nation's leaders to act decisively in the crisis. When Germany threatened to protect Morocco from France in 1905 (uncoded), Theophile Delcassé, the French foreign minister, urged the French cabinet to hold firm:

> If today you yield, you will be compelled always to yield, and you do not know whether you will always have, as you have today, the almost unanimous agreement of the world.[15]

His colleagues and superior did not agree; the Madrid Convention of 1880 had guaranteed the neutrality and sovereignty of Morocco, and it was Delcassé who had sought to have France violate that convention. The climate of international opinion regarding the merits and demerits of the French and German postures was quite clouded, with only the British offering real support to France. Delcassé was forced to resign, and the crisis later ended in something of a stalemate. What is noteworthy, however, is that Delcassé *believed* that "the agreement of the world" was an important component in resisting a threat. Italy appears to have capitulated to British demands in 1923 only *partly* because of the "bad press" she was getting in the League of Nations. More troubling to Mussolini, however, "were two documents, submitted by the Italian Navy in mid-September, which looked upon the possibility of a war with Britain with distinct disfavour."[16]

Evan Luard, J. W. Burton, and others have argued that "foreign opinion" is important to those policymakers who can respond to "a disinterested judge, a form of social conscience, more consistent, because less volatile, than the temperamental promptings of opinion at home."[17] This may be overstating the case. Opinions expressed by persons not party to the crisis may be "less volatile" than opinions in either the target or the threatener nation, but they are not necessarily "disinterested." Indeed, if it can be said that international opinion tends to legitimize some threats under some circumstances while it tends to delegitimize other threats issued under a different set of circumstances (a view shared by Glenn Snyder and Paul Diesing),[18] this tendency may well reflect the vested interests of the nonparticipants. These interests may sometimes condition the type of threat issued or the extent of force used by a threatener to obtain its objectives should the threat fail. Additionally, adverse international opinion may work to undermine the credibility of a particular threat, or it may reinforce the target's willingness to risk action in the hope of gaining protection from the international community. Similarly, supportive international opinion for an issued threat may cause the target to reassess the values attached to a given objective in light of other interests that might be hindered should it continue its action.

For whatever reason, it is certainly worth noting that one predictor of the success or failure of a threat, in both MLE and regression analysis with other independent variables, was the climate of international opinion. Even though support from the international community does not, in this variable, involve any formal commitment to aid the threatener, some targets may view the "moral" support as having the potential to become more concrete if the crisis were to escalate. Thus, international support for a threatener or a target could, on occasion, be counted, at a discount, as part of the capability of an opponent. Such capabilities would represent perceived rather than actual power, but they could nonetheless seriously affect the outcome of a crisis in some instances. In any event, the international community appears to recognize threats that "ought" to be met with some accommodation, as well as those that "ought" to be rejected.

We are less dubious of the causal character of another, more important predictor variable: the degree to which the target's own objectives at the onset of the crisis were of an unlimited or uncompromising nature. This was the most powerful variable in the deck vis-à-vis the "success-failure" variable, with a Kendall's rank-order correlation coefficient of .51 (statistically significant to the .001 level) and standardized MLE and regression coefficients statistically significant to the .05 and .007 levels, respectively. All other things being equal, when the target's goals at the onset of the crisis were unyielding or unlimited, the threat was more likely to fail than when these goals were substantially limited or when the target offered a quid pro quo. Let us offer some examples.

The islanders of Melos simply would not consider relinquishing their sovereignty to Athens in 416 B.C. Thucydides reports their leaders as saying to the Athenian envoys:

> Our resolution, Athenians, is the same as it was before you addressed us. We will not deprive of freedom a city that has been inhabited these seven hundred years; but we put our trust in fortune . . . and . . . men . . . and we will try and save ourselves.

The Athenians, determined to end Melian neutrality in the Second Peloponnesian War, carried out their threat, and "put to death all the grown men whom they took, sold the women and children for slaves, and subsequently sent out five hundred colonists and inhabited the place ourselves."[19]

Potidaean leaders remained absolutely unwilling to tear down their walls as the Athenians directed. They found Spartan allies and rejected the demands, and the result was the outbreak of the Second Peloponnesian War. Philip V of Macedon rejected a Roman ultimatum in 200 B.C., according to the closest student of the affair, "with a curious blend of heroism and stupidity." He might lose all to Rome, but his disdain for her demands sprung from "family pride and the realization that to accept the ultimatum was virtually to surrender his freedom of action in foreign affairs."[20]

In 1415 Henry V of England demanded that France recognize that Normandy and other continental provinces were his domain. The Dauphin did not concede and war ensued. The British force dispatched to threaten the Celestial Kingdom in 1840 had no luck. The Manchu emperor and his counselors miscalculated the strength of Britain, and held too high a regard for his own honor and prestige to yield to British demands. One of his Chinese ministers was provided with first-hand information regarding British capabilities. He was escorted around the largest man-of-war in the squadron, whereupon he sighed and, remembering the haughty reaction his Manchu superior offered all memorials regarding these Western "barbarians," told the British envoys and commanders: "It is very true; you are strong and I am weak. Still, I must fight." Austria's Franz Joseph sensed (correctly) in 1859 that his "dignity and sovereign rights" were being challenged by Piedmont in the Hapsburg domains of Tuscany and Modena, but his desperate threat failed to accomplish its objective, for Piedmont's ambitious monarch, Victor Emmanuel, was committed to an aggressive policy and went so far as to speak of "abdicat[ing] if war is not waged." As a less belligerent Emperor Franz Joseph put it seven years later, contemplating his Prussian enemy, "How can one avoid war where the other side wants it?"[21]

Turkey was no more willing to relinquish to Britain any of its prerogatives in 1922 (the Chanak crisis) than it had been in 1877, when Russia had made a similar (and, with Russia, habitual) demand. In 1899 the British demands that the Boers grant their British "uitlander" residents full-fledged civil and political rights were met with a full-scale Boer mobilization and a vigorous counterultimatum. The Boers were not to limit or yield their objective of total self-determination. Neither was Mexico in 1914, when the United States demanded an abject apology for the "affair of honor" at Tampico. Germany's firm determination to expand eastward in 1939 was as unmovable by British and French threats as Austria's decision to crush Serbia had been unmoved by Russian threats in 1914. Some nations, when told to "get out!" or to "stay out!" will respond, regardless of the costs, with the child's age-old retort: "Make me!"

Conversely, the clear willingness of the Polk Administration and the Senate to negotiate a settlement of the Oregon question in 1846 ensured the success of the British threat of a naval expedition. Similar forces were at work twenty years later. Napoleon III's troops were still struggling to place the Austrian prince, Maximilian, on the throne of Mexico when the United States ended the bloody Civil War. The cost of the operations was troubling to him and to his *corps legislatif*. Public opinion in France had turned against the imbroglio. Thus, when the U.S. secretary of state, William Henry Seward, pressed for the withdrawal of French troops, the target's objectives were neither uncompromising nor unlimited. Napoleon was, after all, more concerned with the impending Austro-Prussian War than with the fate of Maximilian when he cut his losses and announced a staged withdrawal in April 1866.[22] The same may be said of the Prussian willingness to accede to Napoleon III's demand that she withdraw her garrison from Luxembourg in 1867 (uncoded). And the mere mention of Munich evokes the notion of another accommodative moment in history—a moment when the target's prime minister would speak of "how horrible, fantastic, incredible" it was that Britons "should be digging trenches and trying on gasmasks here because of a quarrel in a foreign country between people of whom we know nothing."

Further evidence may be found in the American threat to Britain in 1895 over Britain's border dispute with Venezuela. President Cleveland sent a severely worded note to Lord Salisbury demanding that Britain submit the border dispute to arbitration, and in December he told the Congress that the United States would "resist by every means in its power" Britain's claims to lands the United States determined to belong to Venezuela. He was "fully alive to the responsibility incurred" by this deterrent gesture "and keenly realize[d] the consequences that may follow." At first, Salisbury was unaware of the seriousness with which Americans regarded the dispute, but if the strong language of the president's message to Congress was not enough to change his mind, the warning sounded by his ambassador to the United States, Sir Julian Pauncefote, served to clarify the matter. Pauncefote detected both "in Congress and among the people a condition of mind that can only be described as hysterical." At that time, the Kaiser dispatched his congratulatory telegram to President Kruger of the Transvaal, and Britain's attention turned to what it deemed the more serious affair in South Africa. Canada appeared vulnerable in the event of a conflict with the United States, and Salisbury agreed to submit the border dispute to arbitration. The United States rattled no sabres and deployed no warships, but it got what it wanted—an extension of its Monroe Doctrine—essentially because Britain's ultimate objective was to recruit the United States as a friend, if not a full-fledged ally. More troubled by Germany's interest in South Africa than by America's interest in Venezuela, and with no prestige or sovereignty to speak of at stake, Britain yielded.[23]

In short, some targets are easier to deter or coerce than others, because some targets simply are not as determined or uncompromising as others.[24] Obviously, this does not take us very far, for we have only said that some targets are unyielding, not *why* they are unyielding. They could be convinced that their interests (economic, personal leadership, national honor, ideology, or some other) are too important to suffer them to be encroached on; they could be convinced that they are capable of resisting or brushing aside the threat; or they could act for a combination of these reasons. The Truman Administration was unwilling to yield to Chinese threats that we keep clear of the Chinese border in 1950 for at least two reasons: President Truman wanted to create a unified, non-Communist Korea; and he felt strong political pressures, especially from General MacArthur and the Republicans, to persevere and offer no appeasement to Red China. The drive to the Yalu River presented political opportunities to the administration. Halting that drive in reaction to massive and conspicuous Chinese troop movements and demands was, consequently, never seriously considered, regardless of clear evidence of overwhelming numbers of Chinese troops already south of the Yalu.[25] In the cases described in the two preceding paragraphs, interests (whether of sovereignty, ideology, or simply the preservation of peace) appear to have been more important in shaping the objectives of policymakers in Melos, Piedmont, *fin-de-siècle* Turkey, the Transvaal, Austria-Hungary, Hitler's Germany, and Chamberlain's England than were their perceptions of the capabilities of the threateners. In fact, over half of the states just mentioned literally went out of existence as a result of their "bold resolve!"

Table 3.10
TARGET'S PRIMARY INTEREST TYPE (IN PERCENTAGE OF WEIGHTED CASES)

Threat "Success-Failure" Ranking	Economic	Political Power	Ideological/ Moral	Identification— "Commitment"	Military Security
Total success	73.2	7.8	60.2	23.5	51.0
Sub-stantial success	4.5	20.2	0.0	23.5	10.9
Partial success	11.2	19.6	0.0	27.8	0.0
Failure	11.2	52.4	39.8	25.3	38.1
Total	100.1	100	100	100.1	100
(N) rounded to nearest integer	(11)	(41)	(5)	(7)	(14)

The *type* of interests that targets were unwilling to compromise has significant import for this study. We found that when the target's most important interest at stake in the crisis was its sovereignty or prestige (something we labelled "political power"), the threat was five times as likely to fail as it was when the target's most important interest at stake was economic in character, and twice as likely to fail as it was when the target's most important interests were traditional associations or commitments. (See Table 3.10.) We can detect the particular type of interest at stake when the target's initial posture in the crisis is unyielding by correlating the latter variable with each of several variables that measure the extent to which the target regarded various of its interests (among them, economic viability, military security, ideology, alliance commitments, sovereignty, and prestige) to be at stake in the crisis (A.6, A.22, A.24, A.28, and A.30). Of these, the variable measuring the extent to which the target's political power interests (prestige or sovereignty) were at stake in the crisis was the only one with a statistically significant Kendall rank-order correlation coefficient (.32, significant to the .002 level) when correlated with the variable measuring the extent to which the target was initially unyielding.

Klaus Knorr notes this same trait with regard to the failure of economic threats in the modern age. His analysis found little utility in these threats due to the "pride" and "nationalism" the targets frequently possessed. Thus, Soviet efforts to force Albania back into the Russian camp in 1960 by cutting off trade and aid failed because President Hoxha refused to yield. Albania's economy was weakened, but her sovereignty was not. Similarly, U.S. efforts to force Fidel Castro to adopt measures more acceptable to Washington in 1960 and 1961 (by halting the purchase of Cuban sugar, terminating aid, and placing an embargo on goods bound for Cuba) injured the Cuban economy but did not alter Cuban policies.[26]

Snyder and Diesing believe that when "a state yields on any issue, it is more likely to be because it believes its adversary's interest to be stronger than its own—than because its independent valuation of the stake is low."[27] We found a negative correlation between the *threatener's* perception of the extent to which the target's interests were at stake in the crisis and the success of the threat—that is, when the threatener saw the target's interests in the crisis to be negligible, threats tended to succeed, and vice versa (Kendall's rank-order correlation coefficient − .23, significant to the .02 level). This finding is as Snyder and Diesing had suggested, and it is certainly plausible. But this was *not* true of the target—that is, there was no statistical significance to the correlation of the target's perception of the extent to which the threatener's interests were at stake in the crisis with the success or failure of the threat (Kendall's rank-order correlation coefficient .044). Moreover, neither of these independent variables had the slightest predictive strength when engaged in multiple-variable equations designed to determine the relative strength of various independent variables (multiple regression and maximum likelihood estimation analysis). Why?

Perhaps Snyder and Diesing are wrong in this particular. Perhaps a target nation's "independent valuation of the stake" is more important in determining whether or not it will yield than is its assessment of the strength of "its adversary's interest." The Melians may well have perceived the Athenian interests to be just as substantial as their own without that perception altering their response to the Athenian threat. Theirs was the imagined cry of the Patrick Henrys of the world: "Give me liberty or give me death!" The French leadership in 1415 knew full well that the English had a substantial interest in Poitou and Picardy; they simply were not willing to surrender their own claims to these lands without a fight. Count Cavour and his monarch realized that Austria wanted badly to retain Lombardy in 1859; but that made no difference to them, for they were bent on the creation of an enlarged Piedmont. China realized that Japan's appetite for Korea was as large as her own desire to retain suzerainty there, but she could not bring herself to yield to Japanese demands in 1895. The Truman Administration appears to have sensed the importance to Red China of the UN advance toward the Yalu River in 1951, but the administration could not bring itself to check that advance. There are, of course, instances in which the targets simply misjudged the extent of the threatener's interests (as when India's chief of staff, General Brig Mohan Kaul, told Prime Minister Nehru: "I am convinced that the Chinese will not attack our positions even if they are relatively weaker than theirs"[28]), and such misperception could also lead to the failure of a threat. But an entirely *correct* perception by a target of a high level of threatener interests did not lead to the target's capitulation if the target's *own* resolve, its own "independent valuation of the stake," was high.

Nonetheless, capabilities *are* important, as our next two predictor variables demonstrate. The first, with a Kendall's coefficient of .29 (significant to the .003 level) and standardized MLE and regression coefficients significant to the .09 and .009 levels, respectively, concerns the relative effectiveness of the alliance systems of the contenders. All other things being equal, when the threatener's allies were of more help to their champion than the target's allies were to its fortunes, the threat tended to succeed. Russia supported Austria in her confrontation with Prussia over Hesse-Kassel in 1850, and Prussia had no such support; Prussia experienced the "humiliation of "Olmutz," in part, because of her apprehension that Russia might join with Austria against her. French support of Sardinia clearly was important to Count Cavour's decision to reject Austria's ultimatum in 1859. Russia might have been able singlehandedly to force Japan to back down in 1896 from her voracious gains in Manchuria at China's expense, but Russia's threat acquired a convincing tone when it was repeated by France and Germany. In the Bosnian crisis of 1908–1909 and the Albanian crisis of 1913, the Austrians felt that they could count on Germany, and they had some moral support from other Western powers; little Serbia was unable, in both instances, to get any support from her ally, Russia. In 1956 Britain, France, and Israel were unwilling to dismiss a low-risk Soviet threat during the Suez crisis largely because the United States, their theoretical ally, was exerting considerable influence to check their collective progress against Egypt, while the Soviets, pulling in the same direction, were joined by China. Two years later, when China and her erstwhile ally, the Soviet Union, were at a parting of the ways, a United States threat to China concerning Quemoy looked very formidable indeed. In that same year, the Soviet threat to the West regarding the status of Berlin failed in part because of this same Sino-Soviet rift. In the words of Robert Slusser, an authority on the Berlin crises and Soviet policymakers, "In my view it was Khrushchev's perception of a new option in his policy towards the Chinese Communists which produced the abrupt shift in Soviet policy [that is, backing down]."[29]

Earlier, in 1960, Ecuador sought Soviet aid in its efforts to acquire Andean territory governed by Peru. Unable to acquire any assurances from the Soviets, and faced with a unified OAS, Ecuador yielded. In 1961 Iraq found itself without support in the Arab world for its claim regarding Kuwaiti sovereignty, and a British threat that rallied the Arab world behind Kuwait deterred Iraq. When the

United States moved to deter Idi Amin from attacking Mombasa in the wake of the July 4 raid on Entebbe, Amin did what he could to rally support for his cause in Somalia and Libya, but without success. Subsequently, he backed down. Allies, or the absence of allies, are clearly important in determining the outcome of threats.[30]

The second of these capabilities predictor variables, with a Kendall's coefficient of .38 (significant to the .001 level) and standardized MLE and regression coefficients significant to the .08 level, is quite comparable to the previous one and can be seen in factor 1 of Table A.1 and Plot A.1 where they appear (as variable numbers 28 and 30) to be slightly colinear with it, which makes their strength in the MLE and regression analyses the more impressive, inasmuch as they were probably weakening one another's significance. It appears that when all other things are equal, threats tended to succeed when the target perceived the threatener's ability to inflict serious damage on it to be substantial. One thinks of the Mongol threats to the cities of Khwarazm in A.D. 1218 and 1219. Isolated, one by one, these citadels found the armies of Chenggiz Khan advancing on them. When they beheld "the surrounding countryside choked with horsemen and the air black as night with the dust of cavalry, fright and panic overtook them, and fear and dread spread." The Persian historian Juvaini continues to describe the scene at the opening of the siege of Zarnūg:

At this juncture, the World-Emperor, in accordance with his constant practice, dispatched Dānishmend Hājib upon an embassy to them, to announce the arrival of his forces and to advise them to stand out of the way of a dreadful deluge. Some of the inhabitants, who were in the category of "Satan hath gotten master over them" (Koran 58:20), were minded to do him harm and mischief; whereupon he raised a shout, saying: "I am such-and-such a person, a Muslim and the son of a Muslim. Seeking God's pleasure I am come on an embassy to you, at the inflexible command of Chenggiz Khan, to draw you out of the whirlpool of destruction and the trough of blood.

It is Chenggiz Khan himself who has come with many thousands of warriors. The battle has reached thus far. If you are incited to resist in any way, in an hour's time your citadel will be level ground and the plain a sea of blood. But if you will listen to advice and exhortation with the air of intelligence and consideration and become submissive and obedient to his command, your lives and property will remain in the stronghold of security." When the people, both nobles and commoners, had heard his words, which bore the brand of veracity, they did not refuse to accept his advice, knowing for certain that the flood might not be stemmed by their obstructing his passage nor might the quaking of the mountains and the earth be quietened and allayed by the pressure of their feet.

Later, the Mongols reached the major city of Bukhara and, upon threatening it, were permitted to enter. After plundering the marketplace and destroying the citadel, the Mongols began to levy taxes, and Juvaini reports a conversation between two Khwarazm leaders concerning this "scourge of God":

In that moment, the Emir Imān Jalāl ad-Dīnb. al-Hasan Zaidī, who was the chief and leader of the *sayyids* of Transoxiana and was famous for his piety and asceticism turned to the learned *imān* Rukn-ad-Dīn Imamzada, who was one of the most excellent savants in the world . . . , and said: "*Muluānā*, what state is this? *That which I see do I see it in wakefulness or in sleep, O Lord?*" *Maulānā Imāmzāda* answered: "Be silent: it is the wind of God's omnipotence that bloweth, and we have no power to speak."[31]

This has to be the preeminent case illustrating the importance of perceived capabilities, but one might also consider the case of Pietro de Medici's Florence, confronted by the advancing forces of the French monarch, Henry IV, in 1495. The French were on their way to Naples with the modern world's first standing army, and as they passed through the Florentine marches, they made certain demands on that city-state in order to secure their rearguard and supply lines. Pietro ("the Unfortunate"), the Florentine chief of state, had no effective allies, and no more than a rag-tag smattering of an army. He rode out to see the French and, in the words of George F. Young,

He there saw for the first time what a regular organized army was like, and, if he had not done so before, must have realized at once how futile would be any opposition which Florence could offer to such a force, and that it could only have a result which he was bound at all cost to prevent.[32]

He granted the French the forts they wanted with due speed.

Four centuries later, the Venezuelan crisis appears to have provided another example of the importance of the target's perception of the threatener's capabilities and of the relative unimportance of the *actual* capabilities of the contending parties. Daniel M. Smith speaks of the risks America ran in offering a threat to Britain without "the means to implement it, because if war had come in 1895, the British fleet had an overwhelming superiority and could have inflicted devastation upon America's commerce and coasts." But if this was so (and it appears to have been), the *British* did not believe it, as Thomas Patterson, Kenneth Hagan, and Gary Clifford have pointed out.[33] Rather, the Royal Navy expressed anxieties about its ability to control matters in the Caribbean and the North Atlantic. Britain perceived America's naval and military capabilities to be substantial, especially inasmuch as its Admiralty felt that some British naval power would have to be held in reserve to deter the ambitions of Germany and others elsewhere. British leaders may have exaggerated the risks; in any event, the British had other reasons for avoiding conflict with the United States, as we have seen. But their perception of America's naval capabilities counted in their decision to accommodate.

Other cases that we could discuss, illustrating that the target's decision to capitulate was in large measure due to the absence of allies or to the target's perception of superiority of the threatener's military capabilities, include the Japanese "21 Demands" to China in 1915, the Corfu crisis of 1923, the harassment of Czechia's President Hacha by Hitler in 1939, the U.S. insistence that the Trujillo brothers surrender their authority and leave the Dominican

Republic in 1961, or the Soviet naval show of force to support its demand that Ghana release its merchant vessel in 1969. But perhaps the elaborated cases have already served adequately to illustrate the point: the target's perception of the threatener's military capabilities appears to affect the outcome of a threat.[34]

A few other variables had tolerable statistical scores and are worth mentioning (though they appear less important than those already mentioned). The first of these is quite surprising, and is probably noncausal. It appears that when the target had important international commitments at stake in the crisis, the threat was more likely to succeed than when it did not. (Standardized MLE and regression coefficients significant to the .10 and .02 levels, respectively.) One example of this phenomenon may be found in the British threat to Naples in 1742. Charles, king of the Two Sicilies, was the son of Philip V of Spain, and Philip, who was trying to recover certain central Italian duchies by force, had managed to acquire 12,000 troops from his son's realm for that purpose. The British, allied with Austria against Philip, dispatched a naval squadron to the harbor of Naples, well within range of Charles's palace, "to demand that the king of the Two Sicilies should not only immediately withdraw his troops from acting in conjunction with those of Spain, but that his Sicilian Majesty should, in writing, promise not to give them any further assistance of any kind whatsoever." If not, the British commodore "would make the necessary dispositions to bombard the city, and press his demand by force of arms." Charles's capital was highly vulnerable, his defenses inadequate, and after some hemming and hawing, he wrote down what the British had demanded and sent it out to the commodore.[35]

It would seem that some nations become targets of threats *because* they are allied to an enemy of the threatener and appear to be vulnerable. In addition to the case of Naples, we find that the Spartan threat to Acanthus, the U.S. threat to Napoleon III regarding Maximilian's Mexican empire, and the "humiliation" of Prussia at Austrian hands before her German friends in 1850 fit this description. But we do not want to claim too much for this theory. Discretion demands that we retire from this discussion with the more modest observation that being committed to help others does not appear to help a target resist a threat.

The target's perception of the credibility of the threat was also a tolerable predictor of its success (Kendall's coefficient = .29, significant to the .005 level; regression coefficient significant to the .05 level). Two examples may suffice to illustrate the significance of this rather self-evident variable.

Throughout late July 1914, German policymakers persistently doubted that Russia would go to war with both Austria-Hungary and Germany. One German official noted on July 17 that German policymakers "reckon" that "England is altogether peaceably minded and neither France nor Russia appears to feel any inclination for war." On July 20 another wrote that "in circles here [Berlin], even at the foreign ministry, the opinion prevails that Russia is bluffing and that, if only for reasons of domestic policy, she will think well before provoking a European war." Gottlieb von Jagow, the German foreign minister, wrote on July 18 to Prince Lichnowsky, Germany's ambassador to Britain, that "when all is said and done, Russia is at present not ready for war. . . . In a few years Russia . . . will have built her Baltic Fleet and her strategic railways. Our group will in the meantime grow weaker and weaker. In Russia they probably know this, and for this reason Russia definitely wants peace for a few years longer.'' On July 27 the British ambassador cabled home from Berlin: "I found Jagow . . . optimistic—his optimism being based, as he told me, on the idea that Russia was not in a good position to make war.''[36] German officials were mistaken regarding Russian resolve, of course: Russia mobilized on July 29 and 30, and after an unsuccessful effort to halt this mobilization, Germany went to war.

The British threat to Turkey in the Chanak affair clearly lacked credibility in the eyes of Mustapha Kemal, the Turkish leader, due to the strong public opposition in Britain of that government's policies. Kemal persevered and the threat failed. Two observations seem warranted: (1) When a target can identify a division of opinion or absence of will in the threatener's polity, the threatener's ability to establish credibility appears to become problematic, and the threats may fail. (2) The threat may, in fact, be real (and thus credible), but if the target misunderstands and decides that it is a bluff (as did Germany in 1914), the result may well be tragic.

Another independent variable with potentially predictive qualities (Kendall's coefficient = −.23, significant to the .02 level; standardized MLE and regression coefficients significant to the .07 and .05 levels, respectively) was the degree to which the crisis affected the international system's balance of power. When it did, all other things being equal, threats tended to fail. (One thinks here of Carthage's unwillingness to yield to Rome in 218 B.C.) Obviously, ''tended to'' is as much as can be said, for there are exceptions, but the tendency *is* statistically significant and seems quite logical, and it is correlated with another of our predictor variables: a threat by a major power (as were all of ours) in a highly polarized age, imperilling the world balance of power, tends to increase the likelihood that the target will have more alliance help than will the threatener, as aid would flow to the target from the other camp. (The Kendall's coefficient for these two variables—''alliance effect ratio'' and ''crisis affect on power balance''—was statistically significant to the .05 level.) The fact that Sparta was highly angered and troubled by the policies of Athens in 431 B.C. clearly is central to an understanding of why Potidaea resisted Athenian demands.[37] That is, the highly bipolar atmosphere made it much easier for Potidaea to find a powerful ally and to resist.[38] Another example of this phenomenon is the polarization of the international system in the threat environment of the summer of 1914. Threats by Austria-Hungary and Prussia failed as the respective power camps drew upon their allies for moral and political support and defended their collective interests.

While analysis of the *significant* variables and factors contributes some interesting insights into the character of threats, some attention to those variables and factors that were *not* statistically significant also has some value for our study, for while many of our findings may appear to be truisms or common sense, it is interesting to note that other "common wisdom" factors did *not* seem to be substantiated by our analysis. Among the variables that account for virtually none of the variance in the variable that records the success or failure of each of the seventy-seven threats are the extent of the political power interests of the threatener at stake in the crisis; the degree to which the crisis imperilled the economic viability of either party; the population ratio of the contenders; the actual conventional-force-level ratio of the contenders; the degree to which the forces actually deployed by the threatener were sufficient to enforce the demands if necessary; the degree of clarity with which the threat was communicated; and the relative distance of the contenders from the theatre of operations.

This is not to say that all these variables do not count; some of them clearly do. San Remo cannot possibly threaten the United States militarily. But, then, it would never occur to San Remo to attempt such a thing. ("The mouse roared" only in Hollywood.) As we have seen in the first section of this chapter, nations rarely issue threats unless they feel they have substantial political reasons for doing so and unless they possess sufficient military manpower to make the threat appear credible on that score. Hence, there was rarely much deviation from the norm with those variables. They "counted," in the sense that each was a *sine qua non*, but they were not among those variables that appeared to explain why the threats either succeeded or failed.[39]

The same cannot be said of the variables measuring the threat to economic viability, the clarity of threat communication, tactical flexibility and initiative,[40] the suitability of the forces actually deployed, the effect that terrain might exercise on the fortunes of one side or the other, and the relative distance of the parties from the scene of the crisis. There was sufficient variation in the coded values of these variables theoretically to have accounted for the variation in the success-failure variable. However, they did not. Hence, we can say that neither seizing the initiative, nor economic viability, nor terrain, nor distance, nor elaborate displays of force, nor clearly communicated threats determine the outcome of threats.

We ought to explore the significance of what has just been offered with regard to the last two of these apparently inconsequential variables: shows of force and clarity of communication. First, let us consider the finding with regard to the show of force.

For those who wonder whether the brandishing of one carrier task group, or two, or a task group and two battalions of Marines, or two groups and four battalions will carry the day, we submit that such fine tuning of the threat forces does not appear to matter. Targets can count, and if they do not look upon the threatener's allies and *overall* capabilities with sufficient alarm, and if they are themselves unwilling to be flexible, then all the bristling and sabre-rattling that a coterie of national-security managers can manage will not suffice. How many battalions, moved how fast, to what points, would Napoleon III have needed to force Bismarck and his monarch to "guarantee" that no Hohenzollern would take the Spanish throne in 1870? In the event, Bismarck found the prospect of the war so convenient to his purposes that he appears to have altered the character of Wilhelm's version of Napoleon's demands in order to bring it about! Fine tuning a threat would have been so much wasted effort.

Another example may help illustrate the point: The American military commander in the South, General Ulysses S. Grant, sent some 40,000 men to Texas in the fall of 1865, thus making them available as a "suitable display of force" to menace the French in Mexico. But Secretary of State William Seward had not asked Grant to do this, and he chose not to thrust it before the attention of the French Government. Nor did Seward intend to use the troops. He wrote his minister in Paris, John Bigelow, in March 1865: "If we have a war with [France], it must be a war of her own making . . . We shall defend ourselves if assailed on our own ground. *We shall attack nobody elsewhere*. . . . For us to intervene in Mexico would be only to reverse our principles." Moreover, there is evidence that the French themselves did not regard this "army of observation" with distress. According to one prominent student of the crisis, the French commander in Mexico, Marshal François Bazaine, seemed "more impressed with the unofficial encouragement given [by Washington] to [the Mexican foe of Maximilian, Benito Juarez] than to the danger of hostile action [ordered by Washington]." A spokesman for the government in the Chamber of Deputies spoke slightingly of the force in Texas as a body of northern farmers anxious to be home, who, if they were to be used anywhere, would have to be deployed against intransigent southern rebels.[41]

The French may well have been worried about the powerful American Navy, a navy that was never deployed to menace them but that, nonetheless, in its harbor berths, appeared to be capable of sallying forth and destroying the "flimsy" French warships and cutting the French forces in Mexico off from supplies, relief, or escape.[42] In short, it was not Napoleon's fear of deployed American forces in Texas, but his anxieties about the *total* military capabilities of the reunited states, his preoccupation with European problems, and the credibility of the American position that affected his decision to announce a staged withdrawal of French forces from Mexico.

Secretary of State Philander Knox kept a squadron of U.S. warships off Standard Oil Company's Mexican depot, Tampico, during the Mexican Revolution in 1912 in order to keep the Mexicans "in a salutary equilibrium, between a dangerous and exaggerated apprehension and a proper degree of wholesome fear," as he cynically put it. President Woodrow Wilson continued the policy in 1913 and 1914, when revolution turned to civil war, and he added to the squadron until it outnumbered the combined Mexican, British, and German forces in the area. When the contending Constitutionalist (revolutionary) and Federal (government) forces finally approached Tampico in early April, Admiral Henry Mayo repeatedly warned their commanders to stand clear of American oil-storage facilities. These warnings did not prevent the shelling of such facilities by Federal forces on April 8. Nor did the squadron's presence prevent the arrest of several American naval personnel in Tampico by Federal troops on April 9. Indeed, the seizure of Vera Cruz by force—to compel the Federal president, General Huerta, to apologize for the arrests—did not suffice either! Pressure from Latin American states (the climate of international opinion) finally did manage to convince Wilson that compromise was in order. "Suitable displays of force" had not helped; rather, they provoked Mexicans on both sides of the civil war.[43]

Consider as well the Chinese threat to intervene in the Korean War if U.S. troops were to approach the Chinese border. This threat was accompanied by deliberately conspicuous Chinese troop movements toward the Yalu River, along the river, and, eventually, even across the river. These had little effect on the Truman Administration, for reasons that Alexander George and R. Ned Lebow have made clear.[44] Domestic political pressures, and pressures from General Douglas MacArthur, led Truman and his advisors to press on despite these clear signals from China's rattling sabre.

May not the same be said of President Carter's efforts to secure the release of the American hostages in Iran? Would anyone now claim to know the correct number of carriers or troopships the United States could have moved to Iranian waters that would have forced the Khomeini regime to agree to their release? (Indeed, it would also be hard to find a better example of *a resolute target* of a threat than the Iran tremulously led by this bitterly anti-American leader of the Shiite sect of Islam.)

The movement of military forces is not always irrelevant to the outcome of threats, of course. The Russian mobilization of its reserves on July 29, 1914, certainly affected the German leadership, but in a way that led to war (thus, to the *failure* of the Russian threat to the Central Powers). Germany felt it could not permit Russia to mobilize its armies on its eastern frontier unanswered, for that would give Russia an unacceptable military advantage. Hence, it mobilized its own forces and gave Russia an ultimatum on July 31; when Russia did not respond, Germany declared war (on August 1). The act of mobilization was viewed then in somewhat the same way as strategists today speak of a preemptive strike—that is, both represent movements of such decisive force toward the target that the target feels compelled to unleash its own forces in reaction. Such decisive movements of force are not the show of force that we have been addressing, but in our analysis, they were encompassed in the same variable. Hence, part of the reason that "suitable displays of force" did not account for any of the variance in the success-failure result is due to the fact that certain displays of force are viewed by targets as being suitable only to preemptive warmaking. As such, they are *not* suitable to the task of aiding the threatener to achieve its objectives without recourse to war. Too much of a display of force may thus prompt a target to react violently. And it does not appear to be the case that no display of force is too little. Threats can succeed without a soldier being moved or a ship lifting anchor.

Now let us explore the significance of our finding that the "clarity of threat communication" variables were not associated with the success of threats. Two variables recorded the degree to which the signals regarding the goals and the means were conveyed in a clear and consistent fashion. They appeared to form a single factor (#13 in Table A.1), and were of no statistical significance in the analysis (nor were either of the variables that composed that factor when each was separately substituted for the factor), which is to say that they did not behave as others had predicted they would—that is, vague, ambiguous threat communications were just as likely to succeed as were perfectly clear ones. It is undoubtedly true that some ambiguously delivered threats have led to failure when they cause the target to misperceive the seriousness or credibility of the threatener. For example, Snyder and Diesing point out that Germany misread Britain's determination to aid France in 1914. Lord Grey had indicated that Britain could not remain neutral in the event of war between Germany and France, *though she was not automatically committed to war*. Germany chose to give more weight to the *qualifier* than to the central premise—to her ultimate distress.[45]

Nonetheless, our reading suggests that a clear-cut, bold-faced threat may not have been as effective as one that allowed the target some face-saving way to give in without appearing to have been *forced* to do so. Consider the behavior of the Manchu Court toward the victorious Vietnamese insurgent, Nguyen Hue, in 1770. The court was not interested in becoming embroiled in Vietnam. Previous Chinese governments had found that to be a costly and fruitless business. Nguyen Hue could remain in control—so long as he would submit to China and pay formal tribute. His attack on the Chinese forces supporting the deposed king *must* have been a "mistake." Wouldn't he like to come to Peking and kow-tow? All would be forgiven. Here was a magnificent Chinese Army, with a *very* friendly commander, to escort him there in proper fashion. (Nguyen Hue sent his nephew to offer tribute, and upon that relative's safe return, he himself went to kow-tow.[46] Cool Chinese diplomacy had secured China's modest goals without recourse to arms.

An even more striking example of this phenomenon is that of the Spartan threat to Acanthus in 431 B.C. The Spartan commander, Brasidas, had marched his force all the way through Thessaly by assuring anxious Thessalians that "he came as a friend," an "unexpected visitor." Upon reaching the gates of Acanthus, Brasidas affected surprise. Were not the Acanthans allies now? Did they mean to "stand in the way" of their "freedom"? "I have come here not to hurt but to free the Hellenes. . . . My object in coming is not to obtain your aid by force or fraud, but to offer you mine to help you against your Athenian master." He assured the Acanthans that he did not favor one party of Acanthans against another and would not interfere in their internal affairs. He did not speak of attacking the city itself were he rebuffed, but he did warn the Acanthans of the vulnerability of their vines, and he swore to them that Sparta would never enslave Acanthus or return it to Athens. Submission, by his reasoning, meant independence.[47]

Let us move from one of the earliest threats coded to the most recent one we analyzed in our consideration of threat communications: American officials denied, for the record, that the dispatch of aircraft and naval vessels to the coast of Kenya in July 1976 was other than "routine." However, the *New York Times* reported that Pentagon officials "privately acknowledged" that the visits were designed to deter Uganda's Idi Amin from carrying out his promise of air strikes against the Kenyan port of Mombasa.[48] We cannot say exactly how much this ambiguously conveyed deterrent measure entered into Amin's decision to call off his announced intentions, for there were other levers—including economic ones—that Kenya was using to deter Amin. Amin could have tried to deal with Kenya's blockade militarily, but he did not, and we suspect that the American deterrent gestures had something to do with this. We also suspect, but we cannot be sure, that the ambiguity of the American threat communication allowed Amin to save face, in that he did not have to appear to be yielding to American pressure. All that we can be sure of is the correlation of this type of threat communication and the absence of a Ugandan attack.[49]

Finally, we note that the United States offered the Soviets some saving of face in 1946, when it described the advance of Soviet forces on Teheran as "without authorization" and asked in the United Nations for a joint Iranian-Soviet agreement regarding the withdrawal of Soviet forces. Once again, we cannot say that the accommodating nature of the American (and Iranian) threat in this crisis *caused*, or was instrumental in bringing about, the Soviet withdrawal; all we can say is that the two events are correlated.[50]

When we restricted the cases to those threats that involved an object or area of contention by the adversaries—that is, when we eliminated those threats exclusively concerned with the sovereignty of the target itself—we continued to find that the relative usefulness of the alliance systems[51] was highly significant (MLE and regression coefficients significant to the .06 and .02 levels, respectively) while the degree to which the target's objectives were flexible or limited and the target's perception of the threatener's capabilities diminished in explanatory value. It appears, then, that the correlations between successful threats and these variables are exceptionally strong among threats that deal, not with mere objects or areas of contention, but with questions of actual sovereignty. It was possible for the British successfully to threaten the United States over the Oregon Territory in 1846, where the question was limited to agreement over the precise boundary of a largely unsettled region far from the center of American life on the northwest coast, which the two nations had already agreed in principle to divide; it had not been possible for Britain to bully the United States thirty-five years earlier, during the Napoleonic Wars, for American leaders had then regarded the nation's sovereignty, honor, and vital interest to be at stake in the crisis.[52] President Kennedy was able to secure from the North Vietnamese modest concessions and a status-quo cease-fire in Laos by threatening to move more American units to the region in 1961; President Johnson was unable to secure concessions from the North Vietnamese by periodically threatening to reinstitute "Rolling Thunder" (the bombing of North Vietnam) in 1967. In 1719 Peter the Great felt that, while British sea power was considerable, the British leadership was unlikely to commit its full resources to a war in the Baltic on behalf of its

Swedish ally in the event that the British threat to Russia was ignored. Two and a half centuries later, in 1971, President Nixon faced the same problem when he dispatched a nuclear carrier to Bengalese waters: Indian leaders knew that the commitment of American sea power could severely injure the forces they had just committed in East Pakistan, but they also felt that American intervention was highly unlikely, inasmuch as American interests in the area of contention were modest and America was already withdrawing from another area (Vietnam) of greater interest to it.

Another variable seems to have acquired some predictive power when our analysis was restricted to threats involving areas of contention. All other things being equal, when the threatener imported vital resources from the area being contended for in the crisis, threats tended to succeed (MLE and regression coefficients significant to the .10 and .03 levels, respectively). When a threatener sought to deter a potential rival from acquiring political influence or control of a region rich in resources important to the threatener, it was also generally the case (for understandable reasons) that the threatener regarded itself as having substantial sphere-of-influence interests in the area being contended for,[53] and regarded its economic viability to be imperilled by the crisis.[54] The target in such a threat came to appreciate the threatener's interests more in the course of the crisis[55] (which is also understandable, inasmuch as such threats tended to end successfully). (Typically, these "important resources" in the modern age consisted of crude oil, and perhaps the preeminent example of the phenomenon just described is the British threat to Iraq in 1961 over Iraq's expressed penchant for Kuwait.)

Also interesting, from the standpoint of common wisdom, was the fact that the variable that measured the extent to which the target had sphere-of-influence interest was not statistically relevant to the success or failure of threats involving contended areas. One might have expected the target to be able to muster significant force to defend objects within its sphere of influence, at least to the extent of offsetting whatever gains were anticipated by the threatener. Moreover, the ties between a nation and its sphere of influence would lend credibility to any counterthreat the target might wish to employ. Based on theoretical considerations, then, there would be every reason to expect the targets to enjoy a high degree of success in warding off threats that touched them in their spheres of influence. Yet the correlation of the variable denoting the extent to which the target felt that the area of contention was located in its sphere of influence with the variable denoting the extent to which the threat may be said to have succeeded or failed was weak (Kendall's coefficient = $-.144$). Indicative of this finding was the fact that while many high officials in the United States strongly regarded the Oregon Territory as being in an American sphere of influence in 1846 when Britain delivered its threat to dispatch a strong naval squadron to American waters, the Polk Administration and the Senate were in agreement that a withdrawal from the line of 54° 40′ was quite acceptable. Their objectives were limited. In the case of Japan's "21 Demands" on China in 1915, it was China's lack of allies and its perception of Japanese capabilities that counted—not the fact that Japan was challenging Chinese suzerainty in Manchuria. Other examples might be given of nations, challenged in areas they considered their spheres of influence, capitulating to threats because of weaknesses in their alliance system or for some other reason. But perhaps the point has been made.

PAST AND PRESENT: DISTINCTIONS BETWEEN THREATS ISSUED BEFORE AND AFTER WORLD WAR II

One of the questions we wanted to answer was whether or not any significant differences between the past (defined as the pre-nuclear age) and the present could be detected. Would some variables have accounted for the success of threats before, but not after, the advent of nuclear weapons? The questions posed additional difficulties in using equal-interval factor analysis because of the reduced numbers of cases to be analyzed (forty-five past, thirty-two present). Given the large number of variables, we were unable to identify factors (to eliminate multicolinearity) until we had excluded numerous variables that had identical estimated communality coefficients. Hence, we dispensed altogether with our equal-interval "supportive" statistical techniques. We believe that past and present MLE analyses employing selected "critical" variables[56] and a comparison of Kendall's rank-order correlations of independent variables with the dependent variable for past and present cases are more reliable, and we base the following observations on these analyses.

Needless to say, several of the independent variables that account for much of the variation in the dependent (success-failure) variable for threats issued in the pre-nuclear age are the same as those for the total set of cases. Thus, the degree to which the target's goals were flexible was quite important. The same may be said of the threatener. A threatener bent on having its way in the past caused many a threat to "fail" when war ensued (a phenomenon we referred to in the previous chapter). It appears that some threats were issued with no particular expectation that the demands would be met, but simply to provide a kind of excuse for war. Rome's demands to Carthage in 218 B.C. were of this character, as were the English demands to Holland in 1667 (uncoded), the Italian demands to Turkey in 1911 (uncoded), the Austrian demands to Serbia in 1914,[57] the Italian demands to Greece in 1923, and the German demands to Poland in 1939.

Why did nations bother to make demands they were reasonably sure would be rejected? They wanted what they were demanding (or, on occasion, wanted war *itself*) very badly, but they were reluctant to "break the rules." At least as early as the Hellenistic and Roman periods, it had become customary for nation-states to respect the conditions of peace, and to interrupt it only for cause (*causus belli*), and only after ambassadors—in the case of Rome, members of the "college of fetials"—were sent to the offending party to inform that state of Rome's grievance and to demand redress. These ambassadors would return to Rome, and the Senate would then wait thirty days for the enemy to comply before war could properly be declared.[58] In the event that war was *desired* (to distract the public from domestic disorders, to deal with a treacherous or overly ambitious neighbor, or to provide a young prince with opportunity for fame and fortune), the customs were still to be observed. When M. Fabius Buteo provokingly offered in 218 B.C. to "shake out either peace or war" from the folds of his toga, he probably was hoping that the Carthaginians would respond as they did: "Give us what you will!" He shook out war.[59] Theodore Abel once claimed that of twenty-five major wars, the decision to fight had often been made long before any threat was issued.[60] Not every such war began with a threat, to be sure; but many did. In short, some threats issued in the past were but excuses for war, and, not surprisingly, they resulted in war.

As with the total set of cases, of those involving threats issued in the past, it appeared that when the target felt the threatener's military capabilities to be substantially higher than the target's, the threat generally succeeded. Threats affecting the era's balance of power generally failed, and the credibility of the threat remained a predictor of its success (all three relationships significant to the .05 level or better).

These results offered few new insights and varied little from our analysis of the total set, but other findings were less consistent with our earlier results. The climate of international opinion was not a statistically significant predictor variable in our analysis of the sample of past cases,[61] probably because the climate of international opinion did not carry as much moral or political weight before the days of modern communications, mass media, and United Nations deliberations.

One variable that had not appeared significant in the analysis of both past *and* present cases appeared to be slightly significant in our analysis of the past cases alone. Somewhat intriguing is the mildly significant ($F = 1.4$) relationship between the degree to which the threatener's economic viability was at stake in the crisis and the *failure* of the threat. Recall that we allowed this variable to represent both economic dangers and economic opportunities. But economic expansion and contraction affect the same policy "nerve." British merchants in 1719 feared that war with Russia would *hurt* the economy. Ambitious Japanese expansionists *risked* war to secure political and economic power in Korea and Manchuria in 1895. And in 1898 American businessmen felt that war with Spain was worth risking if it would end the Cuban crisis and its deleterious effect on the American economy.[62] In short, both economic anxieties and economic expectations of the threatener were prominent in those threats that failed. Targets seem not to have let the economic interests of the threatener govern their own decisions, and a threat issued *because* of such interests sometimes ended in war if the target's own objectives simply would not accommodate those economic interests of the threatener.

Let us move on to a consideration of the present cases (our thirty-two threats issued after World War II). Once again, several variables prominent in the full sample of seventy-seven cases were also statistically significant in analysis of threats issued in the present. These included the climate of international opinion, the target's perception of the threatener's capabilities, the degree to which the target's objectives were flexible, and the effect of the alliance systems on the relative capabilities of the parties.[63] The inflexibility of the target, for example, appeared to be central to an understanding of the inability of the Soviets to force the Polish leadership to keep Wladyslaw Gomulka from power, the failure of the efforts of the United States and Turkey to force Syria into a Western alliance in 1957, the failure of the Soviet threats regarding the future of Berlin in 1958, and the failure of the United States to force North Vietnam to withdraw from the South in 1965 and subsequent years. Conversely, the flexibility and limited character of the target's objectives may help us understand the *success* of the American threat to the Soviet Union in October 1973 regarding the movement of Soviet troops into Syria. When targets have made up their minds about what they need or cannot tolerate, it appears very difficult for threateners to change them except by overrunning them militarily.

The relative utility of the alliance networks of target and threatener may merit an illustrative case, too. The Soviet leaders sent troops into motion in Poland, the Soviet Union, and East Germany on October 18, 1956, after the failure of a plot to arrest Gomulka.[64] The next day the top leadership descended on Warsaw and made its demands to the Polish leadership. Polish intransigence was sustained that night by a Chinese communiqué that demonstrated to the Soviets that Poland had friends. That appears to have had something to do with their decision to "discuss" matters, and to accept a number of Polish compromise proposals, requests, and demands.

One variable found to be significant in analyzing the post–World War II cases consisted of the extent to which the ideological or moral interests of the target were at stake in the crisis. It appears that when the ideological or moral interests of the target *were* at stake, threats tended to fail.[65] The Chinese threat to the United States and the United Nations in 1951, as the latter's forces approached the Yalu, failed to halt that advance. The target certainly had strong allies, while the Chinese do not appear to have been able to acquire comparable support from the Soviet Union. Both parties clearly behaved as if ideology was quite relevant and at issue.[66] Conversely, in 1969, the Soviets were able to force Ghana to release one of their merchant vessels after a lengthy period of internment. The incident was largely void of ideological character, and the target (Ghana) was quite unable to call on Britain or the United States to defend its rather unreasonable behavior.

The credibility of the threat was also significant among our modern threats,[67] and the relevance of this variable to the success of threats can be adequately illustrated by a case in which it was so obviously lacking. When the North Koreans seized the *Pueblo* in 1968, the United States was unable to pursue rapidly and to recapture the ship before it reached Pusan Harbor and its crew could be removed. Thereafter, the vaguely threatening statements of Secretary of State Dean Rusk[68] were thoroughly undermined when the United States signaled its willingness[69] to accept the North Korean charge that the ship had been in that nation's territorial waters. The safe return of the crew was more important to American policymakers than was retribution, and we think we may assume that the North Koreans sensed that the United States would not risk the loss of those lives in a military strike. North Korea ignored the American threat to use force and forced the Americans to use apologies.

The *Pueblo* case may also serve as evidence of the significance of another variable: the degree to which the vested interests of the threatener's bureaucracies weakened the leadership's position and prompted the failure of the threat.[70] Due to pronounced interservice competition in the gathering of intelligence information, and to weaknesses in military communications systems (due also largely to bureaucratic competition), the American reaction to the North Korean seizure was too slow with too little, and the United States was forced to "deal" from weakness.

The Cuban missile crisis may also serve to illustrate this phenomenon. A message from the Soviet leader to the American president during the crisis revealed Soviet sensitivity to the presence of American missiles in Turkey. The president was distressed by this news, for he had, some months before, directed the secretary of state to initiate measures to retire these obsolescent (but diplomatically dangerous) missiles. A reticent State Department bureaucracy (sensitive to Turkish preferences) left the missiles untouched, and they provided the Soviets with leverage in the crisis.[71]

A group of related variables were highly correlated with the outcome of threats in the nuclear age: the degree to which the threatener had investments in the area being contended for, the degree to which the threatener had trade markets in that area, the degree to which it imported vital resources from that area, the degree to which the area of contention was militarily or economically dependent on the threatener, and the degree to which the threatener had strong traditional ties with the area of contention. A high scoring of each and all of these variables was associated in a statistically significant fashion[72] with the success of the threat. It was not that the threatener's economic viability had necessarily been imperilled (though in some instances it was),[73] nor that the area of contention was necessarily part of its formal sphere of influence. Rather, the threatener and the area of contention seem linked by a network of what Bruce Russett has called "associational ties." Nations "testing the water" (Iraq in 1961, for example) seem of late to have been deterred from any expansionist measures when the desired areas are clearly tied to the deterring powers. This is what Russett discovered and reported in his study of twelve midcentury deterrent threats.[74] But we find it interesting that this finding is virtually the *opposite* of that which prevailed for our forty-five pre-nuclear threats. For those cases, strong associational ties of threateners and areas of contention were correlated with the *failure* of threats. The different significance of associational ties in the past and present is, we confess, mysterious to us, and it may be purely an accident of our sample size. In any event, our findings suggest that what Russett found to be powerfully predictive of the outcome of deterrent threats in the mid-twentieth century *may* be due either to sample size or to vagaries of the modern threat environment. (In this regard, we note that the recent Falkland Islands crisis does not conform to Russett's and to our present cases' findings.)

One final variable seems to be predictive of the outcome of threats today, though it proved less significant in the past. This was the threatener's perception of the target's overall capabilities. When the threatener felt itself militarily superior in the nuclear age, threats tended to succeed.[75] What is intriguing is not that such a relationship should exist today (for it seems quite reasonable), but that it should have failed to be predictive of success in the past. (Indeed, a modestly significant relationship of the *opposite* sort was observed—that is, in the past, threats tended to *fail* when the threatener saw itself as militarily superior, to succeed when it saw itself as militarily *inferior*.[76] Our only explanation for this curious finding is that target resolve and threatener intransigence were so terribly important in the past that the threatener's perception of the target's capabilities simply did not matter; other, more powerful "motives . . . of passion," as Lord Melbourne called them, were at work.)

Snyder and Diesing have maintained that shows of force in the nuclear age have more "potency" than they did in the past because "the expanded ensemble of crisis maneuvers in the nuclear age" serve "to clarify interests. . . . He who is most willing to run risks would appear to have the most at stake. . . . the skill with which a state manipulates demonstrative short-of-war tactics may have a considerable effect on the outcome."[77]

This certainly sounds plausible and may well describe the Berlin crises, but it does not appear to be applicable in general. As with the past cases, the ratio of the threatener's forces actually deployed in the threat to the target's military forces was of no consequence in each of several selected-variable analyses of the success-failure variable for the post–World War II cases. Neither, for that matter, was the ratio of either the conventional or the nuclear forces available to the contenders.[78] Deployed and deployable force per se does not appear to be nearly as important in determining the success of a threat as are levels of alliance support and target resolve.

If we look only at threats issued by the United States in the past generation ($N = 23$), we continue to find that a climate of international opinion legitimizing the goals of the target (for example, "Rolling Thunder" or the U.S. threat during the Indo-Pakistani War of 1971) is strongly predictive of the failure of the threat (Kendall's coefficient significant to .001 level). Alliance support more useful to the United States than to the target, another familiar variable, continued to be predictive of the success of the threat (Kendall's coefficient significant to the .005 level). But while similarities between our findings in the analysis of this subset and earlier findings predominate, a few differences may be noted. It appears that public opinion in the United States supportive of the policymakers' decision to deliver the threat was not statistically associated with threat success. Some analysts[79] have hypothesized that public support aids the threatener, especially in as open a society as the United States. We find it hard to believe that public support would cause a reduction in the likelihood that the threat will succeed, inasmuch as it signals resolve (and perhaps enhances credibility to the target). But threatener resolve (and even credibility) appears to be less important than target resolve. All the public expressions of outrage over the fate of the *Pueblo* seem to have been of little consequence in North Korea. The United States Government was unable to coerce North Korea, and North Korea was unwilling to budge. Consequently, the fact of strong support for the threats did not prevent America's bluff from being called. Conversely, the threat to the Soviet Union concerning Yugoslavia in 1951 was criticized in the Congress, and it elicited little public attention, to say nothing of support. We do not know whether it actually deterred the Soviets or, for that matter, whether the Soviets ever seriously contemplated using force in Yugoslavia (which is why we did not bestow much ''weight'' to this case). However, we do know that the threat, such as it was, could not be said to have failed, despite the lack of visible public support for it. Public support may not have *caused* American threats to fail[80] (the Gods were not quite that angry with us), but it seems that it has not contributed to their success.

Equally intriguing is another predictive variable, which might be seen as indicating that the more force the United States put on the line in conveying the threat, the less likely the threat was of being successful (Kendall's coefficient $= -.29$, significant to the .08 level). The United States deployed no military forces in threatening Ecuador in 1960, and neither the United States nor its partner, Iran, deployed force comparable to that deployed by the Soviets in 1946 when demanding that the Soviets leave Iran. Yet both threats succeeded: in the former case, probably because of the target's inability to acquire Soviet support and its acknowledgment of America's latent military power; and in the latter case, either because the Soviets were content with what they thought were Iranian oil concessions or because they were ultimately unwilling to test America's threat ''to support the principles of the U.N. Charter'' in the Iranian crisis.[81] Conversely, the American bombing of North Vietnam, ''Rolling Thunder,'' constituted an extreme form of force projection associated with a threat (the resumption of the bombing raids). Heavy as America's hand was in the crisis, Ho Chi Minh's resolve was weightier. Once again, the relationship is almost certainly not causal, but it does permit us to conclude that displays of force did not appear to have been instrumental to the success of American threats in the nuclear age.

A comparison of past and present cases did indicate some differences in their respective success–failure calculi. Threateners may have been more likely to issue threats merely as an excuse for war in the past than they are now.[82] Perhaps the existence of the United Nations forum makes such unreasonable threats counterproductive now. A target's complaint to that body could embarrass and possibly even check the course of a determined, aggressive threatener. Hence, potential ''excuse'' threats emerge instead as surprise attacks. Conversely, ideological disputes may be more likely to begin with threats in the age of arbitration and nuclear "Assured Destruction" than in a past filled with religious wars and acts of racial imperialism, many of which began without concern for such niceties as a *causus belli*. Heretics, infidels, and "fuzzy-wuzzys" were not "deserving" of prior warning. (And a successful attack on one's ideological foe could not result in one's own destruction in the pre-nuclear age; it could today. Hence, we threaten nuclear use rather than preempt.)

But such differences are quite modest compared to the similarities. In both the pre-nuclear and the nuclear ages, the success or failure of a threat was decided by similar issues: the relative utility of the alliance networks, the extent to which the target was flexible, the target's perception of the threatener's capabilities, and the degree to which the crisis affected the era's balance of power. In the past, a target may have been more concerned with the threatener's capabilities than it would be in the present; in the present, a target might be more concerned with the extent to which certain of the threatener's vital interests were at stake in the crisis than it would have been in the past. But these variations do not strike us as being nearly so significant as do our findings that resolve, allies, credibility, and the balance of power count, and that the fine tuning of forces deployed in the threat may not. Moreover, our analysis offers little confirmation of the oft-heard claim[83] that the introduction of nuclear weapons to the world of power politics has substantially altered the equations that determine the success or failure of threats.[84] The possession of nuclear weapons by both a threatener and a target in some of today's threats means (one hopes) that both parties sense that neither can truly "win." But, as Snyder and Diesing have noted,[85] this same sense of the possibility of self-destruction was felt by threatener (Lord Grey) and target (the Kaiser) in 1914, and by another English threatener (Neville Chamberlain) in 1938 and 1939. The "rubble" might not "bounce," but "civilization as we know it" would end just the same. We would do well to recall in particular the tragic vision of Grey and Kaiser Wilhelm, a vision that did not lead Europe back from the brink of that devastating war. Their vision of the cost did not prevent its payment. Nor can threats today rely on high costs for their success or peaceful resolution.

SUCCESS OR FAILURE: A DIFFERENT DEFINITION

Throughout this chapter, "failure" has meant either a threat that ended in war or one that did not end in war but that also did not result in the attainment of any substantial portion of its objectives. There are, of course, other ways to define failure in the threat environment. One of these is, quite simply, to treat as failures those threats that end in war. Defining failure in this fashion, we wondered what variables would predict it.

About four-fifths of the variance between those threats that ended in war and those that did not was accounted for by regression analysis (statistically tolerable because of the dichotomous character of the dependent variable). Four of the predictive variables were quite predictable. First, all other things being equal, when the threatener was not willing to listen to reason—that is, when the threat served essentially as an excuse for war—war tended to ensue (coefficient significant to the .005 level). Second, all other things being equal, when the threatener had the sympathy of the international community, the crisis generally did not end in war (coefficient significant to the .04 level). Third, all other things being equal, a threat adversely affecting the world balance of power tended to lead to war (coefficient significant to the .03 level). Finally, when during the course of the crisis the parties shifted from essentially diplomatic to increasingly military measures and tactics, the crisis tended to end in war (coefficient significant to the .0002 level).

Two other predictive variables were more intriguing. All other things being equal, when the military security interests of the threatener were not at stake in the crisis, but the target's political power interests were, war was likely to ensue (coefficients significant to the .02 and .05 levels, respectively). Philip V regarded his political power to be very much on the line in 200 B.C., when Rome opportunistically challenged his hegemony in Greece. So did Spain, in 1898, when the United States threatened her concerning affairs in Cuba. Rome and the United States correctly surmised that were their targets to balk at their demands, they would have few problems enforcing them. Hence, when the targets did balk, the threateners perceived war as a low-risk military act.

We were surprised to find that several hypothetically important variables were not statistically significant in explaining why some threats ended in war. It did not appear to matter to the target that resort to bloodshed might have devastating consequences. Also inconsequential were the degree of clarity with which the threat was communicated; the ratio of the actual ("objective") forces of threatener and target; and the degree to which the threatener had, previous to the threat, been able to achieve its objectives in the region. Having achieved one's objectives in a given region in the past appears to be no assurance that a threat can achieve one's objectives a second time without one's having to fight for them.[86]

The Long-Range Consequences

The preceding statement has implications for the long-range consequences of threats, for if achieving one's objectives in a given region on one occasion in the past offers no assurances for the present success of an actor's threats, perhaps the success of threats in the present would be no predictor of the future ability of the threatener to manipulate the target. This is what Karsten hypothesized earlier,[87] and it is what we found on analyzing our coded cases:[88] for some time in the ninth century, Franks and Saxons paid *Danegeld* and avoided the Viking fury. But eventually, they tired of this, organized their forces, and stopped the extortion. The king of the Two Sicilies did yield to British demands in 1742, but as soon as the British squadron had left, he "hastened to repair fortifications and coastal defenses," raised new regiments, acquired a naval squadron, and completely ignored the assurances he had made the British.[89] The Austrian threats to Serbia in 1909 and 1913 were successful, but they steeled the will of the Serbs and (more significantly) their Russian allies, and threat led to war in 1914, when Russia stood firm. Yuan Shih-K'ai accepted Japan's "21 Demands" in 1915 with only minor amendments, but the Chinese public reaction was one of outrage,[90] and China was not as ready to yield in 1931 or 1937. Germany acceded to America's insistence that she halt unrestricted submarine warfare in 1915, but two years later, under greater wartime pressure, Germany reinstituted the practice and refused to rescind those orders when President Wilson repeated his warning. In 1923 British pressure in the League of Nations caused Mussolini to loosen his grip on Corfu. But the process was not repeated in 1935 when Mussolini attacked Ethiopia. Britain protested in the League again, but Mussolini recalled the previous "gratuitous and impudent mystification at the expense of Italy" and ignored the protests.[91] Hitler blustered his way into Czechoslovakia without a shot in 1938 but was unable to repeat the feat a year later in Poland. The Soviet Union gained some prestige with its threat to Britain and France during the Suez crisis of 1956, but one of the long-range consequences of that "successful" threat may have been the acquisition by both Britain and France of nuclear weapons. The success of a threat at Time X is no guarantee that the same sort of threat will work at Time X + 1. A nation that capitulates to a threat once may decide that it must pursue the same course of action given similar circumstances in the future, but it is just as likely that such a capitulation leads to a reaction within the nation against those responsible for it and results in a steeling of the will. Under such reactionary circumstances, accommodative gestures are regarded as unsavory and are referred to as acts of "appeasement."

If the outcome of the threat is no predictor of the character of the future relationship between threatener and target, what variables *do* predict such relationships? Inasmuch as our analysis was largely focused on the immediate environment of the threat, we are not prepared to say with any confidence what appears to have shaped the attitude of targets toward threateners in the years following the threat. Any one or more of a number of unobserved impulses or systemic changes could have accounted for a given relationship. All we can say is that there is not a statistically significant correlation between the observed effectiveness of the threatener's actions and its observable ability in the future to threaten that target.[92]

NOTES

1. Following the method delineated on page 130, cases were weighted in order to suppress the importance of those cases in which (1) the threat was imperfectly understood by the target, (2) the target's behavior in a deterrent situation could not be considered a function merely of the threat, but of other stimuli as well, or (3) the nation issuing the threat was primarily interested in war and thus issued an altogether unacceptable threat. The findings reported in this chapter all reflect the analysis of weighted data, except with regard to maximum likelihood estimation (as that algorithm's computer program did not allow for fractional cases).

2. Barry Blechman and Stephen Kaplan, *Force Without War* (Washington, D.C.: Brookings Institution, 1978), pp. 79–83, report a ratio of 3.1 compellent acts to every 2 deterrent ones in the twenty-five cases in their sample of thirty-three instances in which

the United States deployed force for political purposes between 1946 and 1976 where U.S. actions could be characterized either as deterrent or compellent in nature.

3. This is not to say that the targets always perceived the threat accurately; the clearest threat can still be misunderstood, especially by one who does not want to hear what the other side is saying. Cf. Glenn Snyder and Paul Diesing, *Conflict Among Nations* (Princeton: Princeton University Press, 1977), p. 72.

4. One target *was* stronger than its threatener, but only in one sense. We considered the U.S. threat to the French in 1803 as a test case of our findings. In that case, U.S. strength was considerable in the area of contention (Louisiana) due to its proximity to the threatener and its distance from the target. (Kenneth Boulding argues that capabilities become less viable as means of attaining objectives as one increases the distance between the actor and the point of contention, while weaker states enhance the effectiveness of their capabilities when they must extend their power over relatively short distances. *Conflict and Defense* [New York: Harper, 1962], p. 231.)

5. George Kennan, "Europe's Problems, Europe's Choices," *Foreign Policy,* no. 14 (Spring 1974), pp. 14–15.

6. Raymond Gastil, *Foreign Policy,* no. 16 (Fall 1974), pp. 185–86.

7. Peter Karsten, "Response to Threat Perception: Accommodation as a Special Case," in *Historical Dimensions of National Security Problems*, ed. Knorr Klaus (Lawrence, Kans.: University of Kansas Press, 1976), p. 136.

8. Bruce Russett, "The Calculus of Deterrence," *Journal of Conflict Resolution* 7 (June 1963): 97–109. The trade-investment relation to conflict may not be so much *cause* as *effect*, of course; friendly nations may become economic partners (as did Britain and Turkey, on the one hand, and France and Egypt, on the other, in 1838). In either event, they are not likely to be threat adversaries.

9. George Hunt, *The Wars of the Iroquois* (Madison, Wis.: University of Wisconsin Press, 1940), p. 21.

10. Cordell Hull, *The Memoirs of Cordell Hull,* 2 vols. (New York: Macmillan, 1948), 1:365.

11. Kendall's rank-order correlation coefficients for the two variables ($N = 77$) is .402, statistically significant to the .001 level. The varimax rotated factor matrix values of the two variables were .65 and .78 in a factor composed of a number of other variables, all of which had substantially lower coefficients.

12. Ole Holsti, *Crisis, Escalation, War* (Montreal: McGill-Queen's University Press, 1972), pp. 199–200.

13. See appendices 3 and 4 for an example of case-by-case residual data for a maximum likelihood estimate (of the "war/no war" variable), which identifies the cases that conform to the findings and those that are deviant, and for an example of a multiple regression of weighted cases with plots of standardized residuals.

The 58 percent figure is for the seventy-seven unweighted cases; the 68 percent figure, for the seventy-seven weighted cases, an indication of the relative utility of the weighting process.

14. Neville G. A. Maxwell, *India's China War* (New York: Pantheon Books, 1970), pp. 25, 247–48, 364.

15. Quoted in Snyder and Diesing, *Conflict Among Nations,* p. 301.

16. C. J. Lowe and F. Marzani, *Italian Foreign Policy, 1879–1940* (London: Routledge and Kegan Paul, 1975), p. 198. As we shall see, this perception by the target of Britain's threat that Britain's military capabilities were considerable was also predictive of the

threat's success, and appears to have been more causal than the climate of international opinion.

17. D. Evan Luard, *Conflict and Peace in the Modern International System* (Boston: Little, Brown, 1968), p. 304; J. W. Burton, *International Relations* (Cambridge, England: The University Press, 1965), pp. 108–18, 152–60; *Public Opinion and Foreign Policy,* ed. L. Markel (New York: Harper, 1948), pp. 143–213.

K. J. Holsti does not claim that the United Nations has been an effective instrument during periods of high tension, but his evidence suggests that the UN has, in 71 of 116 instances, succeeded in its efforts (via mediation, supervision, intervention, and the like) to resolve conflicts. This may be further evidence of the significance of the climate of international opinion. Holsti, *International Politics,* 3d ed. (Englewood Cliffs, N.J.: Prentice-Hall, 1977), pp. 495–99.

18. Snyder and Diesing, *Conflict Among Nations,* p. 204.

19. *Thucydides' Peloponnesian War,* trans. Richard Crawley (London: Longmans, Green, 1876), pp. 403–4.

20. F. W. Wallbank, *Philip V of Macedon* (Cambridge, England: The University Press, 1940), p. 137.

21. The quote from the Chinese minister is from Peter Ward Fay, *The Opium War, 1840–1842* (Chapel Hill, N.C.: University of North Carolina Press, 1975), p. 222. Those of Franz Joseph and Victor Emmanuel are in C. W. Hallberg, *Franz Joseph and Napoleon III, 1852–1864* (New York: Bookman Associates, 1955), p. 181; and Gordon Craig, *Europe Since 1815* (New York: Putnam, 1971), p. 212.

Stanley K. Hornbeck, a State Department Asian expert, misjudged the likelihood of a Japanese decision for war on November 27, 1941, when he offered five to one odds against the decision by December 1 with the remark: "Tell me of one case in history when a nation went to war out of desperation." Clearly, Hornbeck was unaware of (or had forgotten) the Austrian decision in 1859 and the Melian decision in 416 B.C. (Hornbeck quoted in James C. Thompson, Jr., "The Role of the Department of State," in *Pearl Harbor as History*, ed. D. Borg and S. Okamoto [New York: Columbia University Press, 1973] p. 101.)

22. Henry Blumenthal, *A Reappraisal of Franco-American Relations, 1830–1871* (Chapel Hill, N.C.: University of North Carolina Press, 1959), p. 177; Dexter Perkins, *The Monroe Doctrine, 1862–1867* (Baltimore: Johns Hopkins University Press, 1933), pp. 515–21.

Compare the argument that Bismarck offered in 1850, defending Prussia's capitulation to Austria, Bavaria, and Russia: The issues involved were "petty." The war would not have "a worthy goal." Otto Pflanze, *Bismarck and the Development of Germany* (Princeton: Princeton University Press, 1963), pp. 78, 79.

23. Walter LaFeber, *The New Empire* (Ithaca, N.Y.: Cornell Unviersity Press, 1963), pp. 268, 276; Thomas Patterson et al., *American Foreign Policy* (Lexington, Mass.: D. C. Heath, 1977), p. 191; Kenneth Bourne, *Britain and the Balance of Power in North America, 1815–1908* (London: Longmans, Green, 1967), pp. 325–30. For more on the avoidance of the unnecessary accumulation of trouble when one already has enemies, see Frederick Hartmann, *The Conservation of Enemies* (Westport, Conn.: Greenwood Press, 1982).

24. Needless to say, the threatener often does not know at the time it issues the threat the extent to which the target is willing to yield. Consequently, the fact that this variable is *important* is of limited use to one seeking predictability of outcome, unless one can

acquire sound information regarding the target's resolve. (See chapter 4 for more on this subject.)

25. R. Ned Lebow, *Between Peace and War* (Baltimore: Johns Hopkins University Press, 1981), pp. 82, 174–77; Dean Acheson, *The Korean War* (New York: Norton, 1969), p. 72.

26. Klaus Knorr, *Power and Wealth* (New York: Basic Books, 1973), pp. 16–20, 23, 145–46, 197.

27. Snyder and Diesing, *Conflict Among Nations*, pp. 186, 190.

28. Maxwell, *India's China War*, p. 58.

29. Slusser, in Blechman and Kaplan, *Force Without War*, p. 388.

30. Snyder and Diesing, among others, have noted the role of alliances in crises. *Conflict Among Nations*, pp. 430–40.

31. Juvaini, *History of the World Conqueror*, quoted at length in Berthold Spuler, ed., *History of the Mongols* (Berkeley, Calif.: University of California Press, 1972), pp. 33, 37.

32. George F. Young, *The Medici* (New York: Modern Library, 1933), p. 231.

33. Daniel M. Smith, *The American Diplomatic Experience* (Boston: Houghton Mifflin, 1972), p. 199; Patterson et al., p. 191.

34. Cf. R. C. North, H. E. Koch, and D.A. Zinnes, "Capability, Threat, and the Outbreak of War," in *International Politics and Foreign Policy*, ed. James Rosenau (New York: Free Press, 1961), pp. 469–82.

35. Harold Acton, *The Bourbons of Naples, 1734–1825* (London: Methuen, 1956), pp. 58–59.

36. R. Ned Lebow has assembled the relevant evidence of Germany's misperception in *Between Peace and War*, pp. 121–24. See also Harry F. Young, *Prince Lichnowsky and the Great War* (Athens, Ga.: University of Georgia Press, 1977), p. 110.

37. See Donald Kagan, *The Outbreak of the Peloponnesian War* (Ithaca, N.Y.: Cornell University Press, 1969), p. 285, for a convincing argument to this effect.

38. The same may be said of Poland's ability to recruit British and French guarantees in the teeth of German demands in 1939. Lawrence LaFore, *The End of Glory* (Philadelphia: Lippincott, 1970), pp. 239, 244.

A variable recording the posture assumed by the target's ally(ies) in the crisis was not utilized in the multivariate analysis because of its colinearity with the variable recording the ratio of alliance support to the parties. It was significantly correlated with the success-failure variable, as our analysis suggests it would be (Kendall's rank-order correlation coefficient = 234, statistically significant to the .008 level).

39. Thus, when we regressed the variable recording the *actual* conventional-force ratio of the two parties and the target's *perception* of the threatener's capabilities against the success-failure dependent variable, we found the former to be insignificant (r^2 – .007, standardized regression coefficient = –.20), while the latter was highly significant (r^2 = .194, standardized regression coefficient = .45, F = 18.3).

40. Hence, our study does not support Oran Young's hypotheses regarding the advantage accruing to the power that forces the other side to initiate novel behavior in a crisis. Young, *The Politics of Force* (Princeton: Princeton University Press, 1968), pp. 215, 218, 240.

41. Perkins, *The Monroe Doctrine, 1826–1867*, pp. 466*n*, 487, 490*n*.

42. Henry Blumenthal, *France and the United States* (Chapel Hill: University of North Carolina Press, 1970), p. 112.

Similarly, in 1958 the Soviets appear to have backed down in Berlin for reasons independent of the West's displays of force. After pointing out the role that the Sino-Soviet rift played in the Soviet decision, Robert Slusser added: ". . . 'The use of force' . . . was not central." In Blechman and Kaplan, *Force Without War*, p. 383.

43. Howard F. Cline, *The United States and Mexico* (Cambridge, Mass.: Harvard University Press, 1953), p. 155; Peter Karsten, *The Naval Aristocracy* (New York: Free Press, 1972), pp. 162–63.

44. Alexander George and Richard Smoke, *Deterrence in American Foreign Policy* (New York: Columbia University Press, 1974); Lebow, *Between Peace and War*, pp. 174–77, 182. See also Maxwell, *India's China War*, p. 58, for an account of India's unsuccessful efforts to force China to accept India's definition of their mutual border by advancing unsupported picket outposts.

45. Snyder and Diesing, *Conflict Among Nations*, pp. 315, 496.

46. Truong Buu Lam, "Intervention versus Tribute in Sino-Vietnamese Relations," in *China's Response to the West*, ed. John K. Fairbank (Cambridge, Mass.: Harvard University Press, 1954), pp. 173–74.

This may be evidence of Roger Fisher's claim that the threatener must provide "a yesable proposition" for the threat to succeed. See his *International Conflict for Beginners* (New York: Harper and Row, 1969), pp. 15–59.

47. *Thucydides*, pp. 304–6. This example brings to mind the British threat to China in 1840 regarding the Chinese banning of opium from British India. Captain Charles Elliot, the British negotiator, slowly became conscious of the inflexibility inherent in Chinese-Manchu diplomacy and of that nation's vital (as well as its more expendable) interests. Consequently, Elliot set aside the instructions Lord Palmerston had given him and let the Chinese negotiator save some face in exchange for much of what Britain demanded. "The language in which the demands of her Majesty's Government is pressed can hardly be too profoundly respectful," he counseled Palmerston. "To consult the situation and prejudices of the Chinese Government is as necessary as to awaken their fears." (To Elliot's chagrin, however, Palmerston did not agree, and the treaty Elliot had arranged was rejected.) Fay, *The Opium War, 1840–1842*, p. 310.

48. *New York Times*, July 13, 1976, p. 1; various conversations with Defense and State Department officials. Coral Bell argues that the United States deliberately sent ambiguous (and different) threats to the Soviets and Chinese during the Quemoy crisis of 1958, which helped to deprive the Chinese of Soviet support. *The Conventions of Crisis* (London: Oxford University Press, 1971), p. 75.

49. The U.S. threat to China over Quemoy in 1958 is another example of this phenomenon, as is the silence President Nixon maintained during the "Christmas bombing" coercion of North Vietnam in 1972. As he put it:

> Any public statements [regarding the bombings] on my part would have been directly counterproductive to the possibility of resumed negotiations. If I had announced that we were resuming bombing for the purpose of forcing the North Vietnamese to negotiate, their national pride and their ideological fanaticism would never have allowed them to accept the international loss of face involved in caving in to such an ultimatum. So I did it with the minimum amount of rhetoric and publicity.

RN: The Memoirs of Richard Nixon (New York: Grosset and Dunlap, 1978), p. 736.

50. See Bruce Kuniholm, *The Origins of the Cold War in the Near East* (Princeton: Princeton University Press, 1980), for the best recent discussion of whether the Russianss were deterred.

51. A lack of U.S. support for France and Britain in the Suez crisis in 1956 is an example of this phenomenon.

52. See the argument in Roger H. Brown, *The Republic in Peril: 1812* (New York: Columbia University Press, 1964).

53. The Kendall's rank-order correlation coefficient for the variable representing the degree to which resources imported from the area of contention were important to the threatener and the variable representing the degree to which the threatener regarded itself as having substantial sphere-of-influence interests in the area of contention was .435, significant to the .001 level.

54. The Kendall's coefficient for the ''important resources'' variable and the threatener's ''economic viability'' variable was .26, significant to the .02 level.

55. The Kendall's coefficient for the ''important resources'' variable and the ''change of target appreciation of threatener's interests'' variable was .25, significant to the .02 level.

56. See Robert A. Gordon, ''Issues in Multiple Regression,'' *American Journal of Sociology* 73 (1968):592–615, for a persuasive case for employing such a ''selective'' technique.

57. Some of Austria-Hungary's leadership proposed a more temperate set of demands that would clearly have been agreed to by Serbia, but Foreign Minister Leopold von Berchtold added to the ultimatum terms that Serbia found impossible to accept. Since this was Berchtold's intent, and since he spent a ''sleepless night'' fearful that Serbia *might* accept the demands, the threat served essentially as an excuse for Austrian military action.

58. William Ballis, *The Legal Position of War* (The Hague: M. Nijhoff, 1937), pp. 21–23; Leon Friedman, ed., *The Law of War* (New York: Random House, 1972), pp. 1, 5.

59. T. A. Dorey and D. R. Dudley, *Rome Against Carthage* (London: Seeker and Warburg, 1971), p. 35.

60. T. Abel, ''The Element of Decision in the Pattern of War,'' *American Sociological Review* 6 (1941): 854–55. Abel's article is, however, controversial, and we cite it only suggestively, not as authority.

61. Kendall's coefficient was −.15, significant only to the .13 level, and neither the MLE nor the regression coefficients were statistically significant.

62. LaFeber, *The New Empire*, pp. 379–406, is convincing on this score.

63. Kendall's coefficients for the correlation of each of these variables and the dependent variable were .64 (significant to .001 level), .42 (significant to .002 level), −.22 (significant to .06 level), and .45 (significant to .001 level), respectively.

64. See Paul E. Zinner, ed., *National Communism and Popular Revolt in Eastern Europe* (New York: Columbia University Press, 1956).

65. Kendall's coefficient was −.55, significant to the .001 level, and the regression coefficient was significant to the .04 level. Cf. Stephen T. Ross, *Quest for Victory* (South Brunswick, N.J.: A. S. Barnes, 1973), pp. 22–24, for evidence in the age of the French Revolution.

66. As clear as the Chinese threat may have been from the perspective of the threatener, the threat was highly problematical from the U.S. viewpoint. Initially, the Indians (through whom the Chinese transmitted their threat) in general, and Krishna Menon in particular, were viewed as questionable sources by American decisionmakers. Moreover, verification of the threat devolved to the local commander, Douglas MacArthur. Yet, whatever

problems inhered in the transmission of the threat and in the ability of MacArthur to influence the decisionmaking process can be attributed to the highly charged ideological atmosphere in Washington. The decision to go beyond the 38th parallel indicated an American commitment to "rolling back" the Communists. Walter LaFeber, "Crossing the 38th," in *Reflections on the Cold War,* ed. Lynn Miller and Ronald Pruessen (Philadelphia: Temple University Press, 1974), pp. 71–90; George and Smoke, *Deterrence in American Foreign Policy,* pp. 186–231.

67. Kendall's coefficient was .51, significant to the .001 level.

68. "My strong advice to the North Koreans is to cool it." Trevor Armbrister, *A Matter of Accountability* (New York: Coward-McCann, 1970), p. 258.

69. Secretary of Defense Robert McNamara revealed a willingness to "give" in response to questions posed by panelists on the television program "Meet the Press" shortly after Rusk's remarks.

70. Kendall's coefficient was −.376, significant to the .004 level; and the standardized regression coefficient was significant to the .03 level.

An earlier example of this phenomenon may have been the Chanak crisis of 1922. The Lloyd George coalition government was experiencing substantial political difficulties in Britain when its friend in the Middle East, Greece, withdrew in confusion from its invasion of central Turkey. The Lloyd George government, with a display of dubious judgment, decided that a defense was called for of the postwar "neutral zone" (which the Allies had created around the Bosporus and Dardanelles) against the advancing forces of Mustapha Kemal lest British prestige suffer a blow "of the most disastrous character, producing, no doubt, far-reaching reactions throughout all Moslem countries." The Indian Office, however, sought to mollify Indian Moslems and caused a pro-Turkish telegram to be published, embarrassing Lord Curzon, the foreign secretary, who wrote that "on the eve of the [International] Conference [on the Turkish crisis], my pitch is queered, my hand is shattered, by the declaration from a branch of the British Government." Inaccurate military intelligence led the British to believe that Kemal planned to attack a fortified British position in Chanak on September 30, and on September 29 the cabinet directed General Sir Charles Harrington, the field commander, to deliver an ultimatum with a "short time limit." The military and Lord Curzon's Foreign Office were opposed to the cabinet's policy for several reasons, and General Harrington procrastinated. The Kemal regime appears to have become aware of the divisions within the British ranks, and it held out until more moderate council prevailed in London and a settlement favorable to Kemal was reached. We do not imply that a more unified stand taken by the military and the Foreign Office would have insured the success of the threats. Kemal's own capabilities and goals, and the desertion of Britain's French and Italian allies (to say nothing of rumblings from two Commonwealth partners, Canada and Australia), had a great deal to do with the outcome of the threat. But the fact that Lloyd George's precipitous policies went against the grain of the leaders of those two bureaucracies (and particularly the military commander on the scene) appears to have contributed to the failure of the threat. David Walder, *The Chanak Affair* (London: Hutchinson, 1969); and Nancy Snodgrass, "The Chanak Crisis: A Study in British Diplomacy" (Ph.D. diss., University of Illinois, 1971), pp. 200–204, 282–84, 290, 342–59.

71. The classic account of the "bureaucratic" element in the Cuban missile crisis is Graham Allison, *Essence of Decision* (Boston: Little, Brown, 1971). (Allison provides several other examples of bureaucracy-generated problems during this crisis.) But see

also Stephen Krasner, "Are Bureaucracies Important? (or Allison Wonderland)," *Foreign Policy*, no. 7 (Summer 1972), pp. 159–79.

72. Each Kendall's rank-order correlation coefficient was significant to the .001 level or better.

73. Kendall's coefficient for this variable and the dependent variable for the thirty-two modern cases was .212, significant to the .078 level.

74. Russett, "The Calculus of Deterrence," pp. 97–109.

75. Kendall's rank-order correlation coefficient for this variable and the success-failure variable for nuclear-era cases was –.34, significant to the .01 level.

76. Kendall's coefficient for these variables for our past cases was .24, significant to the .02 level, and the variable's standardized regression coefficient was significant to the .07 level.

77. Snyder and Diesing, *Conflict Among Nations*, pp. 454, 457.

78. It is true that the threat to *use* nuclear weapons is strongly correlated with the success of the threat. On every one of the six occasions in which the threat included an explicit or clear implicit warning that nuclear weapons might be used, the threat could be said to have been at least partially successful. (These six cases were the Soviet threat during the Suez crisis, the American threat to China concerning Quemoy, the Soviet threat concerning Berlin in 1958, the Soviet and American implicit threats to one another during the 1961 Berlin crisis, and the American "alert" during the Arab-Israeli War of 1973.) But these successes might be attributable to such other variables as the degree to which the target's interests and objectives were limited or flexible (the Soviets in Syria, October 1973) or the target's lack of alliance support (the British and French during the Suez crisis, and the Chinese in 1958). Furthermore, after conducting our analysis, we became aware of another nuclear threat (the "madman" threat by the Nixon Administration against North Vietnam in 1969), a threat that *failed*, in that the North Vietnamese did not accede to the U.S. demands despite the threat of the use of nuclear weapons. (H. R. Haldeman, *The Ends of Power* [New York: Times Books, 1978], pp. 81–85, 97; Nixon, *RN*, pp. 393–414; Daniel Ellsberg, in *Protest and Survive*, ed. E. P. Thompson and Dan Smith [New York: Monthly Review Press, 1981], pp. xv, xxv.) Moreover, the current deterrent posture of Assured Destruction means that the superpower target of a superpower threat to use nuclear weapons may doubt the credibility of the threat, since carrying out the threat would be suicidal. This much may be said of nuclear threats: they appear to create at least some anxieties, and they may explain why the threats are at least partially successful. Only one target appears to have cold-bloodedly called the bluff of such a threatener to date, which is fortunate, because this type of threat can "fail" (in the sense of ending in the *use* of the weapons) only once.

79. See, for example, Alexander George et al., *The Limits of Coercive Diplomacy* (Boston: Little, Brown, 1971), p. 224 (based on three case studies).

80. It is possible, however, as Snyder and Diesing have suggested, that strong public pressure supporting a threat can frighten those who are doing the threatening if they fear it may force their hand or provoke the target. Thus, Lord Grey refused to permit fleet maneuvers during the first Moroccan crisis because he feared that strong supportive statements in the British press might trigger a German reaction. Snyder and Diesing, *Conflict Among Nations*, pp. 220–45.

81. Kuniholm, *The Origins of the Cold War in the Near East*, p. 325.

82. Geoffrey Blainey reminds us, in *The Causes of War* (New York: Free Press, 1973), p. 170, of J. F. Maurice's findings in 1883 that only about 8 percent of some 117 wars

between 1700 and 1880 began with a formal declaration of war preceding the attack. But this is not to say that the crises that led to these wars did not begin with the issuance of a formal threat or set of demands by one or the other. Most did. Indeed, as Maurice points out, in only about 38 percent of the instances in which one power attacked the other without declaring war did its leaders expect to take the enemy by surprise.

83. See, for example, Snyder and Diesing, *Conflict Among Nations,* p. 508; Walter Millis, *Arms and Men* (New York: Mentor, 1958), p. 325; and Fred Sondermann et al., *The Theory and Practice of International Relations*, 4th ed. (Englewood Cliffs, N.J.: Prentice-Hall, 1974), p. 291.

84. For related finding of similarities of the pre- and post-nuclear eras, see Charles Gochman and Zeev Maoz, "Serious Interstate Disputes, 1816–1976: Empirical Patterns and Theoretical Insights," unpublished paper, July 1982.

85. Snyder and Diesing, *Conflict Among Nations*, p. 16.

86. Note that we differ with Blechman and Kaplan (*Force Without War,* pp. 109–11) on this score.

87. Karsten, "Response to Threat Perception," p. 159:

> The fact that a state has in the past assumed an accommodative posture is a poor indicator of that state's future behavior when its interests are again deemed to be threatened. Some states engaging in acts of accommodations are simultaneously taking steps to increase their capabilities to deter or defend in the future. As we have said, pure accommodation, unadulterated by other responses to threat perception, is a relatively rare phenomenon. To be sure, the state being accommodated may choose to apply new pressure in the future, basing its expectations on the success it attained in the past, but it appears to be generally true that a state that has engaged in an act of accommodation experiences a steeling of the will after the fact and is not likely to follow such a course in the future.

88. We were only able to estimate such long-term consequences of the threat in about three-fourths of the cases, of course. In some instances, one or the other, or both, parties to the crisis had simply ceased to exist!

89. Acton, *The Bourbons of Naples,* pp. 60–62.

90. Bernadotte Schmitt, *The Coming of War, 1914,* 2 vols. (New York: C. Scribner's Sons, 1914), 1:359; Jerome Ch'en, *Yuan Shih-K'ai* (Stanford, Calif.: Stanford University Press, 1972), p. 195.

91. C. Seton-Watson, *Italy from Liberalism to Fascism* (London: Methuen, 1967), p. 673; Lowe and Marzini, *Italian Foreign Policy,* p. 198. Later, in 1940, Mussolini recalled "some accounts to settle" over Corfu with the Greeks on the eve of his attack on Greece. Seton-Watson, p. 673*n*.

92. Kendall's rank-order correlation coefficient for these variables was .013 (N – 57).

4

Conclusions and Recommendations

There is no terrour, Cassius, in your threats;
For I am arm'd so strong in honesty
That they pass by me as the idle wind,
Which I respect not.

—Shakespeare, *Julius Caesar,* IV.iii

Blandishments will not fascinate us, nor will threats of a "halter" intimidate, for, under God, we are determined that wheresoever, whensoever, or howsoever we shall be called to make our exit, we will die free men.

—Josiah Quincy, *Observations on the Boston Port Bill*

Let us briefly review the findings of our seventy-seven case analysis and test those findings with six new cases. We shall compare those findings with the conventional wisdom (wherever applicable) and project those findings into the future—to wit, by coding several differing scenarios that posit American responses to different sorts of Soviet pressure on Yugoslavia after the death of President Tito. And in the process, we shall speculate on the significance of our findings.

We noted that a target defending deeply felt interests tended to resist a threat of force whereas one that perceived itself to have insufficient military capabilities, or one whose allies were less useful than the threatener's, tended to yield. The fact that the target found itself vulnerable as a result of its international commitments appeared to be a mild predictor of the threat's success, as was the fact that the target regarded the threat as being credible. Threats also tended to succeed if the balance of power was unaffected; if the threatener's key bureaucracies were not at odds with its leadership; and if the threatener had strong ties with the area of contention in the crisis. Conversely, the fact that the area being contended for was in the target's sphere of influence did not appear to matter. Neither did clearly articulated threat messages or a loud rattling of sabres. Most notably, displays of force supportive of the demands being made did not contribute substantially to the success of the threat.

In the past, some threats failed essentially because they were outrageous—mere preludes to formal declarations of war. In the present, some tended to fail because a highly charged ideological atmosphere or a high level of regional tension strengthened the resolve of the target. Threats issued by the United States in the nuclear age tended to fail when they lacked credibility or lacked the sanction of international opinion. The strong support of the American public for the threat, and the deployment of substantial forces in conjunction with the communication of the demands, did not appear to affect the likelihood that the threat would succeed. Past and present threats had much in common.

Upon completing our analysis of the seventy-seven weighted cases, we searched for some additional cases to test our findings, and, with the help of colleagues, we uncovered six good ones:[1] the U.S. threat to France in 1802–1803 concerning Louisiana; the U.S. threat to Mexico in 1845–1846 regarding the annexation of Texas and the American appetite for California and northern Mexico; the U.S threat to Spain in 1854 over Cuba and the *Black Warrior*; the British demand in 1878 that Russia revise the terms of the Treaty of San Stephano; the British threat to France in 1898 regarding the presence at Fashoda of Captain Marchand and his men; and the Chinese threat to India in 1965 to confine its hostilities with Pakistan to the western half of that nation. How well do our findings predict the outcome of these threats? Let us examine them one by one, chronologically, beginning with the American threat to Napoleon in 1802–1803.

THE NEW ORLEANS CRISIS, 1802–1803

Some leaders of the new United States had since the 1780s sought to protect and insure the rights of western farmers and trappers to untrammeled use of the Mississippi River. When in September 1801 Napoleon acquired the Louisiana colony, with its key port, New Orleans, from Spain, President Thomas Jefferson let his distress at this development be known to France. "On the day that France takes possession of New Orleans," the United States would "marry ourselves to the British fleet and nation." The British ambassador to the United States, Edward Thornton, suggested to Jefferson that the two nations make "a common cause" in attacking France and Spain in New Orleans and Florida, and the French ambassador to the United States, hearing of this budding alliance, warned his foreign minister, Talleyrand, in December 1802.[2]

In the same month, the United States Congress passed a resolution empowering the president to call forth up to 80,000 militia if deemed necessary to deal with the French in New Orleans. Editors of many western and southern newspapers called for strong measures to keep the Mississippi open to American traffic, and some called for an immediate descent of western volunteers upon New Orleans.[3]

Napoleon's initial plans were clear enough: he wanted a French colonial empire in the Americas. He dispatched an army to Santo Domingo to suppress the revolt of Toussaint L'Ouverture, and he ordered another force prepared in Holland for Louisiana, which was to occupy and fortify that province for the future. Napoleon appeared ready to take a firm grip on the American continent. Before any French authority could reach New Orleans, however, the Spanish intendant there further enraged the Jeffersonians by deciding to interpret narrowly a provision in the relevant treaty between Spain and the United States; in late 1802 he closed the port of New Orleans to American goods and vessels.[4] The United States Government now threatened France more directly. Jefferson later explained to Horatio Gates that in early 1803 he had 'said with energy'' to the French Government ''what would take place'' in the event that France dispatched soldiers to New Orleans and continued to deny Americans the use of that port.[5]

But Napoleon did not need much convincing of the need to alter his policies. Indeed, by the time word reached him that Jefferson was sending James Monroe as a special envoy to discuss the Louisiana crisis, Napoleon had already cancelled the military expedition to Louisiana and had directed Talleyrand to offer to sell the colony to the United States. Why? Clearly, the possibility of an Anglo-American alliance troubled France. Talleyrand's visit to the United States ten years earlier had convinced him that Britain and the United States were natural allies. When the French ambassador to the United States warned his government that James Monroe would enter directly into negotiations with the British in the event that his mission to Paris proved unsatisfactory, the warning was taken seriously. When Napoleon and Talleyrand explained to the rest of the government the decision to part with Louisiana, their anxiety about the possible alliance of the United States and Britain was quite evident.[6]

The same cannot be said of American sabre-rattling. France displayed no fear of an attack upon New Orleans by westerners descending the Mississippi. No sooner had the new French prefect, Pierre Clément Laussat, reached New Orleans, in April 1803, than he told his government to ignore the ''clamors'' of westerners. He would ''not be duped'' by American preparations. ''There is no region, as is known, where there are so many political barkers as in the United States.'' When his Spanish predecessor had closed New Orleans, ''there were cries of private persons, for the blow strikes the interests of many of the merchants,'' but he reported that boats arriving from the Ohio Valley reported ''quiet.'' The farmers were preoccupied with the activities of the planting season.[7] In any event, Jefferson's militia was not viewed as being a match for any of the more seasoned French troops that Napoleon would send to Louisiana.

The British Fleet was another matter altogether. As Napoleon told his brother, Lucien, ''our navy is so inferior to that of [Britain] that it renders our colonial possession always uncertain.'' Renewal of the war with Britain would mean the certain loss of Louisiana.

Such a war was not inevitable, however. Peace might have been preserved with Britain had Napoleon been willing to negotiate his differences with that nation. On March 1, 1803, King George III expressed his displeasure to Parliament over the continued presence in Holland of French troops that were being gathered for the expedition to New Orleans. The expeditionary force continued its preparation throughout March, but it now had a new destination: England. No troops would go to Louisiana. By early 1803, the French forces in Santo Domingo had been virtually destroyed by disease and guerrilla operations. There would be no Napoleonic empire in the Americas. Napoleon's attention had shifted back to Europe, and in March he decided to reopen the war with Britain. As such, Louisiana would be vulnerable. He would sell it before it was seized by Britain. This was precisely how he and Talleyrand explained the decision to sell to their colleagues.[8] Napoleon's objectives simply did not include Louisiana any longer, and he turned the American threat into a French opportunity: he would use the money paid for the colony to outfit the army he planned to send across the English Channel.[9] In the words of one student of the crisis:

> The belief that combined action by England and the United States would make it impossible for him to occupy New Orleans was an essential factor in the case. The war already determined on with England would, [Napoleon] believed, result in the loss of Louisiana. [However], by cementing the friendship of the United States by the sale of the province, he would deprive England of a probable ally and enrich his treasury with funds for his approaching operations. The vision of a great colonial empire in America gave place in his mind to new European projects.[10]

It was not American militiamen that had caused Napoleon to negotiate; he simply ceased to regard the Americas as worth the bones of any more Languedoc grenadiers. And the threat of an Anglo-American alliance mattered more to him than his promise to Spain in 1801 never to alienate Louisiana. That commitment had probably been offered without Napoleon's realizing the intense interests many Americans had in the Mississippi and the extremes to which they were willing to go to protect those interests. This case, then, appears to confirm our findings, in the sense that the credibility of the threat, the degree to which the target's objectives were flexible, and the degree to which one or the other party was able to gain leverage with formal or informal allies were strongly predictive of the outcome of the crisis.

THE TEXAS ANNEXATION CRISIS, 1845–1846

In 1845 the newly inaugurated American president, James K. Polk, ordered U.S. naval vessels to the Gulf of Mexico and Colonel Zachary Taylor's regiment in Corpus Christi to "deter and prevent Mexico from either declaring war or invading Texas" (as he put it on September 1 to Senator W. S. Archer). The Congress had annexed Texas on March 1, 1845, despite clear signals from the Mexican Government, as early as 1843, that such annexation would make war inevitable. Polk was encouraged in this show of force by a Colonel Atocha, the representative of the former Mexican president, Santa Anna, who maintained that "when [the Mexican Government] saw a strong force ready to strike on their coasts and border, they would, [Atocha] had no doubt, feel the danger and agree to the boundary suggested.'' Secretary of War William Marcy privately noted that the movement of Taylor's men would ''do no hurt and possibly may be of great use.'' He felt ''at no time'' that ''war with Mexico was probable.'' Neither did President Polk; Mexico *might* have been ''mad enough to declare war'' had it not been ''for the appearance of a strong naval force in the Gulf and our army moving in the direction of her frontier on land.'' His special agent in Mexico, William S. Parrot, parroted these views in September 1845: the Mexicans were cowed by the threat of force; they would not send military forces against Taylor.[11]

As we know, these policymakers were quite mistaken about the Mexicans' resolve and about the effectiveness of the American show of force. Mexican forces were dispatched from Matamoros; they crossed the Rio Grande on April 24, 1846, and fired on a detachment of Taylor's dragoons. Rather than deterring Mexico, the American show of force appears to have provoked that nation to a confrontation that may not have been inevitable. Thus, the outcome of the American threat to Mexico in 1845–1846 appears to have been as our findings would have predicted.

THE "BLACK WARRIOR" CRISIS, 1854

Our third test case involves another threat by the United States, this time directed at Spain, in 1854. The incoming Democratic administration of Franklin Pierce had signaled its interest in Cuba during the campaign of 1852 and had alarmed the Spanish, who took two significant steps to protect their colony: they sought a joint communiqué with France and England regarding Spain's future on the island; and they named an antislavery figure, the Marques de la Pezuela, as captain-general of Cuba, signaling their intention to free and arm Cuba's slaves before they would see the island, ''Spanish or African,'' pass from them.

Upon freeing those slaves for whom no valid ownership paper could be produced, Pezuela stirred American southerners to action: Cuba could not be of value to American slave-holding planters with a free black population, and such a population—''another Haiti''—posed something of a threat to the future of the southern slave system itself. The overt filibuster plans of General John Quitman of Mississippi and his Cuban associates for a descent on Cuba, plans that had the approval of the Pierce Administration, were advanced in time. Before they could be consummated, however, two events had transpired to cause the Pierce Administration to withdraw its support for Quitman and his colleagues and to terminate its pressure on Spain to relinquish Cuba: Pezuela's seizure of the *Black Warrior* and the signing of the Kansas-Nebraska Act.

The captain-general seized the American vessel in Havana Harbor in February 1854, without sufficient legal cause, essentially in order to display resolve to Pierce and the filibusters. The president reacted by directing the U.S. minister to Spain, the hawkish Pierre Soulé, to demand an indemnity for the *Black Warrior* affair and to seek ''to detach'' Cuba from Spain, whether by purchase or by orchestrating the downfall of the government in Madrid. Soulé attempted both of these measures, but he also "turned his instructions . . . into a forty-eight-hour ultimatum."[12] This ultimatum the Spanish ignored, and Washington took no action.

Within a month, Pierce signed the Kansas-Nebraska Act, giving the South the chance to acquire Kansas as a slave state via the ballot. The leading student of the *Black Warrior* affair, Basil Rauch, suspects that the administration decided (especially after disastrous elections in the fall) that the uneasy coalition of northern and southern Democrats could not survive a second consecutive victory for slave interests (the acquisition of Cuba), especially following so closely on the heels of the first. In any event, the day after the initialing of the act, Pierce issued a proclamation warning against filibustering and other unlawful violations of neutrality. Later, he repudiated the Ostend Manifesto. Soulé resigned in disgust and the Quitman expedition dissolved.[13]

Once again, the case appears to confirm our findings: the target's determination to have its way in Cuba led it to rebuff the threatener, who was without allies. Moreover, the threatener's domestic political environment included many Whigs and northern Democrats opposed to the acquisition of Cuba, another slave territory, especially if it were accomplished by force. The knowledge of this domestic opposition may have caused the Spanish to assume that the threat was not to be believed. The threatener did brandish force (Quitman's filibusters, such as would descend on and seize Nicaragua under another adventurer, William Walker, two years later), but the brandishing was to no avail.

THE BRITISH THREAT TO RUSSIA, 1878

Our fourth test case flowed from the decisive Russian victory over Turkey in 1877 and January 1878. For over a century, Britain had been Turkey's best European friend. British strategic and Mediterranean interests involved preventing Russia from gaining free access and use of the Turkish Straits of Bosporus and Dardanelles. And her interests and possessions elsewhere in the Middle East and the Indian subcontinent made her "a Muslim power" (as her foreign secretary put it in 1878), necessarily solicitous of the welfare of Constantinople, "the premier Muslim city in the world." When Russian armies began to overcome Turkish resistance in mid-1877, Queen Victoria and her prime minister, Lord Beaconsfield (Disraeli), warned the Tzar to keep his distance from the straits. By early January, the Turks were in disarray, and 100,000 Russian troops had broken through to a line not one day's march (about 10 miles) from Constantinople and the straits. After much deliberation, Beaconsfield ordered a British fleet of thirteen warships to pass through the Dardanelles. Within a month, the Russians agreed to some of the British demands limiting the scope of Turkey's losses and Russia's acquisitions in the southern Balkans and in Armenia.

At first look, then, it appears that the show of force helped the threatener. One analyst of interstate threats, who also studied this crisis, took note of the British Fleet movement and regards the movement to be related to the success of the threat.[14] We can understand why he or anyone else might assume as much, at first look. However, a careful reading of historical studies of the crisis leads to an altogether different conclusion.

In the first place, it happens that the Turkish Government, far from regarding the presence of the British Fleet as a help, desperately tried to convince the British that its appearance would be a hindrance to Turkish efforts to protect Constantinople and the straits from Russia. The Russians were not advancing on Constantinople or the Bulair line (protecting the Dardanelles), and were negotiating an armistice. Moreover, Russia's terms were precisely the same as those they had offered in December, before their string of dazzling military victories. British entry into the Sea of Marmora, a violation of the 1871 convention, would give Russia an excuse, indeed a motive, for resuming the fight, and Turkey could not hope to protect either Constantinople or the key Bosporus and Dardanelles forts in that event. That was what the sultan wrote to Queen Victoria, and that was what Server Pasha, the Turkish foreign minister, told Sir Henry Austen Layard, the British ambassador. But Beaconsfield was adamant, and on February 13 the fleet sailed, without the sultan's firman (permission). "We gave the Russians the pretext for entering the capital and causing the very danger apprehended," Layard wrote in consternation, imploring the cabinet to withdraw the fleet.[15]

In the second place, the British Fleet did not menace the Russians. What its appearance *did* accomplish was to anger the Tzar so that he ordered his brother, Grand Duke Nicholas, commander of the Russian forces in European Turkey, to take Constantinople "by force" as a consequence! Count Gorchakov, the Russian foreign minister, cynically noted that Russia's entry into the Turkish capital could now be justified "with exactly the same object" as Britain's announced excuse: the protection of lives and property. The Tzar and Grand Duke Nicholas learned on February 17 that there was no landing force with the fleet (the British foreign minister, Lord Derby, had told the Russian ambassador, Count Shuvalov, as much two days before). Hence, the only reason that the Grand Duke did not obey his brother and attack the Turks again was his conviction that his army was too weak, ill, and overextended to attack the Turks in their well-fortified positions. Nonetheless, he did deliver an ultimatum to the Turks on February 23, insisting that his army be allowed to advance unmolested to San Stefano, a fishing village on the Sea of Marmora only six miles from Constantinople.[16]

In the third place, the fleet was in greater danger than the Russian army as a consequence of this show of force. British Admiralty officials feared the Russians might deploy Whitehead (self-propelled) torpedoes. In any event, were the Russians to overrun the Turkish defenders on the Bulair line and at Gallipoli, they could control the guns overlooking the Dardanelles and catch the fleet in "a mousetrap," as Beaconsfield himself told the queen.[17] Moreover, the British Government so undervalued the fleet's military significance that it advised the admiral in command on no less than three occasions that he was "not to attempt armed resistance'' in the event of a Russian attack on Constantinople or the Bosporus forts.[18]

Viewed as a show of force to aid a threat, the movement of the British Fleet into the Sea of Marmora was useless (unless it was counterproductive). But, as it happens, that was not the only show of force the British had in mind. In late March, Beaconsfield told Parliament he planned to call up the reserves and to press for some six million pounds of supplemental military appropriations. Thereafter, he ordered 7,000 native Indian troops to Malta, sent the Channel Fleet to the Mediterranean, and prepared two army corps (a total of 72,000 men) for dispatch either to Malta or to Cyprus (which he asked Turkey to cede to Britain). The German ambassador in London told Bismarck that the dispatch of Indian troops was ''political rather than military,'' that it was calculated to produce a deep impression on [the Muslim population of] India,'' and this is confirmed by private statements made by British statesmen. Some 7,000 troops would be of little consequence anyhow, but the two army corps (and possibly the dispatch of the Channel Fleet as well) were another matter. On May 6 Count Shuvalov told the new British foreign secretary, Lord Salisbury, that ''the sending of a *corps d'armes* from England to Malta'' might disrupt the Congress of the Great Powers on the ''Eastern Question,'' plans for which were well under way. Beaconsfield responded himself. Her Majesty's Government ''could not even slightly defer her preparations''; they would ''continue even if a congress should meet.''[19]

The British military plans may have had some impact on Count Shuvalov. As Count Munster, the German ambassador in London, told Bismarck, ''Shuvalov knows England well and sets a high value on her financial and even military forces.''[20] But Shuvalov was not the Tzar. What then led Alexander to give in (as he eventually did) to some of the British demands regarding Bulgaria and Armenia?

The Tzar (and his brother, the Grand Duke) did not require vast movements of ships and men to know of Britain's military capabilities. Only twenty-three years before, Britain had led the way to the Russian Crimea to defend Turkish (and British) interests in a bloody war. When a Russian plenipotentiary seemed oblivious to the risk of war with Britain, Grand Duke Nicholas shouted, ''Are you going to saddle us with another war with England?'' The mere threat of a breaking-off of diplomatic relations with Russia (on February 21) was enough to dissuade the Tzar from further efforts to take Constantinople. The movement of the British Fleet had prompted Alexander to press for that city; the threat of a diplomatic rupture was enough to return his appetite to ''pre-fleet'' conditions. Alexander did not want another Crimean War.[21]

There are other reasons for Russia's willingness to negotiate. As we have said, Russia's military forces were spent. Moreover, her finances were in disarray, a typhus epidemic raged in her cities, and she was experiencing political unrest.[22] Autarchy might deal with these matters, but it had no real control over another—the position taken by the Austro-Hungarian Empire.

Austria-Hungary had ambitions in the Balkans, too, and though it had not joined Russia in the war, it sought a share of the spoils. Count Julius Andrássy, the Austro-Hungarian foreign minister, agreed on May 16 to Lord Beaconsfield's request for "an understanding," and on June 6 Andrássy and Lord Salisbury signed "a general agreement as between gentlemen" concerning Britain's demands regarding Bulgaria and Roumania in exchange for Britain's support of "any proposal on Bosnia brought forward by Austria-Hungary" at the forthcoming Congress on the "Eastern Question" in Berlin. On the same day, the Tzar expressed his fear of "war with England and probably also with Austria-Hungary," and told his ministers that "concessions, however much against the grain, were necessary."[23] Shortly after the Congress of Berlin opened, on June 18 Lord Beaconsfield "presented as a virtual ultimatum" the British demands; in the words of B. H. Sumner, he was "manfully backed up by the Austrians to the consternation of the Russians."[24]

The Russian delegation balked, seeking instructions from St. Petersburg. Beaconsfield thereupon threatened war, ordered the British delegation to pack, and readied a special train for the voyage back to London. Prince Bismarck, chairman of the Congress, told the Russians that Beaconsfield was serious, and (in the words of R. W. Seton-Watson) "lost no time in impressing upon them the need for a timely retreat." The Tzar simultaneously sanctioned the more critical of the concessions that the British had demanded, and Lord Beaconsfield reported to the queen that Russia had "surrendered."[25]

The threat may have been made more credible to Russia by virtue of the several British displays of force—that much we must allow. Hence, this case cannot be viewed as entirely supportive of our findings. But we are confident that these displays of force were not as important as other factors in explaining the Tzar's concessions. Britain's military capabilities were well known to St. Petersburg; her resolve (the threat's credibility) was not doubted in June, though it had been when it essentially consisted of the fleet's movement, in February; her support of Turkey was known to be a long-standing and important component of her policy; her temporary alliance with Austria-Hungary clearly affected Russia's decision, as did Russia's own internal weaknesses. The target's resolve began to wane, not with the appearance of the British Fleet, or even with the talk of British troops, but with the threat of a diplomatic breach and of an Anglo-Austrian understanding. R. W. Seton-Watson, commenting on Russia's lack of concern for Britain's calling up of reserves for the two army corps, expressed a similar view:

> Russia could at this moment [early April] unquestionably have seized Constantinople, blocked the Bosporus and made any British military advance impossible. She did not underestimate British financial resources, but what decided her to compromise was her own precarious internal position and her distrust of Austria-Hungary on her flank.[26]

In short, we can find the same variables accounting for the outcome of this crisis that accounted for most of the seventy-seven cases we analyzed.

THE FASHODA CRISIS, 1898

Our fifth test case had brought France and Britain to the brink of war in 1898. France bristled in the 1880s at the way Britain had established suzerainty in Egypt, a region long of interest to the French. Both nations were expanding their colonial empires throughout the world in the late nineteenth century, and in the 1890s, some French colonists cast longing glances at the Sudan and Upper Nile regions. Egyptian control of the Sudan had lapsed, the French maintained, and France was free to stake a new claim to these headwaters. Not so, said Britain. Sir Edward Grey, undersecretary for foreign affairs, pointedly told the House of Commons in 1895 that a French move into the Sudan would be viewed by Her Majesty's Government as "an unfriendly act."[27] French colonists ignored the threat, and in the summer of 1898, Captain Marchand and a small band of officers and men, after a trying trek, finally reached the Upper Nile at Fashoda and raised a French flag in a deserted Egyptian fort. Almost simultaneously, a much larger combined Anglo-Egyptian force, moving south from Cairo, defeated Sudanese followers of the Mahadi at Omdurman and continued south to confront the tiny French garrison at Fashoda on September 9.

Lord Salisbury, the prime minister, was adamant. He would not discuss the French claims (none of which he granted) until Marchand left the Sudan, which he felt was Egypt's and Britain's by "right of conquest." He showed the French the report of General Sir Herbert Kitchener, the Anglo-Egyptian commander and "Hero of Omdurman," on the untenable nature of Marchand's position at Fashoda. As Kitchener put it, Marchand "seems quite as anxious to return as we are to facilitate his departure," and, he reported, Marchand felt "sure that, under the circumstances, the orders for his retirement [Marchand would later insist that he had said "relief," not "retirement"] would not be delayed."[28]

Theophile Delcassé, the French foreign minister, responded by urging "discussion" before Marchand's departure. He told the British ambassador that "the national honour" of France was at stake. The French Fleet was ordered to Cherbourg in late September, and other channel ports were ordered to be made ready to receive it.[29]

Salisbury enjoyed support; indeed, some pressure for a "tough" stance came from his cabinet, the Commons, and the press. His ambassador to France, Sir Edmund Monson, told Delcassé that Britain would not "retreat." How determined were the French? The Colonial Office seemed adamant enough, but Delcassé's Foreign Office was of two minds: it wanted access to the Upper Nile or renegotiation of the balance of French and British power in the region, if it could be secured peacefully. But the Foreign Office preferred to avoid war with Britain. After all, as one French official told Salisbury in mid-September, "France has only one enemy, namely Germany," the Germany that had taken Alsace-Lorraine in 1871. The view seems to have been the popular one as well. One English account quotes a Frenchman as saying at the height of the crisis: "Why do we want Egypt? The English! *They* aren't Prussians." George Clemenceau, the future French premier, editorialized in his paper *L'Aurore* in October: ''The brutal fact is that France cannot think of throwing herself into a war for the possession of some African marshes, when the German is camped at Metz and Strasbourg.''[30]

Moreover, the Dreyfus affair had reached its zenith, with the embarrassing disclosure of injustice and treason within the French Army. A German editorial regarding the Fashoda crisis observed on September 26 that ''England has her hands free, while the energies of France are paralyzed by the Dreyfus case.''[31] French diplomatic objectives in the Fashoda crisis were not lacking, but they were somewhat limited by considerations of the European balance of power and by the domestic political scene.

They were also limited by virtue of the French perception of her military capabilities relative to Britain. If France remained firm, Kitchener would eventually force Marchand to withdraw, an act that would surely lead to war. French interests on the Upper Nile might still flourish were she to defeat Britain's naval forces and gain control of the Mediterranean Sea. That, however, was quite impossible. French naval strategy had for some time been defensive in nature (the ''Jeune École'' school), and the French naval chief of staff advised Delcassé on October 11 that the fleet was but half the size and quality of Britain's. American naval victories at Manila Bay and Santiago de Cuba ''had just demonstrated [what] lay in store for the weaker force in a modern naval conflict.'' Delcassé wrote to his wife on October 22 of ''the necessity of avoiding a naval war which we are absolutely incapable of carrying on even with Russian help.'' Neither he nor his ambassador to Britain, Paul Cambon, had any real expectations of Russian aid, for the Russians signaled clearly their inability to aid France. ''What to do all by ourselves?'' Cambon wrote Delcassé. On October 23 Marchand's report to Delcassé reached the foreign minister. His position, he wrote, was untenable.[32]

In the next four days (October 24 to October 27), the British noisily put their fleet on a war footing, and on November 2 Delcassé ordered Marchand to withdraw from the Sudan, without France having obtained any significant quid pro quo from Britain. Was this naval show of force as ''significant a part'' of the French capitulation as some believe? R. Ned Lebow, for example, says its ''psychological impact cannot be underestimated.''[33] It probably did help Delcassé to justify his action in the French Assembly, but it does not appear to have been nearly so important to Delcassé himself as other factors. In the first place, in early October, Delcassé had already signaled to Britain his willingness to order Marchand's withdrawal if the British were to ''build him a golden bridge'' to retreat over, involving the discussion of Anglo-French borders in West Africa. Britain would promise nothing, though she eventually did settle such borders to mutual satisfaction. This much Salisbury did say: to permit Delcassé some ''face,'' he would officially state (quite truthfully) that he had never formally demanded Marchand's withdrawal. His threat had been vaguely communicated, permitting Delcassé to avoid humiliation. In the second place, as we have seen, Delcassé clearly did not need the fleet's mobilization to know the dangers that he faced on the high seas. In the third place, Delcassé clearly preferred peace with Britain. His enemy was Germany, and Britain, his enemy's enemy, might some day become his friend. (Indeed, he spoke as early as October 6 of an "entente.") Without allies, means, or resolve, and with a serious domestic crisis (that brought the government down on October 26), France would, in the words of Paul Cambon, "realize the possible."[34] Finally, and conclusively, when Marchand traveled without authority to Cairo (in order to be able to communicate with Delcassé), Delcassé had the excuse he needed: Marchand's position was now obviously untenable, he was insubordinate, and he could be ordered to withdraw. In every element, then, this crisis appears to illustrate our findings regarding the significance of target resolve, target perception of threatener capabilities, threat credibility, the clarity of threat communication, the relative utility of allies, and the relative importance of threatener shows of force.

THE SUBCONTINENT CRISIS, 1965

Our final test case is that of China's threat to India in 1965. When India and Pakistan went to war over Kashmir, China issued threats designed to deter India from attacks on East Pakistan. Inasmuch as China had backed up a threat to India just three years before with a substantial use of force, its threat in 1965 was regarded as quite credible by the Indians. For the same reason, the movement of substantial Chinese forces to the Indian border was not necessary; India could count and was well aware of the numbers of troops that China could invade with, should she choose to. In any event, India did not attack East Pakistan. She appears to have been deterred from doing so both by the fact of the Chinese threat and by her own willingness to limit the conflict to West Pakistan and Kashmir.[35] The key variables once again correlated with the outcome of the threat in the predicted fashion.

Verification of our findings with six test cases does not constitute the kind of "proof" a physicist might demand, but physicists generally rely on other physicists to attempt the verification of their findings, and the laboratory conditions of the natural scientist are not available to students of international relations. We must be content with more modest efforts at replication. Others, analyzing threats that we failed to include among either our original seventy-seven coded or our six verification cases, will be able to judge our findings for themselves.

We have already spoken of the support our study provides for some of the hypotheses advanced by Bruce Russett, Robert C. North, Ole Holsti, Evan Luard, and others. We should now like to comment further on the relationship between our findings and the conclusions of other scholars. In particular, we should like to discuss the extent to which our findings confirm the hypotheses generated by models postulating "rationality" as the basis for decisionmaking.

The key features of models of rational decisionmaking have centered on a favorable cost-benefit ratio for the threatener, the process of communicating threat information to parties involved in the dispute, and establishing the credibility of the threat. Consequently, behavioral hypotheses generated by these models have tended to stress actions that augment these critical aspects of the decisionmaking model. Hence, a successful threat must skew the cost-benefit ratio in the threatener's favor (a development that must be perceived by both parties), it must limit the options available to the target, and it must convince the target that dire consequences would inevitably follow defiance of the demands.

These considerations have led to a great deal of emphasis on the clarity with which the threat is communicated. For the model of rational decisionmaking to be applicable, the threat must certainly be understood. A rational analysis of the prospective costs and benefits faced by the target assumes that the target is fully aware of the behavior demanded of it and of the exact costs threatened in the event of noncompliance with the demands. In this sense, the threat is clearly tied to specific acts to be performed—or not performed—by the target. Some threats are incremental, in that they specify different levels of damage for different types of target responses; some are absolute, in that a refusal to comply triggers the full magnitude of the promised punishment. In any event, it is argued, the link between whatever actions are demanded and the proposed punishment must be clear and fully understood by the target. Despite the apparent logic of such propositions, our study did not provide statistical support for a link between clearly communicated threats and success. Statistical tests on the sample failed to reveal any significant association, and the variable measuring clarity of communication was significant only in the subset of cases containing conflicts that were focused on an identifiable area of contention. Even within this subset, the data offered no support for the above proposition, for success was associated with the *ambiguity* of the threat.

These findings do not necessarily refute or undermine the basic arguments in support of a rational model for decisionmaking. What we may have here are "level of analysis" problems—that is, there are two closely related problems that must be considered. First, scholars who have emphasized rationality as the basis for the decisionmaking process may have applied a definition of clarity that is unnecessarily rigid and formal. Ultimately, clarity is not desired in its own right, but as a precondition that must be met if the target is to be able rationally to choose the proper response. Any vagueness in the linkage between the desired behavior and the proposed damage interjects a degree of uncertainty about the actual costs and benefits inherent in the threat situation and thereby impedes the process of rational decisionmaking. However, a threat that does not specifically make these linkages may be clear enough to modify successfully the target's behavior. Even an ambiguous threat may signal concern and, assuming that the threatener possesses the capability to inflict enough damage, may still induce the target to comply.

Second, the degree of clarity with which a threat is communicated may affect the potential costs that could accrue to both parties. What may be of critical importance is that the ambiguity of the threat is relevant to a phenomenon other than the requirement for full information postulated by the models of rationality-based decisionmaking alone—ambiguous threats allow face-saving. It is clearly cheaper to issue an ambiguous threat. In the event that the target resists, the threatener has much less at stake. The reduced costs to the threatener involve not only the fact that less prestige is at stake in the crisis, but also that there would be less pressure actually to incur the costs of inflicting the proposed damage. This reduction of costs applies with at least equal force to the target. Compliance with the terms of a threat can be explained as the result of factors independent of the threat, or, in some cases, the target may even be able convincingly to feign ignorance of the threat itself. In either case, the target loses less in terms of prestige than would be the case with a more clearly communicated threat.[36]

Ambiguous threats may also contribute to success on occasion by keeping the threat environment more fluid. The lack of clarity may indicate, or even create, a degree of flexibility about both the goals and the means of goal attainment for both parties. If this is the case, one would expect that threats ambiguously communicated would be associated with a high degree of flexibility on the part of the target (which trait we had found to be associated with the success of the threat). And this is exactly what we found—a statistically significant correlation of these two variables (Kendall's coefficient = .21, significant to the .01 level). Clear threats not only limit the options available to the target, but also the alternatives open to the threatener. Whereas theorists such as Schelling and Kahn have argued that it is precisely this restriction of options that provides the essential structure for a successful threat, our findings regarding flexibility and ambiguous threats suggest just the opposite. We do not want to overstate our case, though. Ambiguous threats are not *always* wise. Were a target to be irresolute, a threat imperfectly communicating the threatener's goals or means, overestimated by the target, might lead to a preemptive attack by the target.[37] But clarity is not *essential* to the success of a threat.

Analysts have generally argued that shows of force accompanying a threat are important instruments and often determine the outcome of the threat. For example, one scholar has written that "a military threat is credible only if it implies immediate defeat. Immediate defeat assumes concentration of forces."[38] We are nearly alone in holding that displays of force are largely irrelevant to the outcome of threats, but we did find one study that maintained that, of late, shows of force have not mattered as much as the target's perception of the threatener's "power in being."[39] We would go further and argue that this has always been the case. Repositioning one's force in conjunction with a threat may help one win the war that ensues if the target refuses to yield, but it has rarely been instrumental in bringing about the success of the threat itself.

Most analysts are silent regarding the target's objectives in discussing those factors they believe to determine the outcome of a threat. Thomas Schelling, Herman Kahn, Henry Kissinger, and J. L. Payne all appear to argue that threats can be successful if the threatener confronts an opponent with risks that make further resistance foolhardy. All these analysts assume that the United States is peaceloving and defensive at heart and that it seeks to deter, with demonstration of resolve, an essentially aggressive but opportunistic foe. Since they view the Soviets as fundamentally and essentially opportunistic, these analysts regard the resolute deployment of force as a sensible and virtually certain means of ensuring the success of a threat.[40] They tend to stress *threatener* characteristics (credibility, resolve, displays of force) and tend to deprecate the importance (and seriousness) of *target* goals and interests. And they are not alone in this regard. Adam Yarmolinsky, special assistant to Secretary of Defense Robert McNamara, and his deputy assistant secretary for international affairs noted that during the Cuban missile crisis, American decisionmakers "spent at least 90 percent of [their] time studying alternative uses of troops, bombers and warships" whereas "straightforward diplomatic negotiation seems hardly to have been considered,"[41] even though it eventually was to play a major role in securing the central objective of the American threat and the resolution of the crisis. We find wisdom in Yarmolinsky's more general warning that American crisis management too often is shaped by the neatly packaged quick-force-deployment options that the Joint Chiefs have "at the ready."

Yarmolinsky was describing crisis managers of the 1960s, but there is little reason to believe that much has changed in this imbalance of diplomatic initiatives and force deployments. Twelve persons in foreign-policymaking positions within the U.S. Government in 1977 were willing to answer a number of questions about the international system and the threat environment (see our questionnaire, appendix 2), and we found that these persons displayed considerable unanimity concerning a number of questions bearing on our present subject. They identified military power as more important than economic strength, ideology, technology, or any other factor in the shaping of the international system; they regarded military threats as appropriate and feasible actions for the United States to take in a number of specific hypothetical crises;[42] and they regarded (in their words) "credibility," "firmness," "consistency," and the "visibility" and "availability of U.S. conventional forces" to be the most significant factors in determining the outcome of threats about which they had personal knowledge. Their views seem remarkably akin to those of Schelling, Kahn, Kissinger, and Payne.

We regard this emphasis on threatener behavior as particularly dangerous; after all, there is reason to believe that Soviet analysts may look upon U.S.-Soviet relations in a similarly "loaded" fashion and that they treat us as opportunists to be controlled by shows of resolve.[43] In any event, we have not found the "rationality of irrationality" to have been a determinant of the success of a threat.

Klaus Knorr speaks of "the widespread unwillingness in the underdeveloped world, which has become increasingly nationalist, to bow to the threat of superior force. The world of states," he concludes, "has become less coercible than it used to be." It is certainly true that American "coercive diplomacy" in Indochina failed to take into account the unwillingness of Laotians, Cambodians, and

Vietnamese to yield. In 1974 Douglas Kinnard interviewed over one hundred American generals who had seen service in Vietnam and found that over 55 percent of them agreed that "prior to 1968 the will and determination of the enemy to continue the war . . . was not sufficiently considered." Alexander George, David Hall, and William Simons studied American threats issued during the Laotian crisis, the Cuban missile crisis, and the Vietnam War, and they concluded that "asymmetry of motivation favoring the United States" was one of eight essential preconditions for successful "coercive diplomacy."[44]

But Knorr may be mistaken in suggesting that in the *past*, states were less likely to hold to inflexible goals in the face of "superior force." We noted the behavior of the Abydians in chapter 1, and spoke of the Melians and the Boers in chapter 3. We now add that, as Bruce Russett has pointed out, the American efforts to deter Japanese expansion in 1940–1941 failed "*not* because Japanese leaders really expected to win; but because they saw no alternative to war." Their goals were simply inflexible, and no American "proposal" was going to stop them from trying to realize the Greater East Asian Co-Prosperity Sphere.[45]

What have we learned? Some "truisms" are very true, and a few are very untrue. Perceived capabilities matter, alliance support matters, target resolve matters, and force deployments accompanying the threat do not. We already "knew" about capabilities, allies, and target resolve; we were just as surprised by (and dubious of) our findings regarding force deployments as we suspect the reader is. But we have become believers.

What do we think others might learn? Two lessons in particular seem to be obvious, but nonetheless worth spelling out.

(1) *One is very ill-advised to threaten a power one knows to be (or strongly suspects to be) reluctant to yield.* This, we grant, is not easily ascertained. The intentions of a target nation are generally not known with any certainty until they are no longer "intentions" but, *ipso facto,* actions—that is, until the target has actually responded to the threat by demonstrating its willingness, or unwillingness, to yield.

This may sound like mere hindsight. A target refused to yield; hence, it entered the crisis with high resolve. We were not quite that simplistic in our coding or analysis. Targets can enter a crisis displaying considerable resolve and depart in capitulation, or they can enter a crisis in considerable confusion regarding their objectives, essentially irresolute, and develop resolve for any number of reasons. (Here one thinks of the French attitude upon the dispatch of the *Panther* to Agadir[46] or of the United States and the North Korean attack in 1950.) But, in general, targets that are determined to have their way, or to make you fight to have your way, are not easily swayed by threats. (We repeat some of our evidence of this: the resolve explicitly expressed by the Melians to the Athenians [416 B.C.], the Boers to the British [1899], and the Nazis to the British and the French [1939]; and the sense of relief and satisfaction with which Sardinia greeted the Austrian threat [1859] or with which Germany greeted the French threat [1870].) Conversely, targets that are, for whatever reasons, initially limited in their resolution sometimes *are* responsive, given a threat of war. (Examples that we have offered of this phenomenon include President Polk's handling of the Oregon Territory boundary dispute [1846] and the Chamberlain ministry's handling of the Sudetenland crisis at Munich [1938].) A resolute target can yield to a threat if, for example, it perceives itself to be without allies, in grave physical danger, and if the threat is adroitly communicated. The Florentine Signoria that banished Pietro the Unfortunate and the rest of the Medicis when Pietro yielded to Charles VIII's demands in 1494 appeared quite resolute when Charles's army appeared. It responded to Charles's threats with threats of its own ("if you sound your trumpets, we will sound our bells!"). Charles then reworded his demands, "passing the matter off with a bad joke," and the Signoria agreed to a slightly less humiliating treaty.[47] Charles had compromised, but so had the Signoria, once they had seen the army that had so frightened Pietro Medici, and once Charles had managed to bring himself to deal more diplomatically and gracefully with these proud senators.

The Melians made clear their resolve to the Athenian legates,[48] but one can imagine a different outcome had the Athenian spokesman been more adroit and less offensive, or had the Athenians been able to demonstrate more effectively (possibly with the assistance of a third party) that Sparta would not, could not, come to the Melians' aid. Conversely, while the Polk Administration entered the Oregon Territory dispute with Britain quite willing to compromise, one can imagine that Polk might not have yielded the 54° 40′ claim had the British been more insulting in their language, or had the timing of the threat affected the domestic American political scene more directly (as during an election campaign), or had Polk and his allies in the Senate been less effective manipulators of the political process during the treaty debates. The target may possess a high degree of resolve for a number of reasons (such as prestige, honor, ideological rigidity, personal pique, or an inflated view of its own military capabilities), but for whatever reason, this resolve may determine whether the threatener's bluff is called. And this process is more often a cybernetic than a "rational" one.

Hence, we would think that one would want to have *all the information one might possibly acquire* regarding the willingness of a potential target to yield something it values in order to avoid having one's bluff called or finding oneself inadvertently at war. K. J. Holsti allowed that the success of a threat "seems" to be related to the "degree of commitment" each party had toward their "objectives" in the crisis, but he regarded this variable as "virtually impossible to measure,"[49] and, consequently, he deliberately omitted it from further discussions. What Holsti cannot measure, many policymakers do not even appear to try to measure. Snyder and Diesing did "not find on *the record* more than one or two [out of a possible sixteen] explicit estimates of the adversary's intensity of interest . . . [and] . . . no attempt to estimate the strength of [the adversary's] motives, let alone any comparison of that strength with the strength of one's own motives." Rather, they found that the parties gauged their opponent's "likely resolve" and intentions "from his behavior." R. Ned Lebow also noted that threats were "frequently based on erroneous perceptions of an adversary's resolve.'' He recommended that threateners ''remain sensitive to cues from the environment about the validity of their expectations.''[50]

We agree. It is difficult to determine the degree of a target's resolve, even after all the facts on the historical record are known, but if one makes the effort, the results can be rewarding, for this variable appears to be associated strongly with the outcome of threats. And what is true for the after-the-fact social scientist is true for the here-and-now policymaker. Determining a potential adversary's resolve may be difficult, but it is terribly important, and ought not to be dismissed as indeterminate or imponderable. Paul Schratz, of the Murphy Commission (which made a recent Congressional study of American foreign policy), wrote of the importance of the ''task of *assessing* foreign governments . . . , predicting actions they are likely to take, predicting the effect of proposed U.S. initiatives (and redesigning U.S. actions to achieve the desired impact),'' and he also noted that this task was not being done very well, especially by the State Department.[51] We think that Captain Schratz may be overly sanguine in expecting that measures *can* be ''redesigned'' to get a policymaker what he wants if the target is simply unwilling to ''give,'' but we wholeheartedly agree with him that the business of gathering information about the resolve and objectives of other nations is vital. The political-affairs officer who correctly advises his government of the inflexible goals of the potential recipient of a coercive threat may save much honor, blood, and treasure.[52]

In order to accomplish his task, the political-affairs officer must feel that he is free to be honest and direct. If he has seen others relieved of their posts for saying the ''wrong'' things about ''our enemy'' or ''our ally,'' if he has been warned about such remarks himself, or if his superior prefers ''groupthink'' to thoughtful analysis and second guessing, then this vital source of information may fall silent or, worse, may begin to report inaccurately of the motives and intentions of the potential adversary. This was the case in *fin de siècle* Germany. Bismarck and his successors sought loyal and obedient men for Germany's embassies, but these men lacked a sense of initiative. They carried messages in one direction well enough, but they rarely sent back messages that their superiors did not want to hear. Hence, in 1914, when Count Frederich von Pourtales, Germany's ambassador to Russia, was warned by the Russians that they would not stand by and permit Austria to attack Serbia, Pourtales noted his fear that they were serious in his *diary* but told his government what he knew it wanted to hear: that Russia was probably bluffing! The exceptional German ambassador, Prince Karl Max Lichnowsky, in London, did warn ''against continuing to believe in the possibility of localizing the conflict,'' and did describe accurately Britain's determination to enter the war against Germany, but his reports were given insufficient weight, for his views did not reflect the prevailing opinion in Berlin.[53] Some have argued that American diplomats, since the era of McCarthyism, have been too cautious and one-sided in their reports. To the extent that this is true, it is dangerously wrong.

(2) *One is also ill-advised to place much faith in a show of force*. There may

be no harm and some value in a modest, nonbelligerent military demonstration of resolve (a "probe"), but such demonstrations rarely suffice, and we fear that some policymakers may have lost sight of that amid the rustle of "options" and the roar of jets. Other, more substantial troop movements to distant regions may in some instances be considered a *sine qua non*, demonstrating resolve and credibility and preparing the military for potential future action. But while they are necessary, they are not sufficient conditions for the success of threats, and they may even be counterproductive if they provoke a preemptive reaction on the part of the target.

How might any of this relate to the real world? In 1976 we tried to answer that question by imagining a crisis that might evoke a threat: a struggle over the future of Yugoslavia upon the death of President Tito. We suspended our sense of what was "likely" in order to create a mix of scenarios: President Tito dies. A struggle for power breaks out within Yugoslavia between Croats, Slovenes, and Serbs, and between Stalinists and Euro-Communists. The Soviet Union and the West interfere, with varying degrees of resolve, alliance support, and displays of force. The United States threatens the Soviet Union. (Overall military capabilities were not varied, inasmuch as we did not think it credible to suggest that the capabilities of any of the parties in the theoretical crisis were likely to be terribly different, relative to one another, from what they were when we designed the scenario.)[54]

When we applied the findings of our study to our eight theoretical Yugoslav scenarios, we thought we could predict the outcome of an American threat to the Soviets in four of the eight scenarios. (See Table 4.1.) Obviously, one has to suspend disbelief to imagine some of the things we asked ourselves (and now ask the reader) to imagine, but the point is not that any of these scenarios are *likely*. We deal with the succession question in Yugoslavia only because it is a question that *had* been treated as a potential crisis for some time, and it was a theoretical situation in which the question of alliance support was both relevant and in doubt. (Nevertheless, it is worth noting that of the twelve policymakers we interviewed in 1977, ten believed a threat by the United States pursuant to a Soviet incursion into Yugoslavia upon the death of Marshal Tito "appropriate," and eight believed it also to be "feasible.")

Predictions 1, 2, 4, 6, and 8 will not strike many as being very bold or difficult to make. Perhaps 3, 5, and 7 are a little more interesting. In each of these cases, we have treated the type of force deployment accompanying the American threat as if it were irrelevant. We do not mean to imply that there is no conceivable Yugoslav succession crisis in which an American force deployment would help the United States attain all or some of its objectives. We simply question the demonstrable utility of what we have been calling sabre-rattling.

Rereading this several years later, these observations seem particularly salient to an understanding of what has happened in Poland and the Falkland Islands.

Table 4.1
POSSIBLE YUGOSLAV SCENARIOS WITH PREDICTED OUTCOMES

1	2	3	4
Soviet goals are limited; Soviet resolve is qualified. NATO allies essentially support U.S. posture. U.S. threat is accompanied by a variety of large-scale force deployments. Threat succeeds.	Soviet goals are substantial; Soviets are resolute. NATO allies essentially do not support U.S. posture. U.S. threat is accompanied by only a modest force deployment. Threat fails.	Soviet goals are substantial; Soviets are resolute. NATO allies essentially do not support U.S. posture. U.S. threat is accompanied by a variety of large-scale force deployments. Threat fails.	Soviet goals are substantial; Soviets are resolute. NATO allies essentially support U.S. posture. U.S. threat is accompanied by a variety of large-scale force deployments. Outcome unpredictable. (Most dangerous situation.)
5	**6**	**7**	**8**
Soviet goals are limited; Soviet resolve is qualified. NATO allies essentially do not support U.S. posture. U.S. threat is accompanied by a variety of large-scale force deployments. Outcome unpredictable.	Soviet goals are limited; Soviet resolve is qualified. NATO allies essentially do not support U.S. posture. U.S. threat is accompanied by only a modest force deployment. Outcome unpredictable.	Soviet goals are limited; Soviet resolve is qualified. NATO allies essentially support U.S. posture. U.S. threat is accompanied by only a modest force deployment. Threat succeeds.	Soviet goals are substantial; Soviets are resolute. NATO allies essentially support U.S. posture. U.S. threat is accompanied by only a modest force deployment. Outcome unpredictable.

Neither crisis is fully resolved, but at this date (1983) it appears that our central findings are borne out by both.

POLAND

Solidarity prodded the Polish Communist party toward trade unionism and democracy throughout late 1980 and most of 1981, with widespread popular and international support. Repeated Soviet and Warsaw Pact naval and military maneuvers, clearly designed to threaten Solidarity's leadership, may have checked *some* of the momentum and the more daring demands of the movement, but they clearly did not defuse it or turn it from its conflict course with the party. Solidarity and its supporters (may we not read here "Poland"?) were not deterred by Soviet threats. On the eve of General Jaruzelski's imposition of martial law (December 13, 1981), a French polling organization conducted a scientific sample of 600 Poles, asking whether the Soviet Union would intervene, whether the Polish Army would cooperate if the Soviets did intervene, and whether Poles would "go into the streets" in resistance in the event of intervention. Some 63 percent of Poles surveyed doubted that the Soviets would intervene; 60 percent felt "the Polish Army won't cooperate," and 74 percent answered that Poles would "go into the streets" in resistance.[55] Solidarity and its supporters would not yield to threats, despite repeated Soviet-Warsaw Pact sabre-rattling. A united nation, it appears, will simply ignore the risks that overwhelming military force constitutes if it is unwilling to surrender political, social, and economic rights without being *made* to do so. In Lech Walesa's words: "It is better to die on your feet than live on your knees."

THE FALKLANDS CRISIS

Since the 1830s, British citizens have been virtually the sole inhabitants of the Falkland Islands in the far South Atlantic. The Argentine Republic, however, had also explored and laid claim to the islands, and has long contested British dominion over them. For years, Argentine children have learned that the Falklands (called Las Malvinas by Argentina) were part of the national patrimony. Argentine efforts to persuade Britain to part with the islands at the conference table were fruitless, and on April 2, 1982, 9,000 Argentine troops seized the Falklands. Britain's prime minister, Margaret Thatcher, responded by dispatching naval and military forces and threatening to remove the Argentine invaders by force if they did not withdraw. Argentina refused to comply until her sovereignty over Las Malvinas was acknowledged, and neither party moved from its stated objectives sufficiently to forestall the use of force. Britain regained the islands; hundreds of Argentines and Britons lost their lives, but as of August 1982, Argentina had still not conceded defeat. Why did the British threat fail?

The massive and ponderous movement of the British task force toward the Falklands was as clear a show of force as a theoretician might conjure. Coupled with a British Broadcasting Corporation "disclosure" of two (nonexistent) British nuclear attack submarines said to be operating in the immediate vicinity of the islands, this British armada prompted the Argentines to keep their navy largely at berth in its continental harbor shelters. That is, the Argentines perceived the British to be capable of sweeping the seas. Now, after the fact, we can say that, objectively, the Argentines should have realized that their air force was no match for the British Harrier jets and surface-to-air weapons, but that was clearly not the view Argentina's leadership took at the time. The British threat, coupled as it was with a suitable force deployment, should have convinced a "rational actor" to come to terms, especially since Secretary of State Haig and UN Secretary-General Pérez de Cuéllar worked long and hard to convey messages and propose various compromise solutions to the questions of invasion, occupation, and sovereignty. But neither the Argentine nor the British Government is a good example of a "rational actor." Margaret Thatcher's Conservative party was not ideologically prepared to make any substantial concessions while Argentine troops remained on the islands, and it actually benefited somewhat on the domestic political scene from its firm stand during the crisis. The junta of Argentine generals and admirals who collectively determined Argentine policy was both constitutionally and practically incapable of agreeing to substantial concessions. Hence, the British show of force was ineffective.

Why? Primarily because the target's resolve was very high. Negotiations having failed, Argentina had decided to seize the islands, presenting the British with a fait accompli. The leadership may have hoped the British would acquiesce, but it was also aware that Britain's response might be just as firm as it was. A junta as badly divided by interservice and personal rivalries as was Argentina's could hardly have managed to back down from agreed-upon objectives, especially given the vast popular support this not-otherwise-popular junta enjoyed throughout the period of the threat. We necessarily await the historians' perspective of time and a careful sorting of the facts for a more complete analysis of this crisis,[56] but we believe that such an account is not likely to alter the basic features of our current analysis, nor to cause us to doubt that the Falklands crisis serves as a good illustration of our findings regarding the efficacy of military threats.

We began this study with the assumptions, shared by many others, that force deployments accompanying a threat were important, that the "right" show of force was of considerable assistance to the threatener, and that targets engaged in cost-benefit analysis that largely determined their behavior in crisis. But our analysis did not bear these hypotheses out. Hence, we conclude by repeating our two chief *caveats*: (1) Do not threaten anyone who appears resolute unless what you want from them merits a war or unless you are willing to have your bluff called and your credibility questioned in the future. (2) Do not assume that sabre-rattling, a show of force, is going to be decisive in attaining the goal of your threat; and keep in mind that a show of force *can* become the provocative entr'acte to war.

NOTES

1. Actually, the reader may have noticed in chapter 3 that we mentioned several other threats that we had not coded but that struck us as relevant while we were discussing our

findings. (In each instance, we added the word "uncoded" after the mention of the case.) Thus, in a sense, five threats also served as test cases: the "self-destruct" threat to Philip V by Abydos in 200 B.C.; England's demands on Holland in 1667; the French demand that Prussia remove its garrison from Luxembourg in 1867; the Italian threat to Turkey over Libya in 1911; and the Austrian and French counterthreats in 1792.

The British threat to the Irish peace negotiators in December 1921 to sign an agreement that was not wholly satisfactory to the Irish or "resume whatever warfare they could wage against each other" does not meet all our tests for qualification as a case because Britain had not *quite* recognized Ireland officially as an independent state. But it is worth pointing out that the threat succeeded (the Irish delegates signed) because the targets were not resolute. Unlike some of their compatriots in Dublin, the negotiators (and the majority of the Irish people) were willing to accept freedom under the dominion status that the Lloyd George government was demanding rather than continue to insist on a republic inasmuch as this would mean "apparently certain war." Frank Pakenham, *Peace by Ordeal: The Negotiation of the Anglo-Irish Treaty, 1921* (London: Sidgwich and Jackson, 1972), pp. 240–46, 264–67. No new British troop movements or timely "show of force" was involved.

2. James A. Robertson, ed., *Louisiana Under the Rule of Spain, France, and the United States,* 2 vols. (Cleveland, Ohio: Arthur H. Clark, 1911), 2: 20–21; Frederick Jackson Turner, "The Significance of the Louisiana Purchase," *Review of Reviews* 27 (May 1903):578–84; Lloyd Gardner, Walter LaFeber, and Thomas McCormick, *The Creation of the American Empire* (Chicago: Rand McNally, 1975), pp. 68–70; E. Wilson Lyon, *Louisiana in French Diplomacy, 1759–1802* (Norman, Okla.: University of Oklahoma Press, 1934), p. 180.

3. Lyon, *Louisiana in French Diplomacy,* pp. 178–79, 182–83; Turner, "Louisiana Purchase."

4. Turner, "Louisiana Purchase," p. 580.

5. Jefferson to Gates, July 11, 1803, *The Writings of Thomas Jefferson*, 10 vols., ed. Paul Leicester Ford (New York: G. P. Putnam's Sons, 1892–1900), 8:250.

6. Lyon, *Louisiana in French Diplomacy,* pp. 45, 200–203, 215; Robertson, *Louisiana Under Rule,* 2: 63.

7. Robertson, *Louisiana Under Rule,* 2: 31–32.

8. Lyon, *Louisiana in French Diplomacy,* pp. 140, 197, 200–201, 215; Robertson, *Louisiana Under Rule*, 2: 63.

9. Lyon, *Louisiana in French Diplomacy*, p. 202; Robertson, *Louisiana Under Rule*, 2: 63.

10. Turner, "Louisiana Purchase," p. 581.

11. Milo M. Quaife, *The Diary of James K. Polk* (Chicago: A. C. McClurg, 1910), 1: 228–29; Norman Graebner, "The Mexican War: A Study in Causation," *Pacific Historical Review* (1980), pp. 405–11.

12. Basil Rauch, *American Interests in Cuba, 1848–1855* (New York: Columbia University Press, 1948), p. 284.

13. Ibid., pp. 283–95.

14. Readers will have to take our word for this. The analyst mentioned was simply discussing the case with Karsten. It would be unfair to that person to be named here, as his views were not the "sober second thought" of book or article.

15. B. H. Sumner, *Russia and the Balkans, 1870–1880* (Oxford: Clarendon Press, 1937), p. 374; Barbara Jelavich, *The Ottoman Empire, the Great Powers, and the Straits*

Question, 1870–1887 (Bloomington, Ind.: Indiana University Press, 1973), pp. 99, 100, 102; R. W. Seton-Watson, *Disraeli, Gladstone, and the Eastern Question* (London: F. Cass, 1962), pp. 315–17.

16. Jelavich, *The Ottoman Empire*, p. 105; Sumner, *Russia and the Balkans*, pp. 378, 381, 388; Seton-Watson, *Disraeli, Gladstone*, pp. 332, 414; Richard Millman, *Britain and the Eastern Question* (Oxford: Clarendon Press, 1979), p. 394.

17. Sumner, *Russia and the Balkans*, p. 388*n*; Millman, *Britain and the Eastern Question*, p. 365.

18. Millman, *Britain and the Eastern Question*, pp. 394, 435; Sumner, *Russia and the Balkans*, p. 384.

19. Seton-Watson, *Disraeli, Gladstone*, pp. 324, 376, 394; Millman, *Britain and the Eastern Question*, pp. 398, 399, 428, 595.

20. Seton-Watson, *Disraeli, Gladstone*, p. 367.

21. Ibid., pp. 323, 330.

22. Ibid., p. 414.

23. Millman, *Britain and the Eastern Question*, pp. 434, 440; Sumner, *Russia and the Balkans*, pp. 496, 499. (The last passage quoted is Sumner's paraphrasing of the Tzar, via Count Gorchakov, the foreign minister.)

24. Sumner, *Russia and the Balkans*, p. 520.

25. Seton-Watson, *Disraeli, Gladstone*, p. 448; Sumner, *Russia and the Balkans*, pp. 520–24; A. Lobanov-Rostovsky, *Russia and Europe, 1825–1878* (Ann Arbor, Mich.: University of Michigan Press, 1954), pp. 297–98.

26. Seton-Watson, *Disraeli, Gladstone*, p. 397.

27. Morrison B. Giffen, *Fashoda: The Incident and Its Diplomatic Setting* (Chicago: University of Chicago Press, 1930), p. 20. Cf. the remarks of the British ambassador to France, Lord Dufferin, June 29, 1894 ("a most serious conflict"), cited in Mekki Shibeika, *British Policy in the Sudan, 1882–1902* (Oxford: Oxford University Press, 1952), p. 337. See also Shibeika, pp. 343–44.

28. G. N. Sanderson, *England, Europe, and the Upper Nile, 1882–1880* (Edinburgh: University Press, 1965), pp. 271, 334, 337.

29. Sanderson, *England, Europe*, p. 342; Giffen, *Fashoda*, p. 76.

30. Sanderson, *England, Europe*, pp. 342, 396, 400; Giffen, *Fashoda*, pp. 57, 154; Raymond Songtag, *European Diplomatic History, 1871–1932* (New York: Century, 1933), p. 528; T. W. Riber, "A Survey of British Policy During the Fashoda Crisis," *Political Science Quarterly* 44 (1929): 65–70; R. Arie, "L'Opinion publique en France et l'affaire de Fachoda," *Rev. Hist. Cols.* 41 (1954): 329–67; Anon., "The Failure of Our Foreign Policy," *The Contemporary Review* (April 1898).

31. Giffen, *Fashoda*, p. 109. Cf. Roger G. Brown, *Fashoda Reconsidered: The Impact of French Domestic Politics on Policy in Africa, 1893–1898* (Baltimore: Johns Hopkins University Press, 1969).

32. Sanderson, *England, Europe*, pp. 355, 369; Christopher Andrew, *Theophile Delcassé and the Making of the Entente Cordiale* (London: Macmillan, 1968), p. 102; Brown, *Fashoda Reconsidered*, p. 78. Delcassé had just served as the mediator to the Spanish-American conflict.

33. R. Ned Lebow, *Between Peace and War* (Baltimore: Johns Hopkins University Press, 1981), pp. 323, 326.

34. Sanderson, *England, Europe*, p. 380; Brown, *Fashoda Reconsidered*, p. 120.

35. Assad Homayoun, "Pakistan-China Relations up to 1970" (Ph.D. diss., Georgetown University, 1972), pp. 110–12, 116–18.

36. George Kennan made a comparable point in his famous essay "Sources of Soviet Conduct," *Foreign Affairs* 25 (July 1947): 580.

> The main element of any United States policy towards the Soviet Union must be that of a long-term . . . containment of Russian expansive tendencies. It is important to note, however, that such a policy has nothing to do with outward histrionics; with threats of blustering or superfluous gestures of outward "toughness." While the Kremlin is basically flexible in its reaction to political realities, it is by no means unamenable to considerations of prestige. Like almost any other government, it can be placed by tactless and threatening gestures in a position where it cannot afford to yield even though this might be dictated by its sense of realism. . . . For these reasons, it is a *sine qua non* of successful dealing with Russia that the foreign government in question should remain at all times cool and collected and that its demands on Russian policy should be put forward in such a manner as to leave the way open for a compliance not too detrimental to Russian prestige.

37. For a good discussion of this subject (and analysis of the 1973 "Red Alert" crisis), see Joseph J. Kruzel, "Military Alerts and Diplomatic Signals," in *The Limits of Military Intervention*, ed. Ellen Stern (Beverly Hills, Calif.: Sage, 1977), pp. 84–99.

38. Lawrence Farrar, "The Limits of Choice: July, 1914, Revisited," *Journal of Conflict Resolution* 16 (1972): 18. See also Blechman and Kaplan, *Force Without War* (Washington, D.C.: Brookings Institution, 1978), who argue that shows of force have "a beneficial effect" on outcomes (p. 519), despite their own evidence: that the *larger* the shows of force, the *less* successful the outcome (pp. 98–99); and that treaty commitments are better predictors of success than show of force (p. 115).

39. Norman Padelford et al., *The Dynamics of International Politics,* 3d ed. (New York: Macmillan, 1976), p. 406: "A show of force in the old sense has been affected by technological advances . . . the use of military power through show of force is coming increasingly to rely on the onlooker's estimate of the power in being, coupled with statements of resolution, or even of threat, by the possessor."

40. Thomas Schelling, *The Strategy of Conflict* (Cambridge, Mass.: Harvard University Press, 1960); Herman Kahn, *On Thermonuclear War* (Princeton: Princeton University Press, 1961); Henry Kissinger, *American Foreign Policy* (New York: Norton, 1974), p. 15; J. L. Payne, *The American Threat* (Chicago: Markham, 1970).

41. Adam Yarmolinsky, *The Military Establishment* (New York: Harper and Row, 1971), pp. 34, 127. Cf. Tad Szulc, quoting a Department of Defense (DOD) official critical of Henry Kissinger's emphasis on force during the EC-121 crisis: "Henry always wanted to use Defense Department hardware, not realizing the problems." *The Illusion of Peace* (New York: Viking Press, 1978), p. 82.

42. It may be of interest to know that when asked to identify regions where American threats were likely to be most effective, most of the policymakers interviewed mentioned threats issued in Europe (ten of twelve) and the Middle East (eight of twelve), whereas when asked where such threats might be ineffective, nine of the twelve mentioned Africa.

43. See, for example, John Lenczowski, *Soviet Perceptions of U.S. Foreign Policy* (Ithaca: Cornell University Press, 1982), pp. 156ff.

44. Klaus Knorr in James Rosenau et al., *World Politics* (New York: Free Press, 1976), p. 385; Douglas Kinnard, "The Vietnam War in Retrospect . . . ," *Journal of Political and Military Sociology* 4 (1976): 17–28; A. George, D. Hall, and W. Simons, *The Limits of Coercive Diplomacy* (Boston: Little, Brown, 1971), pp. 218–20.

45. Bruce Russett, "Pearl Harbor: Deterrence Theory and Decision Theory," *Journal*

of Peace Research 2 (1967): 88–105. None of the American measures in 1940 or 1941 designed to check Japanese aggression in China and Indo-China was, strictly speaking, in the nature of threats or ultimata; the U.S. Government was quite careful in avoiding such statements as late as November 26, 1941, when it offered its last "proposal" to the Japanese. But if the United States did not formally threaten Japan, it embargoed oil and scrap metal, froze Japanese assets in the United States, sent U.S. warships on calls to Philippine, New Zealand, and Australian ports, bolstered U.S. defenses in Guam, and moved the Pacific Fleet from San Diego to Pearl Harbor. We finally decided that these were not so much threatening gestures as defensive reactions, and we chose not to code this case. But it does illustrate the fine dividing line between a "threat" and a "defensive reaction." Others, reasoning only slightly differently than did we, might have concluded that the United States *did* "threaten" Japan (and, indeed, several scholars have so argued). In any event, Japan, given its own interests and long-range objectives, *felt* threatened by the United States. (See John E. Wiltz, *From Isolation to War, 1931–1941* (New York: Appleton-Century-Crofts, 1968), pp. 116–26; John L. Snell, *Illusion and Necessity* (Boston: Houghton Mifflin, 1963), pp. 78, 82–85; and Nobataka Ike, ed., *Japan's Decision for War* (Stanford, Calif.: Stanford University Press, 1967), for arguments we found persuasive with regard to these questions.)

46. Charles Lockhart, *The Efficacy of Threats in International Interaction Strategies*, Sage Professional Papers in International Studies, vol. 2, series No. 02-023 (Beverly Hills, Calif., 1973), p. 26.

47. G. Young, *The Medici* (New York: Modern Library, 1933), p. 246.

48. Thucydides, *The History of the Peloponnesian War*, trans. R. Crawley (London: Longmans, Green, 1876), pp. 401–3.

49. K. J. Holsti, *International Politics* (Englewood Cliffs, N.J.: Prentice-Hall), p. 176. This seems to be what Glenn Snyder and Paul Diesing had in mind when they wrote, "If each party *knew* what the other intended to do—in simple terms: yield, stand firm, or fight—and also knew its own intentions in the light of that knowledge, there could be no crisis. . . . Thus it is largely because of the lack of complete information that crises occur at all." And elsewhere: "The assessment of comparative resolve in crisis between nuclear powers is a highly subjective matter." *Conflict Among Nations*, pp. 8, 47.

50. Snyder and Diesing, *Conflict Among Nations*, p. 496; Lebow, *Between Peace and War*, pp. 270–71. Arthur N. Gilbert and Paul G. Lauren also comment on the difficulty one side may have in "managing a crisis" when the other side is unyielding in its objectives. ("Crisis Management: An Assessment and Critique," *Journal of Conflict Resolution* 24 [December 1980]: 641–64.)

51. Paul Schratz, "National Decision-Making and Military Intervention," in Stern, *The Limits of Military Intervention*, p. 357.

52. We do not want to sound overly sanguine about the ease with which political-affairs officers or intelligence officers can manage to get at the truth regarding a target's goals and objectives, or the ease with which they can persuade policymakers of the accuracy of their findings. We know that there are always many voices with many "truths." But the effort must be made. For an excellent analysis of the problems in intelligence gathering and policymaker use of such findings, see Richard K. Betts, "Analysis, War and Decision," *World Politics* 31 (October 1978): 61–89.

53. Harry F. Young, *Prince Lichnowsky and the Great War* (Athens, Ga.: University of Georgia Press, 1977), p. 108; Lebow, *Between Peace and War*, pp. 125–28, 153–83,

155, 301–2; Luigi Albertini, *The Origins of the War of 1914,* 3 vols., ed. and trans. Isabella M. Massey (London: Oxford University Press, 1952), vol. 2.

54. We repeat our offer of copies of this scenario for a nominal fee. Write c/o Prof. Peter Karsten, Dept. of History, Univ. of Pittsburgh, Pittsburgh, Pa. 15260.

55. Reported on "ABC News," Dec. 16, 1981. See also Neal Ascherson, *The Polish August* (London: Penguin Books, 1982).

56. For one good account of the crisis, see Lawrence Freeman, "The War of the Falkland Islands, 1982," *Foreign Affairs* 61 (Fall 1982): 196–210.

Appendix 1

The Statistical Analysis: A Continuation of Chapter 2

Let us begin with a *caveat* with regard to our coding measures: Few of the variables for which values were assigned are purely interval in character—that is, the intervals between the coded numbers do not represent equal measures of precise numeric data. They are, strictly speaking, ordinal, not interval, variables, and the use of ordinal variables in such statistical exercises as factor analysis or regression are treated by some with suspicion, if not disdain.

Clearly, we had to determine the type of scaling to be used in the coding process. Only some of our data were truly adaptable to interval scaling; most were suited to ordinal ranking, and some data were simply nominal. Some methodological "purists" have argued in favor of restricting any statistical analysis of ordinal data to the use of non-parametric statistics. In practice, this leads to an almost exclusive reliance on interval data for complex questions in international relations. Only interval data—given the restrictive nature of these assumptions—are adaptable to certain forms of multivariate analysis (for example, multiple regression, factor analysis, and so on). Those who favor this sort of approach emphasize "objective" as opposed to "perceptual" or subjectively determined variables, as the latter may be "inefficient and uneconomical." That is, the variables are too vague or too difficult to measure to be really useful.[1]

We have come to reject the purist position for two reasons. First, the reliance on interval data may be too exclusive a criterion in that it can force the researcher to eliminate relevant information from the analysis. In extreme cases, one could reduce the study to a set of measurable but trivial sets of data.[2] The purist aversion to perceptual and subjective data precludes factors that a number of analysts consider critical in determining the outcome of a crisis.[3] For example, may we not ask whether threats succeed or fail due to the threatener and the target leaderships' *perceptions* of strength rather than relying on objective measures of actual force levels alone (as do Singer, Small, and Bueno de Mesquita)?[4] We regard subjective estimates of factors such as credibility, perceived capabilities, resolve, and a number of similar concepts that appear frequently in the literature as too important to discount.

Second, reliance on interval data may be deceptive. One of the supposed advantages of interval over ordinal data is that the former record information in a more complete and precise fashion. Yet the nature of our study is such that the informational value of the scales is reversed—the ordinal rankings enable us to assemble a higher quality and more thorough data base. One reason for this is that upon careful examination, the interval scales available for this study—and similar scales used in other studies—appeared to be only superficially interval in some important respects. For example, an indicator such as troop size, when used to represent military power, may be as much an ordinal as an interval scale. One does not find a hypothesis drawn so finely as to suggest that minute variations in the number of a nation's troops are predictive of the resolution of a crisis. Rather, the number of men under arms is a cipher for the much broader concept of military power. Since armies of the same size can vary substantially in terms of capability, the data may be analogous to a categoric mean, around which the actual information may cluster. The ordinal nature of the data would be even more noticeable if one were to reorganize such troop-size figures into categories in order to eliminate statistical distortions caused by abnormal distributions[5] of the data. The use of such a scale could be quite inaccurate, since it does not explicitly include information relevant to a determination of military power. Thus, using an indicator such as the number of troops—even if such an indicator may be reasonably accurate in a general sense—could generate rankings that do not depict the actual balance of forces. China would be "higher" than Great Britain during the 1840s. Similarly, an evaluation of the relative power of the French and Prussians immediately before the Franco-Prussian War would *have* to include some consideration of the Prussians' superior staff system, reserve training, and logistical advantages, *inter alia*, in the rankings.[6]

Our choice of an ordinal ranking scheme was chosen to avoid the problems mentioned above and to increase the comparability among the cases in the study. Purely interval data posed two problems in terms of the latter criterion. First, we were dubious about the quality of the data as a source of valid comparison. Second, pure interval data were simply not available for all the cases due to the wide historical and geographical range of the study. Thus, we would have had to eliminate cases, use different modes of statistical analysis for various subsets of cases—posing additional problems concerning comparability—or select a coding scheme that was universally applicable.

Hence, we took three steps designed to enhance the credibility of our results. First, we created variables that represented scales that *did* reflect equal intervals—that is, when we coded such things as the degree to which the target had economic trade interests in the area being contended for, we identified that degree on a 1–10 high-low scale as a percentage of all the target's foreign markets (0–10, 3–9, 6–8, 9–7, 12–6, and so on). Markets, investments, troop units, distances, and the like can be counted. Other variables are not as easily coded. Coding the worst-case extent of physical risk a target's leadership felt it would suffer in the event that the crisis resulted in war is an example of a more difficult exercise. Here, we asked what percentage of the nation's blood and treasure the target's leadership felt might be lost (0–10, 10–9, 20–8, and so on). Some variables represented a ratio scale, one of the more appealing statistical ways of organizing one's data, inasmuch as it provides a central zero-value reference point ("equal"). And in every instance of coding all these ordinal variables, a conscious effort was made to provide and utilize scales that reflected an *equal* rank ordering (typically envisioned in percentage terms). Thus, when we did subject the data to such statistical measures as posit equal intervals, we did so based on our assumption that the distances between each unit of measurement in each of our ordinal variable scales approximated equal intervals.[7]

Nonetheless, we recognize that our attempts to create equal intervals is not likely to be accepted by all. Hence, we took a second step. We substituted statistical measures that do *not* assume equal intervals for those that do, wherever possible. In correlational analysis, Kendall's rank-order correlation coefficient was the appropriate statistic.[8] A glance back at Table 2.2 might lead one to ask whether some of our variables are colinear; some certainly could be highly correlated. When we correlated each independent variable with all others, we did find almost sixty with suspicious Kendall rank-order correlation coefficients (.2 or higher) with at least one other independent variable. Factor analysis of the independent variables is one good statistical measure of multicolinearity. Hence, we subjected some fifty-eight of the independent variables to equal-interval factor analysis. These factors (with Eigen values of over 1.2, each accounting for at least 3 percent of the effect) are represented (by their varimax rotated factor matrix) in Table A.1.

But another form of factor analysis has emerged—smallest-space analysis (SSA)—which does not require that the variables possess values of equal interval; it requires only that they be ordinal in character.[9] So we subjected the same fifty-eight independent variables to this technique (utilizing Kendall's rank-order correlation coefficient as our "distance coefficient"). Those versed in smallest-space analysis know that the number of "dimensions" required to represent the variables in their smallest relational Euclidean space without excessive "stress" or "alienation" sometimes runs well over the easily envisioned three. Ours ran to six dimensions (some fifteen separate vector plots). We do not intend to subject the reader to such a morass, but we find the simple two-dimensional plot sufficiently representative of the more complex one to reproduce it (Plot A.1) in order that its geometric depiction of the interrelationship of these variables may be compared to the matrix derived from the equal-interval factor analysis. For example, consider factor 1, in Table A.1: It is composed of several variables (those with relatively high coefficient values [over .43]): Nos. 10, 20, 21, 22, 24, 25, 26, 27, 29, 30, 55, 57, and 58. Note that four of these variables (10, 29, 57, and 58) appear at the far left center of Plot A.1, and the other nine (20, 21, 22, 24, 25, 26, 27, 30, and 55) appear at the far right center of the plot. Note also that the four variables appearing in the far left center of the plot have negative coefficients in the equal-interval factor matrix and that those to the far right center have positive ones. This tells us that these two groups of variables are highly colinear (but in an inversely related manner). It also tells us that the equal-interval statistical test for factors has yielded results closely approximated by the ordinal test—evidence that equal-interval assumptions we might make about these independent variables appear viable.

Smallest-space analysis is still the more appropriate statistical measure of multicolinearity of the two. Hence, we made use of its results to reduce the number of variables to a more manageable size. But SSA cannot identify and mathematically re-create factors (via factor-score coefficients) because it is not based on equal-interval assumptions in the fashion of conventional factor analysis. Thus, we were forced to a trial-by-error method of substituting, and experimenting with, some colinear variables during the next step, the maximum likelihood and regression analysis, in our search for statistically significant independent variables that best served to predict the variance in the dependent success-failure variable. In a few instances, however, we were able to identify on the SSA plot a single variable, within a cluster (factor) of variables to replace them all. In another instance, we composed a variable that scaled the clustered variables (the factor). (This scale represented the ratio of the objectively identified actual overall capabilities of the contending parties.) But other colinear variables were not as easy to eliminate or scale. Hence, the need for substitution and experimentation—that is, in multivariate statistical analysis run A, we included independent variable *X* (which seemed from our SSA to be

Plot A.1

SMALLEST-SPACE ANALYSIS OF FIFTY-EIGHT INDEPENDENT VARIABLES

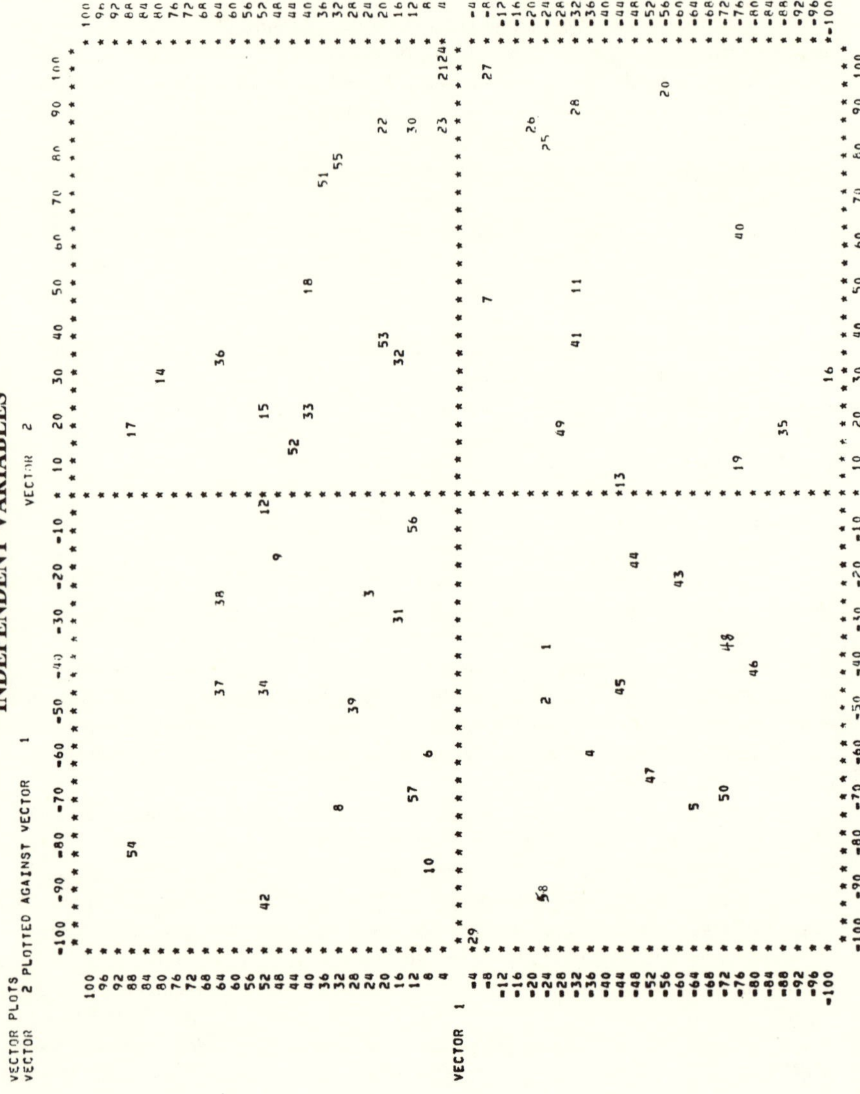

Table A.1
FACTOR MATRIX (FOR THE FIRST FIVE FACTORS) OF FIFTY-EIGHT INDEPENDENT VARIABLES

Variables		Factor 1	Factor 2	Factor 3	Factor 4	Factor 5
1	(1)*	0.02143	0.07756	0.33233	-0.13889	0.05651
2	(24)	-0.16666	-0.06855	-0.07208	0.18159	0.19168
3	(25)	-0.26422	0.25755	0.26001	-0.06075	-0.09672
4	(27)	-0.12753	-0.09368	0.26326	0.14248	0.13440
5	(28)	-0.17291	-0.33943	0.28501	-0.14918	0.26917
6	(29)	-0.29979	0.27372	0.29932	0.14154	0.09961
7	(30)	0.38987	-0.06988	-0.03972	0.08035	-0.12031
8	(31)	-0.11579	0.14733	0.70719	0.04878	-0.10711
9	(32)	-0.02549	0.06287	0.12370	-0.04329	-0.15831
10	(33)	-0.41520	0.13695	0.57349	0.09960	0.34791
11	(34)	0.35591	-0.18193	0.23659	0.00027	0.19744
12	(76)	-0.17820	0.42446	0.11562	-0.07727	0.12156
13	(77)	-0.02289	-0.03753	0.14003	-0.24543	-0.05590
14	(78)	0.02324	0.01314	0.41307	-0.19376	-0.28468
15	(79)	-0.08326	0.76862	0.16599	-0.08204	-0.04332
16	(36)	-0.06279	0.00283	-0.16637	-0.87423	-0.09512
17	(80)	-0.00728	0.04677	-0.03459	0.86913	-0.01509
18	(37)	0.25735	0.59672	-0.04075	0.11436	0.00885
19	(38)	0.12128	-0.20276	-0.13025	-0.17434	0.03847
20	(41)	0.61950	-0.08266	0.00036	-0.07124	0.02018
21	(43)	0.67057	-0.00276	0.02744	0.06369	0.16175
22	(44)	0.39425	0.19139	-0.20959	0.20790	0.14083
23	(45)	0.39253	0.20133	-0.36463	0.08124	0.01972
24	(46)	0.76952	0.06537	-0.01875	0.03557	0.07402
25	(48)	0.47507	-0.17880	-0.11469	0.07776	0.20536
26	(49)	0.38321	0.20396	-0.11408	0.03343	0.06463
27	(40)	0.88337	0.10368	-0.13635	0.00562	0.08979
28	(50)	0.30648	0.11146	-0.28295	-0.26494	0.03451
29	(82)	-0.84491	-0.15307	0.18193	0.03934	0.18560
30	(83)	0.54094	0.27803	0.04303	0.09676	-0.11646
31	(64)	-0.13001	0.09403	-0.10564	0.03089	0.09401
32	(65)	0.06242	0.14652	-0.00645	0.04226	0.05192
33	(66)	-0.01290	0.23304	0.16166	-0.10020	-0.07008
34	(67)	-0.28439	-0.03657	0.15135	-0.04416	-0.05171
35	(35)	-0.00438	-0.12153	-0.02631	-0.15264	-0.01498
36	(85)	0.05949	0.16425	0.11034	0.22631	0.09485
37	(56)	-0.15732	0.07535	0.04526	0.09830	0.00842
38	(57)	0.07377	0.10373	0.01311	0.02242	-0.01243
39	(58)	-0.18174	-0.02266	-0.06284	0.17037	-0.03531
40	(59)	0.02150	0.14611	-0.59260	-0.30286	-0.02876
41	(60)	0.03831	0.06096	-0.00476	0.00881	0.03821
42	(61)	-0.23640	-0.00779	-0.01078	0.04524	-0.01308
43	(90)	-0.14725	-0.03391	-0.02892	0.00064	-0.06681
44	(91)	-0.07983	0.00434	-0.12775	-0.07148	0.37338
45	(93)	0.03786	0.01690	-0.00634	0.04628	0.92219
46	(92)	-0.10958	-0.19342	-0.17721	-0.15725	-0.07780
47	(86)	0.12832	-0.16583	0.05574	0.06163	0.40757
48	(89)	0.00222	0.07888	-0.13559	-0.19115	0.04707
49	(88)	0.09171	-0.09504	-0.00596	-0.02556	0.20249
50	(84)	0.17869	0.56984	-0.09436	0.08931	-0.05902
51	(22)	-0.06434	0.29570	0.00547	0.05823	0.01315
52	(21)	0.30170	0.08539	-0.12196	0.15711	0.07679
53	(72)	-0.14089	-0.07542	-0.02087	-0.06595	0.05025
54	(74)	0.30724	0.18706	0.09589	0.11685	-0.08320
55	(7)	0.00671	0.35670	0.13377	0.00727	0.25005
56	(8)	-0.63452	0.31838	0.18793	-0.02534	0.31545
57	(62)	-0.14709	-0.08471	-0.15469	0.10238	0.28243
58	(63)	-0.60071	0.12097	-0.08920	0.04946	0.11962

* The numbers in parentheses are those of the ordinal variable list in Table 2.2. These variables appear in Table A.1 and Plot A.1 with different numbers (1–58).

colinear with variable *Y*). In run B, we replaced variable *X* with variable *Y* to see if that substitution resulted in any significant difference in the predictor rank-ordering, strength, or statistical significance of any of the important variables.

Testing for "coder reliability," we asked three scholars expert in specific cases independently to code a total of five of our cases. The resulting "coder reliability coefficient" (based on over 1,200 comparative decisions) was .85, high enough to lend credence to our group-consensus method.[10]

The data were analyzed, using several programs (SPSS, Minissa-II, and Crawtran-Probit). All seventy-seven cases were included in a first run, correlating and cross-tabulating each independent variable with the one measuring the success or failure of the threat. The purpose of this run was simply to generate a profile of the cases. Which variables contained little internal variation? Which ones reveal wide variations in intensity or degree? Which ones, that is, could be said to be "constants" and which truly variable? (See chapter 3, part 1.)

We also weighted the cases on three separate scales. We wanted to suppress the importance of those cases in which the threat was not clearly understood by the target, in which the nation(s) issuing the threat was primarily interested in war all along and thus deliberately issued an altogether unacceptable threat, or (in deterrence cases) when we were not certain that the target's lack of aggressiveness was a function of the deterrent threat itself. We were interested in knowing why threats either succeeded or failed, and the introduction, at full strength, of such cases would simply reduce our ability to get a clear answer to our question. A target that did not even perceive the threat was no target at all; a target that never intended to take any action was not in any sense "deterred" by a deterrent threat, no matter how impressive that threat might have been; demands issued merely as an excuse for a dearly sought-after war were more provocation than threat and would tell us little of the physiognomy of threats. Consequently, we weighted each case on a 1–5 scale for each of these three conditions and then multiplied all cases by .013 (to return to an approximation of the number seventy-seven, in order that tests for statistical significance would not be based on an artificially inflated *N*).

How were we to *know* whether a target was deterred by a threat unless the target indicated as much publicly, unless the target's archives had been successfully mined by industrious historians, or unless the target's leaders later published revealing autobiographies? In some cases, especially recent threats seeking to deter the Soviet Union, the evidence was sparse or ambiguous. Had the Soviets withdrawn their forces from Iran in 1946 because they feared a collision with the United States and Britain, because they preferred a cooperative course of action within United Nations guidelines, or because the Iranian premier's conditional offer of oil concessions appeared to give Stalin all that he had really hoped to obtain from Iran? The answer seemed to us to be a combination of these three motives, but we gave the case only a mid-range weight on the appropriate scale because we could not say with confidence that the Soviets had been deterred by the possible use of American force.

The threat the United States posed to North Korea after the North Koreans shot down an EC-121 spy plane in early 1969 was designed to deter them from repeating the action. A U.S. task force entered the Sea of Japan on April 18. Armed escorts accompanied future EC-121 flights, and the North Koreans did not attack any of these. But we know that on April 23 the North Koreans broadcast a response to the American actions. They would "not sit with folded arms, but will take resolute measures for safeguarding our sovereignty as ever."[11] How "deterred," then, was North Korea by the U.S. threat? Our answer was that we were uncertain (a 3 on a 5-point ordinal scale).

Similar problems existed in assessing Soviet interests, intentions, resolve, and perceptions throughout our analysis, just as they exist for every analyst of Soviet policy. We consulted the views of others, examined the relevant evidence ourselves, and then came to a collective judgment about how each variable was to be coded, but we admit that the problem remains. Until more data are forthcoming, our judgments regarding Soviet behavior are simply judgments, and we have, consequently, given less weight to some of these cases in our analysis.[12]

Regression analysis assumes a linear relation between independent and dependent variables. But such relationships could be nonlinear, and a few hypotheses, such as the one involving the suitability of the forces deployed in conveying the threat, posit a curvilinear relation between this relevant variable and the variable recording success or failure of the threat. That is, in the case of the suitability-of-force variable, one hypothesis contends that the success of the threat is made more likely by the deployment of *sufficient* forces than by the deployment of *either* insufficient *or* more than sufficient force.[13] Consequently, we cross-tabulated each independent variable against the dependent variable and checked each for curvilinearity. The dependent variable has only four values; hence, it is difficult to call *any* configuration "curvilinear." But cross-tabs, "breakdowns," and "dummy variable" regression did not reveal any clear candidates for a "curvilinear" label.[14] Hence, regression seemed the appropriate multivariate analysis to employ in order to detect those variables and factors that might predict the outcome of a threat were our variables strictly equal-interval in nature. We have argued that our independent variables are sufficiently close to the equal-interval rule to warrant regression analysis, but we are not as confident about the dependent success-failure variable. It is ordinal, possessing four rank-ordered conditions: failure (force used or bluff called); no force used and threatener's objective partially obtained; no force used and objectives substantially obtained; and no force used and objectives totally obtained. Hence, we also utilized a statistical method comparable to regression (in that it identifies predictor variables after multivariate analysis of dependent and independent variables)—namely, maximum likelihood estimation (MLE). This algorithm does not require that the dependent variable be equal-interval (as in regression). It calculates the probability (or likelihood) of observing the values of the independent variables taken in our particular cases for any given set of values that the dependent variable parameters might assume.[15]

We backed up our smallest-space/maximum-likelihood analyses (ordinal assumptions) with equal-interval factor analysis and multiple regression. The results were almost always quite similar to those derived from smallest-space/maximum-likelihood, but will be reported only as supplementary and suggestive information because of the equal-interval assumption implicit in the statistical measures involved.[16]

Readers interested in obtaining copies of our codebook and data cards (for a nominal fee) may do so by writing to us in care of Professor Peter Karsten, Department of History, University of Pittsburgh, Pittsburgh, Pa. 15260.

NOTES

1. J. David Singer, "The Level-of-Analysis Problem in International Relations," in *The International System*, ed. Klaus Knorr and Sidney Verba (Princeton: Princeton University Press, 1961), p. 88. But see Singer's current reconsideration, *Explaining War* (Beverly Hills, Calif.: Sage, 1973), p. 17.

2. One of the authors (Karsten) had an opportunity to participate in an attempt to develop a fairly sophisticated research model designed to test the hypothesis "deterrence works," during a National Security Education Seminar in 1972 (Charles Kegley and Rich Sinnrich were the research group leaders). Karsten and his associates found, to their distress, that their efforts to maintain scientific purity had trivialized the set of hypotheses derived from the original proposition.

3. See, for example, Richard Cottam, *Foreign Policy Motivation* (Pittsburgh: University of Pittsburgh Press, 1977), and Manus Midlarsky, *On War: Political Violence in the International System* (New York: Free Press, 1975).

4. See, for example, Bruce Bueno de Mesquita, *The War Trap* (New Haven, Conn.: Yale University Press, 1981), chap. 3.

5. Jack E. Vincent, *Factor Analysis in International Relations* (Gainesville, Fla.: University of Florida Press, 1971), pp. 23 ff., has a brief and lucid description of the problems associated with abnormal distributions.

6. J. David Singer offered a similar critique of a "methods textbook" reliance on equal-interval data searches that ignore the "cruder, but perhaps equally accurate and more valid, indicator in ordinal or nominal form." Singer, *Explaining War,* p. 17.

7. For good arguments on behalf of the legitimacy of these sorts of assumptions in interval-based statistics, see Richard P. Boyle, "Path Analysis and Ordinal Data," *American Journal of Sociology* 75 (1970): 461–80; and Sanford Labovitz, "The Assignment of Numbers to Rank Order Categories," *American Sociological Review* 35 (1970): 516–20. Cf. James C. Lingoes, ed., *Geometric Representatives of Relational Data: Readings in Multidimensional Scaling* (Ann Arbor, Mich.: Mathesis Press, 1977); and S. Labovitz, "Statistical Usage in Sociology: Sacred Cows and Ritual," *Sociological Methods and Research* 1 (1970): 13–38.

8. Our data had many "tied cases" (that is, cases in which the value assigned for a given variable was the same as the one assigned for that variable in one or more other cases). Hence, Kendall's coefficient was preferable to Spearman's *rho* (another nonparametric correlation coefficient that does not treat "tied cases" as conservatively as does Kendall's coefficient).

9. See Lingoes, *Geometric Representations*, passim, and J. C. Lingoes, ed., *The Guttman-Lingoes Nonmetric Series* (Ann Arbor, Mich.: Mathesis Press, 1973).

10. Our group-consensus technique was not the one employed by our experts, of course, inasmuch as the cost of bringing three or more experts together for such coding sessions to duplicate our techniques was prohibitive. But by explaining and defining our variables and answering all queries, we think it is possible that our experts approximated our methodology.

11. Tad Szulc, *The Illusion of Peace* (New York: Viking Press, 1978), p. 86.

12. For a good discussion of the problems implicit in the study of Soviet crises management and decisionmaking, and a review of the literature, see John O. Steinbruner, Arnold Horelick, and A. Ross Johnson, *The Study of Soviet Foreign Policy: Decision-Theory-Related Approaches* (Beverly Hills, Calif.: Sage, 1975).

13. See Bernard Brodie, *Strategy in the Missile Age* (Princeton: Princeton University Press, 1959), pp. 264-304. An alternative hypothesis would be that the more force deployed, the more effective would be the threat. (The nul hypothesis would then be that there is no relationship at all between the actual deployment of forces during the crisis and the outcome of the crisis.)

14. Michael Wallace found a curvilinear relationship between polarization in the international system and the outbreak of war; utilizing the Correlates of War data, he noted

that both low and high polarizations were correlated with war while only moderate polarization correlated with a low incidence of warfare. (M. Wallace, "Alliance Polarization, Cross-Cutting, and International War, 1815-1964," *Journal of Conflict Resolution* 17, no. 4 [1973].) The Correlates of War study does not examine specific threats per se as we have; rather, it surveys crises and wars in the entire international system over a span of a century and a half. Hence, the data bases are not identical. But we also coded systemic polarity and the occurrence or nonoccurrence of war, and our analysis of the correlation of these two variables reveals no such curvilinearity. The degree of systemic polarization appears to be curvilinearly related to the *frequency* of threats and crises themselves, not to their outcomes.

15. For a good discussion of maximum likelihood (and a comparison of this technique to regression), see John Aldrich and Charles Cnudde, "Probing the Bounds of Conventional Wisdom," *American Journal of Political Science* 19 (1975): 571–608.

16. We thank P. R. Krishnaiah of the Department of Mathematics and Statistics at the University of Pittsburgh; Phil Sidel, Aly Abdoulliel, and Klaus Teuter of Pitt Social Science Computer Research Institute; and Regionald Baker, former editor of the *Historical Methods Newsletter,* for their advice regarding our methodology, but we absolve them of any responsibility for it.

Appendix 2

A Questionnaire on the Political Utility of Threats to Use Force Put to Twelve Upper-level U.S. Foreign-Policy Officials (in State, ACDA, and DOD) in 1977

Your response will never be identified with your name or organization, nor will your views ever be made public, except as part of an aggregate sample.

Position/Affiliation (Optional) ______________________________

Date ______________________________

Last 2 Positions/Assignments/Affiliations (Optional) ______________________________

____

____

____

I. GENERAL WORLD VIEWS

1) Which three factors are most important (in rank order, 1st, 2nd and 3rd) in the shaping of the international system?
   - (a) Economic strength?
   - (b) Technological developments?
   - (c) Nationalistic movements?
   - (d) Military power?
   - (e) Internal transformations in states?
   - (f) Ideologies?
   - (g) Other (Define)?

2) Is the credibility of U.S. commitments to come to the defense of other nations on the rise, stable, or declining?
   - (a) As *you* see it?

     10 9 8 7 6 5 4 3 2 1 0
     Rising Stable Declining
   - (b) As *European allies* see it?

0 1 2 3 4 5 6 7 8 9 10
Declining Stable Rising

(c) As *potential adversaries* see it?
10 9 8 7 6 5 4 3 2 1 0
Rising Stable Declining

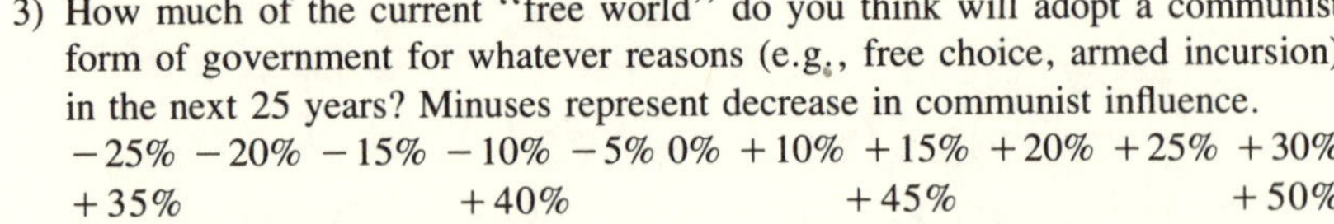

3) How much of the current "free world" do you think will adopt a communist form of government for whatever reasons (e.g., free choice, armed incursion) in the next 25 years? Minuses represent decrease in communist influence.
−25% −20% −15% −10% −5% 0% +10% +15% +20% +25% +30%
+35% +40% +45% +50%

4) Is the best strategy for avoiding war to "stand up" to hostile powers, or to seek an accommodation with them?

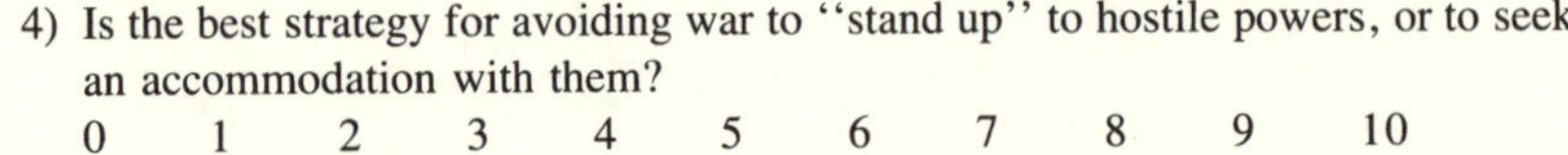

0 1 2 3 4 5 6 7 8 9 10
Not Accommodative Essentially Accommodative

5) How seriously do you believe that the Soviet Union threatens American interests abroad?
+5 +4 +3 +2 +1 0 −1 −2 −3 −4 −5
Substantially Not Significantly

6) How effective do you think American military threats against the Soviet Union generally are in crisis?
+5 +4 +3 +2 +1 0 −1 −2 −3 −4 −5
Effective Ineffective

II. SPECIFIC BELIEFS ON THE POLITICAL UTILITY OF THREATS TO USE FORCE

One of the purposes of this questionnaire is to gain some insight into the "political utility of threats to use force" in the nuclear age. By that phrase is meant those advantages and disadvantages attending the explicit demonstration by the U.S. of military capabilities and a willingness to use them to obtain something in the international arena after 1950. (A list of cases used by researchers at the Center for Arms Control and International Security Studies at the University of Pittsburgh appears at the end of this questionnaire.)

1) Is the threat to use force for political ends morally objectionable?

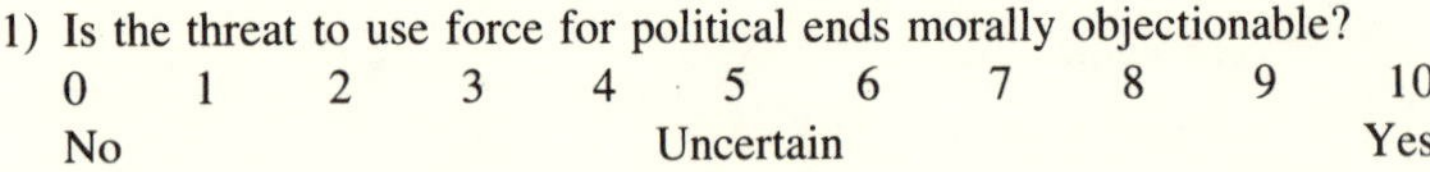

0 1 2 3 4 5 6 7 8 9 10
No Uncertain Yes

2) Currently, in which areas of the globe are U.S. interests such that the political utility of threats would be most effective?

3) In which would they currently be ineffective?

III. FACTORS AFFECTING OUTCOMES OF THE POLITICAL USE OF THREATS

1) Can you briefly describe for me one or two instances of the political utility of threats in which (a) you were involved, or (b) you have some substantial knowledge? (Optional)

(c) What were the most important factors affecting the outcome in this case (these cases)?

(d) If one element in the U.S. policy with respect to this political use of threats could have been changed, what would you have changed, and why?

2) I would like to ask you to imagine a number of hypothetical, but potential crises which impinge to one degree or another on U.S. interests. In which ones would you regard a threat by the U.S. to use force as politically appropriate and/or militarily feasible responses? (Please circle one number for appropriateness and one number for feasibility on each part.)

(a) Another Arab oil embargo

+3 +2 +1 0 −1 −2 −3 +3 +2 +1 0 −1 −2 −3
Appropriate Inappropriate Feasible Not Feasible

(b) Panamanian attack on Canal Zone forces

+3 +2 +1 0 −1 −2 −3 +3 +2 +1 0 −1 −2 −3
Appropriate Inappropriate Feasible Not Feasible

(c) Soviet military incursion into Yugoslavia after death of Tito

+3 +2 +1 0 −1 −2 −3 +3 +2 +1 0 −1 −2 −3
Appropriate Inappropriate Feasible Not Feasible

(d) Full-scale insurgency in Rhodesia

+3 +2 +1 0 −1 −2 −3 +3 +2 +1 0 −1 −2 −3
Appropriate Inappropriate Feasible Not Feasible

(e) North Korean raids upon, shelling of, South Korea

+3 +2 +1 0 −1 −2 −3 +3 +2 +1 0 −1 −2 −3
Appropriate Inappropriate Feasible Not Feasible

Appendix 3

Case-By-Case Residuals for Maximum Likelihood Estimates of War/No War

Probit Threats

OBSERV		DEP VAR. Y	Y HAT	PROBABILITY	RESIDUAL	CLASSIFICATION
1	*	0.00000E+00	-0.52804E-01	-0.52804E-01	0.52804E-01	0.00000E+00
2	*	0.00000E+00	-0.12843	-0.12843	0.12843	0.00000E+00
3	*	0.00000E+00	-0.83628E-02	-0.83628E-02	0.83628E-02	0.00000E+00
4	*	0.00000E+00	-0.13694E-01	-0.13694E-01	0.13694E-01	0.00000E+00
5		0.00000E+00	0.73547	0.73547	-0.73547	1.0000
6	*	1.0000	0.55791	0.55791	0.44209	1.0000
7		0.00000E+00	0.62888	0.62888	-0.62888	1.0000
8	*	0.00000E+00	0.10612	0.10612	-0.10612	0.00000E+00
9	*	0.00000E+00	-0.53069E-02	-0.53069E-02	0.53069E-02	0.00000E+00
10	*	1.0000	1.1668	1.1668	-0.16680	1.0000
11	*	1.0000	0.76607	0.76607	0.23393	1.0000
12	*	0.00000E+00	0.23373E-01	0.23373E-01	-0.23373E-01	0.00000E+00
13	*	0.00000E+00	0.20149	0.20149	-0.20149	0.00000E+00
14	*	0.00000E+00	-0.13575	-0.13575	0.13575	0.00000E+00
15	*	0.00000E+00	-0.92660E-01	-0.92660E-01	0.92660E-01	0.00000E+00
16	*	0.00000E+00	-0.64519	-0.64519	0.64519	0.00000E+00
17	*	0.00000E+00	0.53136E-01	0.53136E-01	-0.53136E-01	0.00000E+00
18	*	0.00000E+00	-0.31932E-02	-0.31932E-02	0.31932E-02	0.00000E+00
19	*	0.00000E+00	0.71385E-01	0.71385E-01	-0.71385E-01	0.00000E+00
20	*	0.00000E+00	0.10965	0.10965	-0.10965	0.00000E+00
21	*	0.00000E+00	0.17170	0.17170	-0.17170	0.00000E+00
22	*	0.00000E+00	-0.11862E-01	-0.11862E-01	0.11862E-01	0.00000E+00
23	*	0.00000E+00	0.62140E-01	0.62140E-01	-0.62140E-01	0.00000E+00
24	*	0.00000E+00	-0.64423E-01	-0.64423E-01	0.64423E-01	0.00000E+00
25	*	0.00000E+00	0.16127	0.16127	-0.16127	0.00000E+00
26		1.0000	0.48849	0.48849	0.51151	0.00000E+00
27	*	1.0000	0.83226	0.83226	0.16774	1.0000
28	*	1.0000	0.64876	0.64876	0.35124	1.0000
29	*	0.00000E+00	0.97696E-01	0.97696E-01	-0.97696E-01	0.00000E+00
30	*	0.00000E+00	0.15087	0.15087	-0.15087	0.00000E+00
31	*	0.00000E+00	0.27345	0.27345	-0.27345	0.00000E+00
32	*	0.00000E+00	0.93336E-01	0.93336E-01	-0.93336E-01	0.00000E+00
33	*	1.0000	0.93163	0.93163	0.68371E-01	1.0000
34	*	1.0000	0.84762	0.84762	0.15238	1.0000
35	*	1.0000	0.82215	0.82215	0.17785	1.0000
36	*	1.0000	1.0101	1.0101	-0.10102E-01	1.0000
37	*	1.0000	0.59322	0.59322	0.40678	1.0000
38	*	1.0000	0.55358	0.55358	0.44642	1.0000
39	*	0.00000E+00	0.19150	0.19150	-0.19150	0.00000E+00
40	*	0.00000E+00	-0.88835E-01	-0.88835E-01	0.88835E-01	0.00000E+00
41	*	1.0000	0.89696	0.89696	0.10304	1.0000
42	*	0.00000E+00	-0.29496	-0.29496	0.29496	0.00000E+00

```
•
43  *  0,00000E+00  0,21380      0,21380      -0,21380      0,00000E+00  I     *                        I
44  *   1,0000       1,1273       1,1273      -0,12734       1,0000      I                             *I
45  *   1,0000      0,86853      0,86853       0,13147       1,0000      I                        *     I
46  *  0,00000E+00  0,39029      0,39029      -0,39029      0,00000E+00  I          *                   I
47  *   1,0000      0,70564      0,70564       0,29436       1,0000      I                   *          I
48  *   1,0000       1,3241       1,3241      -0,32409       1,0000      I                             *I
49     0,00000E+00  0,65160      0,65160      -0,65160       1,0000      I                  *           I
50  *   1,0000      0,78905      0,78905       0,21095       1,0000      I                      *       I
51  *  0,00000E+00  0,48041      0,48041      -0,48041      0,00000E+00  I             *                I
52  *   1,0000       1,1919       1,1919      -0,19186       1,0000      I                             *I
53  *  0,00000E+00  0,21461      0,21461      -0,21461      0,00000E+00  I     *                        I
54  *  0,00000E+00  0,76409E-01  0,76409E-01  -0,76409E-01  0,00000E+00  I  *                           I
55  *   1,0000      0,83135      0,83135       0,16865       1,0000      I                       *      I
56  *   1,0000      0,55101      0,55101       0,44899       1,0000      I               *              I
57  *  0,00000E+00  -0,22604     -0,22604      0,22604      0,00000E+00  I*                             I
58      1,0000      0,40019      0,40019       0,59981      0,00000E+00  I           *                  I
59  *  0,00000E+00  0,43734      0,43734      -0,43734      0,00000E+00  I            *                 I
60  *  0,00000E+00  -0,31738     -0,31738      0,31738      0,00000E+00  I*                             I
61  *   1,0000      0,93325      0,93325       0,66752E-01   1,0000      I                          *   I
62  *   1,0000      0,76972      0,76972       0,23028       1,0000      I                     *        I
63  *   1,0000      0,98540      0,98540       0,14602E-01   1,0000      I                           * I
64  *  0,00000E+00  0,47469E-01  0,47469E-01  -0,47469E-01  0,00000E+00  I *                            I
65  *  0,00000E+00  -0,18584     -0,18584      0,18584      0,00000E+00  I*                             I
66  *  0,00000E+00  0,20435      0,20435      -0,20435      0,00000E+00  I     *                        I
67  *  0,00000E+00  0,19212      0,19212      -0,19212      0,00000E+00  I    *                         I
68  *  0,00000E+00  -0,17804     -0,17804      0,17804      0,00000E+00  Ir                             I
69  *   1,0000      0,74952      0,74952       0,25048       1,0000      I                    *         I
70  *   1,0000      0,54567      0,54567       0,45433       1,0000      I               *              I
71  *  0,00000E+00  -0,18841     -0,18841      0,18841      0,00000E+00  I*                             I
72  *  0,00000E+00  -0,30049E-02 -0,30049E-02  0,30049E-02  0,00000E+00  I*                             I
73  *  0,00000E+00  0,21693      0,21693      -0,21693      0,00000E+00  I     *                        I
74  *  0,00000E+00  0,27349      0,27349      -0,27349      0,00000E+00  I       *                      I
75  *   1,0000       1,0947       1,0947      -0,94654E-01   1,0000      I                             *I
76  *   1,0000      0,88328      0,88328       0,11672       1,0000      I                         *    I
77  *   1,0000       1,0679       1,0679      -0,67934E-01   1,0000      I                             *I


                          TOTAL  0=25  25=5  5=75  75=1
        DEP, VAR, = 0      47     39     5     3     0
        DEP, VAR, = 1      30      0     2     8    20
```

Appendix 4

Multiple Regression Results for Seventy-Seven Weighted Cases with Residual Results

MULTIPLE REGRESSION RESULTS FOR SEVENTY-SEVEN WEIGHTED CASES WITH RESIDUAL RESULTS

Dependent variable: VAR249

Summary table

Variable	Multiple R	R square	Rsq change	Simple R	B	Beta
VAR142	0.14576	0.02125	0.02125	0.14576	0.2405721D-01	0.01759
VAR298	0.16626	0.02764	0.00640	-0.10094	0.6247431D-01	0.06798
VAR296	0.22499	0.05062	0.02298	-0.08831	-0.6649048D-01	-0.11443
FACTOR5	0.22560	0.05089	0.00027	-0.02419	0.5146726D+00	0.09594
FACTOR6	0.22567	0.05093	0.00003	-0.00899	0.3815161D+00	0.06294
FACTOR8	0.23598	0.05568	0.00476	0.02702	0.6393261D-03	0.00013
VAR134	0.25954	0.06736	0.01168	0.12972	-0.1256677D+00	-0.08063
VAR245	0.37328	0.13934	0.07198	0.27394	0.1827242D+00	0.08959
VAR225	0.37455	0.14029	0.00095	-0.04816	-0.5198958D-01	-0.04689
VAR052	0.38911	0.15141	0.01112	-0.21984	0.1763979D-01	0.04340
VAR147	0.50369	0.25370	0.10229	0.41436	0.2324885D+00	0.18563
VAR221	0.50845	0.25853	0.00482	-0.15849	-0.1043735D+00	-0.07049
VAR064	0.50900	0.25908	0.00056	0.03516	0.2262736D-01	0.05039
VAR100	0.71972	0.51800	0.25892	-0.59394	-0.6676876D+00	-0.65044
VAR299	0.72679	0.52822	0.01022	-0.24546	-0.1363704D+00	-0.15860
VAR206	0.72840	0.53057	0.00235	-0.03203	0.4978548D-01	0.01959
VAR143	0.77189	0.59581	0.06524	0.27220	0.2368765D+00	0.20323
VAR224	0.82015	0.67265	0.07683	0.28849	0.6567701D+00	0.33321
VAR257	0.82159	0.67502	0.00237	0.01061	-0.2806546D-01	-0.06051
(Constant)					0.2829941D+01	

```
* * * * * * * * * * * * * * * * * * * * * *  M U L T I P L E   R E G R E S S I O N  * * * * * * * * * * * * * * * * * * * * * *

Dependent variable:  VAR249

          Observed   Predicted                                Plot of standardized residual
SEQNUM      VAR249      VAR249     Residual            -2.0      -1.0       0.0       1.0       2.0

     1    3.000000    2.120235     0.8797646                                 :           *
     2    2.000000    1.405275     0.5947250                                 :       *
     3    4.000000    3.317072     0.6829277                                 :         *
     4    2.000000    3.036043    -1.036043                    *              :
     5    4.000000    4.325662    -0.3256623                            *    :
     6    4.000000    1.410410     2.539590                                  :                     X
     7    2.000000    2.841551    -0.8415515                     *           :
     8    1.000000    1.569996    -0.5699963                         *       :
     9    1.000000    1.926915    -0.9269154                    *            :
    10    4.000000    4.960957    -0.9609569                    *            :
    11    4.000000    2.908718     1.091282                                  :              *
    12    2.000000    2.106685    -0.1066846                                *:
    13    4.000000    3.983247     0.1675319E-01                             *
    14    1.000000    1.477666    -0.4776659                          *      :
    15    4.000000    3.654665     0.3453349                                 :    *
    16    2.000000    1.622225     0.3777751                                 :    *
    17    3.000000    2.319043     0.6809569                                 :         *
    18    3.000000    2.465558     0.5344418                                 :      *
    19    2.000000    1.335368     0.6646323                                 :        *
    20    2.000000    2.935452    -0.9354517                    *            :
    21    2.000000    2.739044    -0.7390440                       *         :
    22    1.000000    1.830622    -0.8306217                     *           :
    23    2.000000    2.660263    -0.6602629                        *        :
    24    4.000000    3.606558     0.3934420                                 :     *
    25    3.000000    3.438473    -0.4384734                           *     :
    26    4.000000    4.106830    -0.1068304                                *:
    27    4.000000    4.679540    -0.6795397                       *         :
    28    4.000000    3.231996     0.7680043                                 :          *
    29    3.000000    2.190900     0.8091000                                 :          *
    30    1.000000    1.244492    -0.2444924                              *  :
    31    2.000000    2.137189    -0.1371391                               * :
    32    1.000000    1.019672    -0.1967191E-01                             *
    33    4.000000    2.976815     1.023185                                  :             *
    34    4.000000    4.348813    -0.3488127                            *    :
    35    4.000000    2.617673     1.382327                                  :                  *
    36    4.000000    3.283134     0.7168564                                 :         *
    37    4.000000    2.364823     1.635177                                  :                     X
    38    3.000000    3.500657    -0.5006565                          *      :
    39    1.000000    1.819319    -0.8193188                      *          :
    40    1.000000    1.236220    -0.2362197                              *  :
    41    4.000000    3.310481     0.6895187                                 :         *
    42    2.000000    1.910410     0.8959033E-01                             :*
    43    2.000000    1.490853     0.5191473                                 :      *
```

* MULTIPLE REGRESSION *

Dependent variable: VAR249

Plot of standardized residual: -2.0 -1.0 0.0 1.0 2.0

SEQNUM	Observed VAR249	Predicted VAR249	Residual
44	4.000000	2.649779	1.350221
45	4.000000	3.901148	0.9885195E-01
46	1.000000	2.037286	-1.037286
47	4.000000	2.667877	1.332123
48	4.000000	4.866759	-0.8667592
49	3.000000	4.415713	-1.415713
50	4.000000	2.022150	1.977850
51	3.000000	3.477648	-0.4776477
52	4.000000	3.192714	0.8072863
53	1.000000	1.854052	-0.8540520
54	1.000000	1.988584	-0.9885837
55	4.000000	4.030505	-0.3050513E-01
56	4.000000	4.603921	-0.6039207
57	1.000000	1.977876	-0.9778756
58	4.000000	3.558234	0.4417661
59	2.000000	2.226164	-0.2261645
60	1.000000	0.4772615	0.5227385
61	4.000000	3.688274	0.3117261
62	4.000000	3.109111	0.8908888
63	4.000000	3.581027	0.4189727
64	2.000000	2.946406	-0.9464063
65	2.000000	1.966939	0.3306051E-01
66	2.000000	1.710137	0.2898630
67	3.000000	2.837804	0.1621963
68	1.000000	1.573228	-0.5732284
69	4.000000	2.974376	1.025624
70	4.000000	3.022528	0.9774722
71	2.000000	2.260179	-0.2601791
72	1.000000	1.664727	-0.6647266
73	1.000000	1.827337	-0.8273375
74	1.000000	0.9390804	0.6091958E-01
75	4.000000	4.285063	-0.2850632
76	4.000000	4.122390	-0.1223897
77	4.000000	4.017466	-0.1746556E-01

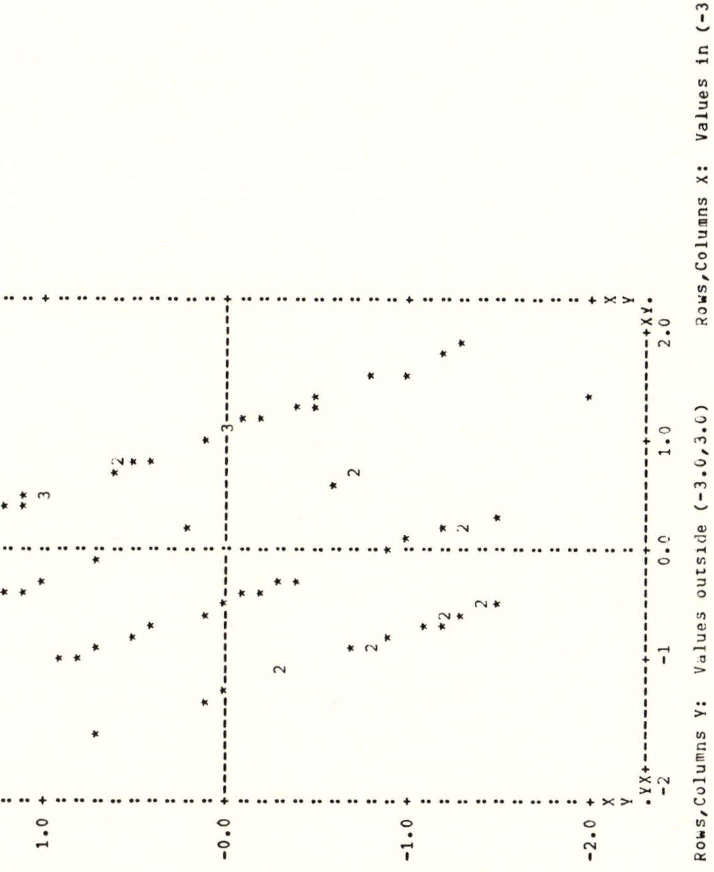
Rows,Columns Y: Values outside (-3.0,3.0)
Rows,Columns X: Values in (-3.0,-2.05) or (2.05,3.0)

Select Bibliography of Sources Used in Case Analysis

ATHENS VERSUS POTIDAE, 431, B.C. AND SPARTA VERSUS ACANTHUS, 431 B.C.

The Cambridge Ancient History. Edited by J. B. Bury et al. Cambridge, England: Cambridge University Press, 1923–39. Vols. 4–7.

Henderson, Bernard. *The Great War Between Athens and Sparta*. London: Macmillan, 1927.

Kagan, Donald. *The Outbreak of the Peloponnesian War*. Ithaca, N.Y.: Cornell University Press, 1969.

Schaefer, Hans. *Staatsform und Politik*. Leipzig: Dieterich, 1932.

Thucydides. *The History of the Peloponnesian War*. Translated by Richard Crawley. London: Longmans, Green, 1876.

ATHENS VERSUS MELOS, 416 B.C.

The Cambridge Ancient History. Edited by J. B. Bury et al. Cambridge, England: Cambridge University Press, 1923–39. Vols. 4–7.

Henderson, Bernard. *The Great War Between Athens and Sparta*. London: Macmillan, 1927.

Kagan, Donald. *The Outbreak of the Peloponnesian War*. Ithaca, N.Y.: Cornell University Press, 1969.

———. *The Peace of Nicias and the Sicilian Expedition*. Ithaca, N.Y.: Cornell University Press, 1981.

Schaefer, Hans. *Staatsform und Politik*. Leipzig: Dieterich, 1932.

Thucydides. *The History of the Peloponnesian War*. Translated by Richard Crawley. London: Longmans, Green, 1876.

ROME VERSUS CARTHAGE, 218 B.C.

Badian, Ernst. *Foreign Clientelae, 264–70 B.C.* Oxford: Oxford University Press, 1958.

Dorey, T.A., and Dudley, D. R. *Rome Against Carthage*. London: Seeker and Warburg, 1971.

Livius, Titus. *Ab urbe Condita Libri*. Books 21–45. Lipsiae: B. Teubner, 1926.

Polybius. *The Histories [of Rome]*. Translated by W. R. Paton. 6 vols. London: W. Heinemann, 1922–27.

Sanctis, Gaetano de. *Storia dei Romani*. 4 vols. Turin and Florence: Fratelli Bocca, 1907–53. Vol. 3.

Scullard, Howard. *A History of the Roman World from 753 to 146 B.C.* 2d rev. ed. London: Methuen, 1951.

ROME VERSUS MACEDON, 200 B.C.

Badian, Ernst. *Foreign Clientelae, 264–70 B.C.* Oxford: Oxford University Press, 1958.

Dorey, T. A., and Dudley, D. R. *Rome Against Carthage*. London: Seeker and Warburg, 1971.

Livius, Titus. *Ab urbe Condita Libri*. Books 21–45. Lipsiae: B. Teubner, 1926.

Polybius. *The Histories [of Rome]*. Translated by W. R. Paton. 6 vols. London: W. Heinemann, 1922–27.

Sanctis, Gaetano de. *Storia dei Romani*. 4 vols. Turin and Florence: Fratelli Bocca, 1907–53. Vol. 3.

Scullard, Howard. *A History of the Roman World from 753 to 146 B.C.* 2d rev. ed. London: Methuen, 1951.

Wallbank, Frank W. *Philip V of Macedon*. Cambridge, England: Cambridge University Press, 1940.

VIKINGS VERSUS FRANCE, A.D. 845

Brentano, Frantz Funck. *The Earliest Times*. New York: G. P. Putnam's Sons, 1927.

Kendrick, Thomas. *A History of the Vikings*. New York: C. Scribner's Sons, 1930.

Musset, Lucien. *Au Moyen Age Les Peuples Scandinaves*. Paris: Presses Universitaires de France, 1951.

MONGOLS VERSUS KHWARAZM, 1218–19

Juvaini. *The History of the World-Conqueror*. Translated by John Boyle. 2 vols. Cambridge, England: Cambridge University Press, 1958.

Spuler, Bertold. *History of the Mongols*. Berkeley: University of California Press, 1972.

ENGLAND VERSUS FRANCE, 1415

Lot, Ferdinand. *La France des Origines à la Guerre de Cent Ans*. 16th ed. Paris: E. Champion, 1948.

Perroy, Edouard. *The 100 Years War*. London: Eyre and Spottiswoode, 1951.

Seward, Desmond. *The Hundred Years War*. London: Constable, 1978.

FRANCE VERSUS FLORENCE, 1495

Petrie, Sir Charles A. *Earlier Diplomatic History, 1492–1713*. London: Hollis and Carter, 1949.

The Renaissance, 1493–1520. Edited by George R. Potter. Cambridge, England: The University Press, 1957.

Young, George F. *The Medici*. New York: Modern Library, 1933.

BRITAIN VERSUS RUSSIA, 1719

Grey, Ian. *Peter the Great: Emperor of All Russia*. Philadelphia: Lippincott, 1920.

Mediger, Walther. *Meckleburg, Russland und England-Hannover, 1706–1721*. Hildesheim, Germany: Lax, 1967.

Michael, Wolfgang. *England Under George I*. 2 vols. London: Macmillan, 1939. Vol. 2.

Schuyler, Eugene. *Peter the Great*. 2 vols. New York: Russell and Russell, 1967.

Sumner, B. H. *Peter the Great and the Emergence of Russia*. London: English University Press, 1950.

BRITAIN VERSUS KING OF TWO SICILIES, 1742

Acton, Harold. *The Bourbons of Naples (1734–1825)*. London: Methuen, 1956.

Mahan, Alfred Thayer. *The Influence of Sea Power upon History, 1660–1783*. Boston: Little, Brown, 1890.

Valesecchi, Franco. *L'Italia nel Settecento dal 1714 al 1788*. Milan: Milione, 1959.

CHINA VERSUS VIETNAM, 1770

Deveria, Gabriel, *Histoire des Relations de la Chine avec l'Annam—Vietnam du XVIe au XIXe Siècle*. Paris: E. Leroux, 1880.

Lam, Truong, Buu. "Intervention versus Tribute in Sino-Vietnamese Relations." In *China's Response to the West*, edited by John K. Fairbank. Cambridge, Mass.: Harvard University Press, 1954.

PRUSSIA VERSUS AUSTRIA, 1778

Atkinson, Christopher T. *A History of Germany, 1715–1815*. London: Methuen, 1908.

Padover, Saul K. *The Revolutionary Emperor: Joseph the Second, 1741–1790*. New York: R. O. Ballou, 1934.

BRITAIN VERSUS EGYPT, 1839–40

Anderson, Matthew S. *The Eastern Question, 1774–1923*. London: Macmillan, 1966.

Dodwell, H. H. *The Founder of Modern Egypt: A Study of Mohammed Ali*. Cambridge, England: Cambridge University Press, 1931.

Mowat, R. B. *History of European Diplomacy, 1815–1914*. London: E. Arnold, 1923.

Webster, Charles. *The Foreign Policy of Palmerston*. Cambridge, England: The University Press, 1951.

BRITAIN VERSUS CHINA, 1840–41

Costin, William C. *Great Britain and China, 1833–60*. Oxford: Oxford University Press, 1937.

Fay, Peter W. *The Opium War*. Chapel Hill: University of North Carolina Press, 1975.

Holt, Edgar. *The Opium Wars in China*. Chester Springs, Pa.: Dufour Editions, 1964.

Kuo, Pin-chia. *A Critical Study of the First Anglo-Chinese War*. Shanghai: Commercial Press, 1935.

Waley, Arthur. *The Opium War Through Chinese Eyes*. London: Allen and Unwin, 1958.

BRITAIN VERSUS UNITED STATES, 1846

The Cambridge History of British Foreign Policy, 1789–1919. 3 vols. Cambridge, England: The University Press, 1922–23.

Graebner, Norman A. *Empire on the Pacific: A Study in American Continental Expansion*. New York: Ronald Press, 1955.

Jacobs, Melvin. *Winning Oregon: A Study of an Expansionist Movement*. Cladwell, Idaho: Caxton Printers, 1938.

Jones, W. D., and Vinson, J. C. "British Preparedness and the Oregon Settlement." *Pacific Historical Review* 22 (1953):353–64.

Jones, Wilbur. *Lord Aberdeen and the Americas*. Athens, Ga.: University of Georgia Press, 1958.

McCormack, Eugene I. *James K. Polk: A Political Biography*. Berkeley: University of California Press, 1922.

Merk, Frederick. *Manifest Destiny and Mission in American History*. New York: Knopf, 1963.

———. *The Monroe Doctrine and American Expansionism, 1843–49*. New York: Knopf, 1966.

———. *The Oregon Question: Essays in Anglo-American Diplomacy and Politics*. Cambridge, Mass.: Harvard University Press, 1967.

Pratt, J. W. "James K. Polk and John Bull." *Canadian Historical Review* 24 (1943):341–49.

Sellers, Charles G. *James K. Polk: Continentalist, 1843–1846*. Princeton: Princeton University Press, 1966.

Van Alstyne, R. W. *The Rising American Empire*. New York: Quadrangle, 1960.

AUSTRIA, RUSSIA VERSUS PRUSSIA, 1850

Bismarck's Autobiography. Translated by A. J. Butler. 2 vols. New York: Harper and Bros., 1898. Vol. 1.

Clark, Chester W. *Franz Joseph and Bismarck*. Cambridge, Mass.: Harvard University Press, 1934.

Darmstedter, F. *Bismarck and the Creation of the 2nd Reich*. London: Methuen, 1948.

Pflanze, Otto. *Bismarck and the Development of Germany*. Princeton: Princeton University Press, 1963.

BRITAIN, FRANCE VERSUS RUSSIA, 1853

Anderson, Matthew S. *The Eastern Question, 1774–1923*. London: Macmillan, 1966.

Marriott, J.A.R. *The Eastern Question*. Oxford: Oxford University Press, 1940.

Puryear, V. J. *England, Russia, and the Straits Question*. Berkeley: University of California Press, 1931.

Rumm, Agatha. "Crimean War." *New Cambridge History*. Vol. 10. Cambridge, England: The University Press, 1960. P. 458 ff.

Temperly, H.W.V. *England and the Near East: The Crimea*. London: Cass, 1936.

AUSTRIA VERSUS KINGDOM OF SARDINIA, 1859

Delzell, Charles F., ed. *The Unification of Italy, 1859–1861*. New York: Walker, 1965.

Hallberg, C. W. *Franz Joseph and Napoleon III, 1852–1864*. New York: Bookman Associates, 1955.

Smith, Denis Mack. *Cavour and Garibaldi*. Cambridge, England: The University Press, 1954.

Taylor, A.J.P. *The Hapsburg Monarchy, 1809–1918*. London: H. Hamilton, 1948.

PRUSSIA, AUSTRIA VERSUS DENMARK, 1863

Katzenstein, Peter J. *Disjointed Partners: Austria and Germany Since 1815*. Berkeley: University of California Press, 1976.

Mosse, W. E. *The European Powers and the German Question, 1848–1871*. Cambridge, England: The University Press, 1958.

Steefel, Lawrence. *The Schleswig-Holstein Question*. Cambridge, Mass.: Harvard University Press, 1932.

Westergaard, Waldemar. *Denmark and Sleswig*. London: G. Cumgerlege, 1946.

UNITED STATES VERSUS FRANCE, 1865–66

Case, Lynn. *French Opinion on the United States and Mexico, 1860–1867*. Washington, D.C.: American Historical Association, 1936.

Daunway, Clyde A. ''Reasons for the Withdrawal of the French from Mexico.'' *Annual Report of the American Historical Association for 1902*. Washington, D.C., 1903. Pp. 315–28.

Perkins, Dexter. *The Monroe Doctrine, 1826–1867*. Baltimore: Johns Hopkins University Press, 1933.

Schroeder, Seaton. *The Fall of Maximilian's Empire as Seen from a United States Gunboat*. New York: G. P. Putnam's Sons, 1887.

PRUSSIA VERSUS AUSTRIA, 1866

Clark, C. W. *Franz Joseph and Bismarck*. Cambridge, Mass.: Harvard University Press, 1934.

Friedjung, Heinrich. *The Struggle for Supremacy in Germany, 1859–1866*. London: Macmillan, 1935.

Pflanze, Otto. *Bismarck and the Development of Germany*. Princeton: Princeton University Press, 1963.

Steefel, Lawrence. *The Schleswig-Holstein Question*. Cambridge, Mass.: Harvard University Press, 1932.

FRANCE VERSUS PRUSSIA, 1870

Eyck, Erick. *Bismarck and the German Empire*. London: Allen and Unwin, 1950.

Howard, Michael. *The Franco-Prussian War*. New York: Macmillan, 1961.

Robertson, Charles C. *Bismarck*. New York: H. Holt, 1919.

Spencer, Frank. ''Historical Revision No. CXXII: Bismarck and the Franco-Prussian War.'' *History*, N.S. Vol. 40 (1955): 319–25.

Thompson, James M. *Louis Napoleon and the Second Empire*. Oxford: Oxford University Press, 1954.

Wolf, John B. *France, 1814–1919*. New York: Harper and Row, 1963.

RUSSIA VERSUS TURKEY, 1877

Anderson, Matthew S. *The Eastern Question*. London: Macmillan, 1966.

Rupp, G. H. *A Wavering Friendship: Russia and Austria, 1876–1878*. Cambridge, England: Cambridge University Press, 1941.

Stojanovic, M. D. *The Great Powers and the Balkans, 1875–1878*. Cambridge, England: Cambridge University Press, 1939.

Sumner, B. H. *Russia and the Balkans, 1879–1880*. Oxford: Oxford University Press, 1937.

Wirthwein, Walter G. *Britain and the Balkan Crisis, 1875–1878*. New York: Columbia University Press, 1935.

BRITAIN VERSUS EGYPT, 1882

Farnie, D. A. *East and West of Suez*. Oxford: Oxford University Press, 1969.

Lowe, C. J. *Reluctant Imperialists: British Foreign Policy 1878–1902*. London: Macmillan, 1967.

Robinson, R. E., and Gallagher, John. *Africa and the Victorians*. New York: St. Martin's Press, 1961.

Sanderson, G. N. *England, Egypt, and the Upper Nile, 1882–1898*. Edinburgh: The University Press, 1965.

JAPAN VERSUS CHINA, 1895
AND
GERMANY, FRANCE, RUSSIA VERSUS JAPAN, 1896

Jensen, Marius. *Japan and China, 1894–1972*. Chicago: Rand McNally, 1975.

Malazemoff, Andrew. *Russian Far Eastern Policy, 1881–1904*. Berkeley: University of California Press, 1958.

Young, L. K. *British Policy in China*. Oxford: Oxford University Press, 1970.

UNITED STATES VERSUS SPAIN, 1898

Beale, Howard K. *Theodore Roosevelt and the Rise of America to World Power*. Baltimore: Johns Hopkins University Press, 1956.

LaFeber, Walter. *The New Empire: An Interpretation of American Expansion, 1869–1898*. Ithaca, N.Y.: Cornell University Press, 1963.

May, Ernest R. *Imperial Democracy: The Emergence of America as a Great Power*. New York: Harcourt, Brace, and World, 1961.

Pratt, Julius W. *Expansionists of 1898*. Baltimore: Johns Hopkins University Press, 1936.

BRITAIN VERSUS BOERS, 1899

DeWet, C. R. *Three Years War*. New York: C. Scribner's Sons, 1902.

Holt, Edgar. *The Boer War*. London: Putnam, 1958.

Kesteven, G. R. [pseud.]. *The Boer War*. London: Chatto and Windus, 1970.

Ward, A. W., and Gooch, G. P., eds. *The Cambridge History of British Foreign Policy*. 3 vols. Cambridge, England: The University Press, 1922–23. Vol. 3.

BRITAIN VERSUS GERMANY, 1911

Barlow, Ima. *The Agadir Crisis*. Chapel Hill: University of North Carolina Press, 1940.

Berghahn, V. R. *Germany and the Approach of War*. New York: St. Martin's Press, 1973.

Fischer, Fritz. *War of Illusions*. New York: Norton, 1975.

Marder, A. J. *From Dreadnought to Scapa Flow*. Vol. 1. New York: Oxford University Press, 1961.

Steinberg, Jonathan. *Yesterday's Deterrent*. New York: Macmillan, 1966.

Woodward, E. L. *Great Britain and the German Navy*. Oxford: Clarendon Press, 1935.

AUSTRIA VERSUS SERBIA, RUSSIA, 1908–9 AND AUSTRIA VERSUS SERBIA, 1913 AND AUSTRIA VERSUS SERBIA, 1914

Bridge, F. R. *Great Britain and Austria-Hungary, 1906–1914*. London: Weidenfeld and Nicolson, 1972.

———. *From Sadowa to Sarejevo*. Boston: Routledge and Kegan Paul, 1972.

Helmreich, E. C. *The Diplomacy of the Balkan Wars, 1912–1913*. Cambridge, Mass.: Harvard University Press, 1938.

Langer, William. *Explorations in Crisis*. Cambridge, Mass.: Harvard University Press, 1969. Chaps. 2 and 3.

Schmitt, Bernadotte. *The Annexation of Bosnia, 1908–1909*. Cambridge, England: Clarendon Press, 1937.

———. *The Coming of War*. 2 vols. New York: C. Scribner's Sons, 1930.

RUSSIA VERSUS AUSTRIA, GERMANY, 1914

Albertini, Luigi. *The Origins of the War of 1914*. Translated by I. Massey. 3 vols. London: Oxford University Press, 1952–57.

Bridge, F. R. *From Sadowa to Sarejevo*. Boston: Routledge and Kegan Paul, 1972.

Choucri, Nazli, and North, Robert C. *Nations in Conflict: National Growth and International Violence*. San Francisco: W. H. Freeman, 1975.

Fay, Sidney B. *The Origins of the World War*. 2 vols. New York: Macmillan, 1947.

Geiss, Immanuel. *July 1914, The Outbreak of the First World War: Selected Documents*. London: Batsford, 1967.

Holsti, Ole. *Crisis, Escalation, War*. Montreal: McGill-Queen's University Press, 1972.

Nomikos, Eugenia, and North, Robert. *International Crisis: The Outbreak of World War I*. Montreal: McGill-Queen's University Press, 1976.

UNITED STATES VERSUS MEXICO, 1914

Calvert, Peter. *The Mexican Revolution, 1910–1914: The Diplomacy of Anglo-American Conflict*. Cambridge, England: Cambridge University Press, 1968.

Cline, Howard F. *The United States and Mexico*. Cambridge, Mass.: Harvard University Press, 1963.

Haley, P. E. *Revolution and Intervention: The Diplomacy of Taft and Wilson with Mexico, 1910–1919*. Cambridge, Mass.: M.I.T. Press, 1970.

Quirk, Robert. *An Affair of Honor: Woodrow Wilson and the Occupation of Veracruz*. Lexington, Ky.: University of Kentucky Press, 1962.

JAPAN VERSUS CHINA, 1915

Akagi, Roy E. *Japan's Foreign Relations, 1542–1936*. Tokyo: Hokuseido Press, 1936.

Ch'en, Jerome. *Yuan Shih-K'ai*. Stanford, Calif.: Stanford University Press, 1972.

LaFarque, Thomas E. *China and the World War*. Stanford, Calif.: Stanford University Press, 1937.

LaTourette, Kenneth Scott. *A History of Modern China*. London: Macmillan, 1954.

Tchen, Hoshien. *Les relations diplomatiques entre la Chine et le Japon de 1871 à nos jours*. Paris: Editions de "La Vie Universitaire," 1921.

Young, Arthur Morgan. *Japan in Recent Times*. New York: W. Morrow, 1929.

UNITED STATES VERSUS GERMANY, 1916

Albertini, Luigi. *The Origins of the War of 1914*. 3 vols. London: Oxford University Press, 1952–57.

Buehrig, Edward H. *Woodrow Wilson and the Balance of Power*. Bloomington, Ind.: Indiana University Press, 1955.

Link, Arthur S. *Wilson: Vol. 3: The Struggle for Neutrality, 1914–1915*. Princeton: Princeton University Press, 1960.

———. *Wilson: Vol. 4: Confusion and Crisis, 1915–1916*. Princeton: Princeton University Press, 1964.

———. *Wilson: Vol. 5: Campaigns for Progressivism and Peace, 1916–1917*. Princeton: Princeton University Press, 1968.

May, Ernest R. *The World War and American Isolation*. Cambridge, Mass.: Harvard University Press, 1959.

Schmitt, Bernadotte. *The Coming of War*. 2 vols. New York: C. Scribner's Sons, 1930.

Smith, Daniel. *Robert Lansing and American Neutrality*. Berkeley: University of California, 1958.

BRITAIN VERSUS TURKEY, 1922

Lowe, C. J., and Dockerill, M. L. *The Mirage of Power*. Vol. 2. London: Routledge and Kegan Paul, 1972.

Nicolson, Harold. *Curzon: The Last Phase, 1919–1925*. Boston: Houghton Mifflin, 1934.

Snodgrass, Nancy. "The Chanak Crisis." Ph.D. diss., University of Illinois, 1971.

Walder, David. *The Chanak Affair*. London: Hutchinson, 1969.

ITALY VERSUS GREECE, 1923

Lowe, C. J., and Marzani, F. *Italian Foreign Policy, 1870–1940*. London: Routledge and Kegan Paul, 1975.

Seton-Watson, Christopher. *Italy from Liberalism to Fascism, 1870–1925*. London: Methuen, 1967.

GREAT BRITAIN VERSUS ITALY, 1923

Lowe, C. J., and Marzani, F. *Italy's Foreign Policy, 1870–1940*. London: Routledge and Kegan Paul, 1975.

Reynolds, Philip A. *British Foreign Policy in the Interwar Years*. London: Longmans, Green, 1954.

Seton-Watson, Christopher. *Italy from Liberalism to Fascism, 1870–1925*. London: Methuen, 1967.

GERMANY VERSUS BRITAIN, 1938 AND GERMANY VERSUS CZECHIA, 1939 AND BRITAIN VERSUS GERMANY, 1939

Aster, Sidney. *1939: The Making of the Second World War*. London: Deutsch, 1973.

Gilbert, M., and Gott, R. *The Appeasers*. Boston: Houghton Mifflin, 1963.

Hildebrand, Klaus. *The Foreign Policy of the Third Reich*. Berkeley: University of California Press, 1973.

Jackel, Eberhard. *Hitler's Weltanschauung*. Middletown, Conn.: Wesleyan University Press, 1972.

Medlicott, W. N. *British Foreign Policy Since Versailles*. 2d ed. London: Methuen, 1968.

Middlemas, R. Keith. *Diplomacy of Illusion*. London: Weidenfeld and Nicolson, 1972.

Rich, Norman. *Hitler's War Aims*. Vol. 1. New York: Norton, 1972.

Ripka, Hubert. *Munich: Before and After*. New York: H. Fertig, 1969.

Taylor, A.J.P. *The Origins of the Second World War*. New York: Atheneum, 1961.

Wheeler-Bennett, J. W. *Munich: Prologue to Tragedy*. New York: Duell, Sloan, and Pearce, 1962.

UNITED STATES, IRAN VERSUS USSR, 1946

Gaddis, J. L. *The United States and the Origins of the Cold War, 1941–1947*. New York: Columbia University Press, 1972.

Kuniholm, Bruce R. *The Origins of the Cold War in the Near East: Great Power Conflict and Diplomacy in Iran*. Princeton: Princeton University Press, 1980.

Paterson, Thomas. *Soviet-American Confrontation*. Baltimore: Johns Hopkins University Press, 1974.

Rosenberg, J. Phillip. "The Chesire Ultimatum: Truman's Message to Stalin in the 1946 Azerbaijan Crisis." *Journal of Politics* 41 (August 1979): 933–40.

Ulam, Adam. *Expansion and Coexistence: The History of Soviet Foreign Policy, 1917-1967*. New York: Praeger, 1974.

UNITED STATES, YUGOSLAVIA VERSUS USSR, 1950–51

Armstrong, Hamilton F. *Tito and Goliath*. New York: Macmillan, 1951.

Calvocoressi, Peter. *Survey of International Affairs, 1951*. London: Oxford University Press, 1954.

Campbell, John C. *Tito's Separate Road*. New York: Harper and Row, 1967.

Clissold, Stephen. *Yugoslavia and the Soviet Union, 1939–1973: A Documentary Survey*. New York: Oxford University Press, 1975.

Djilas, Milovan. *Conversations with Stalin*. New York: Harcourt, Brace, and World, 1962.

CHINA VERSUS UNITED STATES, 1951

Acheson, Dean. *The Korean War*. New York: Norton, 1969.

Rees, David. *Korea: The Limited War*. New York: St. Martin's Press, 1964.

Spanier, John. *The Truman-MacArthur Controversy and the Korean War*. Cambridge, Mass.: Belknap Press, 1959.

Whiting, Allen S. *China Crosses the Yalu*. New York: Macmillan, 1960.

UNITED STATES VERSUS CAMBODIA, 1956

Sihanouk Varman, Norodom. *My War with the CIA*. New York: Pantheon, 1973.

Smith, Roy. *Cambodia's Foreign Policy*. Ithaca, N.Y.: Cornell University Press, 1965.

SOVIET UNION VERSUS POLAND, 1956

Brzezinski, Zbigniew. *The Soviet Bloc: Unity and Conflict*. Rev. ed. Cambridge, Mass.: Harvard University Press, 1967.

Ulam, Adam. *Expansion and Coexistence: The History of Soviet Foreign Policy, 1917–1967*. New York: Praeger, 1974.

Wolfe, Thomas W. *Soviet Power and Europe, 1945–1970*. Baltimore: Johns Hopkins University Press, 1970.

Zinner, Paul E., ed. *National Communism and Popular Revolt in Eastern Europe*. New York: Columbia University Press, 1956.

SOVIET UNION VERSUS GREAT BRITAIN, FRANCE, 1956

Finer, Herman. *Dulles Over Suez*. Chicago: Quadrangle, 1964.

Laquer, Walter. *The Soviet Union and the Middle East*. New York: Praeger, 1959.

Love, Kenneth. *Suez: The Twice Fought War*. New York: McGraw-Hill, 1969.

Smolansky, O. M. "Moscow and the Suez Crisis: A Reappraisal." *Political Science Quarterly* 80 (1965): 581–605.

Thomas, Hugh. *The Suez Affair*. London: Weidenfeld and Nicolson, 1967.

UNITED STATES, TURKEY VERSUS SYRIA, 1957

Capitanchik, David B. *The Eisenhower Presidency and American Foreign Policy*. New York: Humanities Press, 1969.

Eisenhower, Dwight D. *Waging Peace, 1956–1961*. Garden City, N.Y.: Doubleday, 1965.

Hammond, Paul Yates. *The Cold War Years: American Foreign Policy Since 1945*. New York: Harcourt, Brace, and World, 1969.

Kerr, Malcolm H. *The Arab Cold War*. New York: Oxford University Press, 1969.

Seale, Patrick. *The Struggle for Syria*. London: Oxford University Press, 1965.

BERLIN CRISES, 1958, 1961

Bell, Coral. *Negotiations from Strength: A Study on the Politics of Power*. New York: Knopf, 1963.

Drummond, Roscoe, and Gaston Coblentz. *Duel at the Brink: John Foster Dulles' Command of American Power*. Garden City, N.Y.: Doubleday, 1960.

Eisenhower, Dwight D. *The White House Years: Waging Peace, 1956–1961*. Garden City, N.Y.: Doubleday, 1965.

Horelick, Arnold, and Rush, Myron. *Strategic Power and Soviet Foreign Policy*. Chicago: University of Chicago Press, 1965.

Mander, John. *Berlin: Hostage for the West*. Baltimore: Penguin Books, 1962.

Richardson, James L. *Germany and the Atlantic Alliance: The Interaction of Strategy and Politics*. Cambridge, Mass.: Harvard University Press, 1966.

Schick, Jack M. *The Berlin Crisis, 1958–1962*. Philadelphia: University of Pennsylvania Press, 1971.

Slusser, Robert M. *The Berlin Crisis of 1961*. Baltimore: Johns Hopkins University Press, 1973.

———. "The Berlin Crises of 1958 and 1961." In Blechman and Kaplan, *Force Without War*. Washington, D.C.: Brookings Institution, 1978. Pp. 343–85.

Ulam, Adam. *Expansion and Coexistence: Soviet Foreign Policy, 1917–1967*. New York: Praeger, 1974.

UNITED STATES VERSUS UNITED ARAB REPUBLIC, 1958

Aqwani, M.S., ed. *The Lebanese Crisis, 1958*. New York, 1965.

Campbell, John C. *Defense of the Middle East: Problems of American Foreign Policy*. New York: Harper, 1960.

Eisenhower, Dwight D. *The White House Years: Waging Peace, 1956–1961*. Garden City, N.Y.: Doubleday, 1965.

Halpern, Manfred. *The Politics of Social Change in the Middle East and North Africa*. Princeton: Princeton University Press, 1963.

Meo, Leila. *Lebanon, Improbable Nation: A Study in Political Development*. Bloomington, Ind.: Indiana University Press, 1965.

Qubain, Fabian I. *Crisis in Lebanon*. Washington, D.C.: Middle East Institute, 161.

UNITED STATES VERSUS CHINA, 1958

Greene, Fred. *United States Policy and Security of Asia*. New York: McGraw-Hill, 1968.

Gurtov, Melvin. "The Taiwan Strait Crisis Revisited: Politics and Foreign Policy in Chinese Motives." *Modern China* 2 (January 1976): 49–103.

Hinton, Harold C. *Communist China in World Politics*. Boston: Houghton Mifflin, 1966.

Hsieh, Alice L. *Communist China's Strategy in the Nuclear Era*. Englewood Cliffs, N.J.: Prentice-Hall, 1962.

Thomas, John R. "Soviet Behavior in the Quemoy Crisis of 1958." *Orbis* 6 (1962): 38–64.

Tsou, Tang. "Mao's Limited War in Taiwan Strait." *Orbis* 3 (Fall 1959): 332–50.

———. "The Quemoy Imbroglio: Chiang Kai-shek and the U.S." *Western Political Quarterly* 12 (December 1959): 1075–91.

Whiting, Allen. "New Light on Mao, Quemoy, 1958: Mao's Miscalculations." *China Quarterly* 62 (June 1975): 263–70.

UNITED STATES VERSUS ECUADOR, 1960

Green, David. *The Containment of Latin America*. Chicago: Quadrangle Books, 1971.

New York Times, November–December 1960.

Slater, Jerome. *The OAS and United States Foreign Policy*. Columbus, Ohio: Ohio State University Press, 1967.

Zook, David. *Zarumilla-Maranon: The Ecuador-Peru Disputes*. New York: Bookman Associates, 1964.

UNITED STATES VERSUS DOMINICAN REPUBLIC, 1961

Kurzman, Dan. *Santo Domingo: Revolt of the Damned*. New York: Putnam, 1965.

Lowenthal, Abraham. *The Dominican Intervention.* Cambridge, Mass.: Harvard University Press, 1972.

Schlesinger, A. M., Jr. *A Thousand Days: John F. Kennedy in the White House.* Boston: Houghton Mifflin, 1965.

Slater, Jerome. *Intervention and Negotiation: The United States and the Dominican Revolution.* New York: Harper and Row, 1970.

———. "The Organization of American States, and the Dominican Republic, 1961, 1969." *International Organization* 18 (1964): 268–91.

UNITED STATES VERSUS NORTH VIETNAM, 1961

Fall, Bernard. *Anatomy of a Crisis.* Garden City, N.Y.: Doubleday, 1969.

Hilsman, Roger. *To Move a Nation.* Garden City, N.Y.: Doubleday, 1967.

Rostow, Walt W. *The View from the Seventh Floor.* New York: Harper and Row, 1964.

Schlesinger, Arthur, Jr. *A Thousand Days: John F. Kennedy in the White House.* Boston: Houghton Mifflin, 1965.

Zasloff, Joseph, and Langer, Paul F. *North Vietnam and the Pathet Lao.* Cambridge, Mass.: Harvard University Press, 1970.

GREAT BRITAIN VERSUS IRAQ, 1961

Everyman's United Nations.

Koburger, C. W. "The Kuwait Confrontation of 1961." *U.S. Naval Institute Proceedings,* C (Jan. 1974), pp. 42–49.

Shwadran, Benjamin. "The Kuwait Incident," parts 1 and 2. *Middle Eastern Affairs* 13 (January and February 1962).

Wainhouse, David. *International Peacekeeping at the Crossroads.* Baltimore: Johns Hopkins University Press, 1972.

UNITED STATES VERSUS SOVIET UNION, 1962

Abel, Elie. *The Missile Crisis.* Philadelphia: Lippincott, 1966.

Allison, Graham. *Essence of Decision.* Boston: Little, Brown, 1971.

Divine, Robert, ed. *The Cuban Missile Crisis.* Chicago: Quadrangle Books, 1971.

Horelich, Arnold. "The Cuban Missile Crisis: An Analysis of Soviet Calculations and Behavior." *World Politics* 16 (1964): 363–89.

Kennedy, Robert. *Thirteen Days.* New York: W. W. Norton, 1969.

Pachter, Henry M. *Collision Course.* New York: Praeger, 1963.

Pope, Ronald R., ed. *Soviet Views on the Cuban Missile Crisis.* New York: University Press of America, 1982.

CHINA VERSUS INDIA, 1962

Dalvi, John. *Himalayan Blunder.* Bombay: Jaico, 1969.

Fisher, Margaret W., Rose, Leo E., and Hattenback, Robert. *Himalayan Background: Sino-Indian Rivalry in Ladakh.* New York: Praeger, 1963.

Gittings, John. *The World and China.* New York: Harper and Row, 1974.

Manhekar, D. R. *The Guilty Men of 1962.* Bombay: Jaico, 1968.

Maxwell, Neville. *India's China War.* New York: Pantheon Books, 1970.

Van Eekehen, W. F. *Indian Foreign Policy, and the Border Dispute with China.* The Hague: Martinus Nijhoff, 1967.

UNITED STATES VERSUS NORTH VIETNAM, 1965

Cooper, Chester. *The Lost Crusade: America in Vietnam, 1970*. New York: Dodd, Mead, 1970.

Halberstam, David. *The Best and the Brightest*. New York: Random House, 1972.

Hilsman, Roger. *To Move a Nation*. Garden City, N.Y.: Doubleday, 1967.

Hoopes, Townsend. *The Limits of Intervention*. New York: D. McKay, 1969.

Thompson, James C. *Rolling Thunder*. Chapel Hill: University of North Carolina Press, 1980.

UNITED STATES, YUGOSLAVIA VERSUS SOVIET UNION, 1968 AND SOVIET UNION VERSUS CZECHOSLOVAKIA, 1968

Ermath, Fritz. *Internationalism, Security and Legitimacy: The Challenge to Soviet Interests in Eastern Europe, 1964–1968*. Santa Monica, Calif.: Rand Corp., 1969.

Kessing's Contemporary Archives.

Remington, Robin. *The Warsaw Pact: Studies in Communist Conflict Resolution*. Cambridge, Mass.: Harvard University Press, 1971.

Roberts, Adam. *Nations in Arms*. New York: Praeger, 1976.

Windsor, Philip. "Yugoslavia, 1951 and Czechoslovakia 1968." In *Force Without War*, edited by Barry M. Blechman et al. Washington, D.C.: Brookings Institution, 1978. Pp. 440–515.

UNITED STATES VERSUS NORTH KOREA, 1968, 1969

Armbrister, Trevor. *A Matter of Accountability*. New York: Coward-McCann, 1970.

Kissinger, Henry. *White House Years*. Boston: Little, Brown, 1979.

Nixon, Richard. *RN: The Memoirs of Richard Nixon*. New York: Grosset and Dunlap, 1978.

Szulc, Tad. *The Illusion of Peace*. New York: Viking Press, 1978.

UNITED STATES VERSUS SYRIA, 1970

Alroy, Gil Carl. *The Kissinger Experience: American Foreign Policy in the Middle East*. New York: Horizon Press, 1975.

Laquer, Walter. *Confrontation*. New York: Quadrangle, 1974.

Mangold, Peter. *Superpower Intervention in the Middle East*. New York: St. Martin's Press, 1977.

Nixon, Richard. *RN: The Memoirs of Richard Nixon*. New York: Grosset and Dunlap, 1978.

Quandt, William B. *Decade of Decisions: American Policy Toward the Arab-Israeli Conflict, 1967–1976*. Berkeley: University of California Press, 1977.

UNITED STATES VERSUS INDIA, 1971

Barnds, William J. *India, Pakistan, and the Great Powers*. New York: Praeger, 1972.

Brown, W. Norman. *The United States and India, Pakistan, Bangladesh*. Cambridge, Mass.: Harvard University Press, 1972.

Burke, S. M. *Mainspring of Indian and Pakistani Foreign Policies*. Minneapolis: University of Minnesota Press, 1974.

Choudhury, G. W. *India, Pakistan, Bangladesh, and the Major Powers*. New York: Free Press, 1975.

Gapta, Ramesh Chand. *United States Policy Towards India and Pakistan*. Delhi: H. Prakashan, 1977.

Haendel, Dan. *The Process of Priority Formulation: U.S. Foreign Policy in the Indo-Pakistani War*. Boulder, Colo.: Westview Press, 1977.

Kissinger, Henry. *White House Years*. Boston: Little, Brown, 1979.

Martin, Edwin W. *Southeast Asia and China: The End of Containment*. Boulder, Colo.: Westview Press, 1977.

New York Times, Dec. 1972; Jan. 1973.

Selden, Mark. *Remaking Asia*. New York: Pantheon Books, 1974.

Szulc, Tad. *The Illusion of Peace*. New York: Viking Press, 1978.

UNITED STATES VERSUS SOVIET UNION, 1973

Griffith, William E. *The Soviet Empire: Expansion and Detente*. Lexington, Mass.: Lexington Books, 1976.

Kohler, Fay P., et al. *The Soviet Union and the October 1973 Middle East War: The Implications for Detente*. Coral Gables, Fla.: University of Miami, 1974.

Kruzel, Joseph I. "Military Alerts and Diplomatic Signals." In *The Limits of Military Intervention*, edited by Ellen Stern. Beverly Hills, Calif.: Sage, 1977.

Quandt, William B. *Soviet Policy in the October 1973 War*. Santa Monica, Calif.: Rand Corp., 1976. R-184.

Sivachev, Mikolai Vasilevich. *Russia and the United States*. Chicago: University of Chicago Press, 1979.

UNITED STATES VERSUS CAMBODIA, 1975

Caldwell, Malcolm, and Lek, Tan. *Cambodia in the Southeast Asian War*. New York: Monthly Review Press, 1973.

Gordon, Bernard K. "Cambodia and Laos." In *Divided Nations in a Divided World*, edited by Gregory Henderson et al. New York: D. McKay, 1974.

Head, Richard G., et al. *Crisis Resolution: Presidential Decision Making in the Mayaguez and Korean Confrontations*. Boulder, Colo.: Westview Press, 1978.

New York Times.

Rowan, Roy. *The Four Days of Mayaguez*. New York: Norton, 1975.

Sihanouk Varman, Norodom. *War and Hope*. New York: Pantheon, 1980.

Simon, Sheldon W. "The Role of Outsiders in the Cambodian Conflict." *Orbis* 19 (Spring 1975): 209 ff.

UNITED STATES, KENYA VERSUS UGANDA, 1976

Africa Digest

Africa Recorder

New York Times

U.S. State Department files

Index

About the Authors

PETER KARSTEN is Professor of History and Sociology at the University of Pittsburgh, Chairman of the Department of History, and Co-director of the International Security Studies Program. He is the author of *Law, Soldiers, and Combat* (Greenwood Press, 1978), *Soldiers and Society* (Greenwood Press, 1978), and other books, as well as articles published in numerous periodicals.

PETER D. HOWELL is Instructor of History and Economics at Robert Morris College in Pittsburgh and is a Ph.D. candidate in History at the University of Pittsburgh.

ARTIS FRANCES ALLEN is a Fellow of the University of Lancaster (England) and a candidate for the Ph.D. with the Graduate School of Public and International Affairs at the University of Pittsburgh.